ROUTLEDGE LIBRARY EDITIONS: RUSSIAN AND SOVIET LITERATURE

Volume 11

THE RUSSIAN HORIZON

THE RUSSIAN HORIZON
An Anthology

Edited by
N. GANGULEE

LONDON AND NEW YORK

This edition first published in 2021
by Routledge
2 Park Square, Milton Park, Abingdon, Oxon OX14 4RN

and by Routledge
52 Vanderbilt Avenue, New York, NY 10017

Routledge is an imprint of the Taylor & Francis Group, an informa business

First published in 1943 by George Allen & Unwin Ltd

All rights reserved. No part of this book may be reprinted or reproduced or utilised in any form or by any electronic, mechanical, or other means, now known or hereafter invented, including photocopying and recording, or in any information storage or retrieval system, without permission in writing from the publishers.

Trademark notice: Product or corporate names may be trademarks or registered trademarks, and are used only for identification and explanation without intent to infringe.

British Library Cataloguing in Publication Data
A catalogue record for this book is available from the British Library

ISBN: 978-0-367-68495-2 (Set)
ISBN: 978-1-003-15462-4 (Set) (ebk)
ISBN: 978-0-367-72401-6 (Volume 11) (hbk)
ISBN: 978-0-367-72402-3 (Volume 11) (pbk)
ISBN: 978-1-003-15465-5 (Volume 11) (ebk)

Publisher's Note
The publisher has gone to great lengths to ensure the quality of this reprint but points out that some imperfections in the original copies may be apparent.

Disclaimer
The publisher has made every effort to trace copyright holders and would welcome correspondence from those they have been unable to trace.

THE RUSSIAN HORIZON

An Anthology compiled by
N. GANGULEE
Formerly Professor of Calcutta University

with a Foreword by
H. G. WELLS

"It takes more than intelligence to understand Russia, and she cannot be measured with a two-foot rule."
TIUTCHEV

London
GEORGE ALLEN & UNWIN LTD

First published in 1943

for
the defenders of freedom
everywhere

All rights reserved
Printed in Great Britain by T. and A. CONSTABLE LTD,
at the University Press, Edinburgh

CONTENTS

Chapter		Page
	FOREWORD	8
	INTRODUCTION	11
1	GLIMPSES INTO TSARIST RUSSIA	20
2	THE DREAM OF A NEW RUSSIA	45
3	THE BIRTH OF SOVIET RUSSIA	68
4	THE IDEOLOGICAL BASIS OF SOVIET RUSSIA	100
5	THE ROAD TO FULFILMENT	113
6	SOVIET FOREIGN POLICY	158
7	THE TESTAMENT OF FAITH IN SOVIET RUSSIA	173
8	THE RUSSO-GERMAN WAR (1941)	196
9	SOVIET RUSSIA AND HER ALLIES	225
10	THE NEW HORIZON	253
	NOTES ON RUSSIAN AUTHORS QUOTED	266
	ACKNOWLEDGMENTS	273
	INDEX TO AUTHORS	276

FOREWORD

I HAVE been asked by my friend Dr. Gangulee to contribute a few words by way of introduction to this compilation. I do so very readily, although I find myself rather out of harmony with its unrestrained eulogy. My attitude towards the Russian Revolution has always mingled criticism with admiration, and at the present time particularly do I feel the need to restrain enthusiasm and insist upon hard clear understanding between East and West in regard to the future. No one, I think, has been more consistently interested and sympathetic with the mighty Russian experiment. When my sons went to Oundle School, I insisted that they should learn Russian in addition to the school French and German, which they spoke already fairly well. Sanderson, the great Headmaster of Oundle, fell in with my idea. He added a competent Russian teacher to his staff, the first Russian teacher at any English public school. I went to Russia in the winter of 1913-14 and saw something of the Cadets and that belated and half-hearted Duma that used to meet in the Taurida Palace. I witnessed Gorki's distressful visit to America in 1906, and I saw him as the rather critical and trusted friend of Lenin in 1920, and idolised in 1934. I talked to Lenin, who spoke good English, when I visited Russia with my Russian-speaking son in 1920, and I had three hours with Stalin (and an interpreter) in 1934, when my son made a two months' tour of the scientific centres of the country and did some mountaineering in the Caucasus. All these encounters and experiences are faithfully described in my *Autobiography*. I made certain criticisms and forecasts, and I see no reason in what has happened since to modify them.

I submit these credentials because I think they establish my right to be explicit and critical about the rôle of Russia in the intense conflict between a new birth of society and narrower and grimmer forces, that may yet abort the last hopes and creative struggle of mankind. I doubt if this great crisis of suffering is frustrated, there will remain sufficient mental and moral vitality in our race to go on with further efforts. That is a quantitative question to which no conclusive reply is possible. It is a question of how many clear-headed righteous men are to be found in the world.

In spite of my admiration and affection for Russia and things Russian, I do not see why we should sacrifice too much to mutual congratulations at the present time. Russia has been and is a mighty experiment in equalitarian collectivism, but it is only part of the world experiment in equalitarian collectivism that our species has to make if it is to survive. The Russian experiment has the unavoidable weaknesses of any first experiment, and unhappily it has been saddled with and blinkered by the immense conceit and profound historical ignorance of the more mediocre elements in the Communist Party, which for a time threatened to become a very serious obstacle to that generous world-wide revolutionary reconstruction of human affairs, without which we shall certainly fall through disaster after disaster to the ultimate night of mankind. The primary ignorance which the Communist Party would have imposed upon us is due to the assumption that human history began with a series of financial operations, very variable and unsystematic in their nature, which Marx misinterpreted and called the "Capitalist *System*"—whereas, in the period following the Black Death, there was a vigorous communistic movement in Western Europe, as equalitarian and as sound as anything Russia has produced. Marx appears to have been totally ignorant of Wat Tyler and John Ball and the proletarian disturbances of the fifteenth and sixteenth centuries. And Russia seemed to be forgetting altogether that the ideology of its revolution came to it from the West, and even so was by no means the best the West could have given it, and that a constant exchange with the freer range of thought and speculation of the Western world is still absolutely necessary to carry on the unifying work that lies ahead.

Against any such understanding, which would rob it of its dogmatic authority, the Communist Party fought with a passionate intensity, as malignantly defensive in its way as the large-scale operations of the Roman Catholic Church. "Fought" I can write and not "fights," because a gesture of immense sanity, the dissolution of the doctrinaire Comintern, has come from Russia, and made a fundamental change in the world outlook. There is nothing so urgent in the world now as the need to thrust aside all such intolerances, and for the new war-tempered generations of Russia, China, the West and vernacular India, which is the only India that matters, to get to plain and frank speech with one another.

Such are my reactions to Dr. Gangulee's cloud of witnesses and testimonials. Good, I say, but let us get on with it. The human task becomes plainer and more hopeful, but it still remains to be done. Day breaks over the Russian horizon. I should have said this Evensong of Dr. Gangulee was premature only a few months ago. As an Evensong it is still, I think, premature, but as a Morning Hymn of confident aspiration, it has my warmest appreciation and I am only too happy to join in his chorus.

H. G. WELLS.

INTRODUCTION

We are living in a very singular moment of world history. Not merely because we are in the midst of another world war, but it is a moment of crucial crisis that involves every aspect of spiritual and material civilisation. It seems that we are on the threshold of a new epoch.

The unprovoked attack on the Union of Soviet Socialist Russia by Hitler's Germany on June 22, 1941, the prompt declaration of Anglo-Soviet Alliance that followed it, and the subsequent collaboration of China and of the United States of America with Soviet Russia, are events of great significance. We must remember that Germany attacked the Union of Soviet Socialist Republics in fear of her achievements as a powerful Socialist state. "The eight million square miles of Russian earth are not as bare of the modern machine as they were fifteen years ago. They stir with a life and an effort which testify to a new age, a new strength. Five more years of peace and industrial development, and Russia might easily have become an impregnable military fortress. But Hitler denied her this period of respite," writes Maurice Hindus. Indeed, the Nazis regarded the emergence of the Union of Soviet Socialist Republics as "the war on Europe" and sought to inspire the bourgeoisie states with the supreme mission of defending Europe against Russian Communism.

The world to-day stands in astonishment and admiration before the Russian spirit which has roused the millions of the Russian peoples as one man against the invader. Not a quisling, not a coward, not even a laggard could be found among them; no fifth column to sabotage their sublime effort to defend the Soviet land; and above all, no conflict of interests divides the Russian workers and peasants and their Government. Their spirit is like steel—strong and supple, and with it they are well prepared to face the storms of history.

While the Anglo-Soviet Alliance has been so enthusiastically received by the peoples of both countries, it is realised that there must be something more than this collaboration necessitated only by the exigencies of war. If Soviet Russia and Britain together with their allies are to play a significant rôle both in war and peace, there must be a true alliance of the spirit. Without it, this wartime alliance cannot be forged into an effective instrument wherewith to carry out the tasks of the post-war world. Sir Stafford Cripps, on his return from Moscow, declared his conviction that it was now essential to turn, to quote his own words, "our forced association as common enemies of Hitler into a willing co-operation in the reconstruction of Europe after the war."

That Russia's contribution to a reconstructed international politics will be great once she gains a decisive victory over German Fascism is becoming clear to perceptive minds. The British Government have already declared their intention to foster the spirit of sincere collaboration with the Union of Soviet Socialist Republics after the war, and an overwhelming majority of the British public desire it. The Trade Union movements of both countries realise the necessity of strengthening the bonds of sympathy and comradeship between the workers. The Russian Trade Delegation came to Britain to establish personal contacts with British working men and women. The delegates visited factories and noted British methods of wartime production.

But this spirit of close collaboration with Soviet Russia cannot grow without removing that ignorance and suspicion which have so long vitiated her relations with Britain. The fear of what is implied by the expression "Russian encroachment" has not disappeared, and there is a considerable volume of opinion that regards permanent alliance of capitalist states with the Union of Soviet Socialist Republics as anathema.

"In the course of the last twenty years," observes M. Maisky at the opening of the Russian Course for Teachers organised by the Board of Education, "for reasons upon which I have no desire to dwell, my country was subjected to a very regrettable misrepresentation in the world at large. Thus the people of my country were separated from the rest of the world, including Great Britain, by a wall of ignorance and suspicion. To destroy this wall, to clear the air, to make the peoples outside the Soviet Union understand my country better, is a matter of highest importance, especially now. On this to a very large extent depends the possibility of close collaboration between our two countries during the war and after the war, when our common foe has been utterly crushed and annihilated. And without such collaboration between the Soviet Union and Great Britain, with the friendly co-operation of the United States, there is no hope of mankind's establishing a just and durable peace."

The purpose of this anthology is to present a picture of the Union of Soviet Socialist Republics with a view to fortifying the hopes of permanent understanding between that country and her present allies. Beginning with a chapter on Tsarist Russia, I have tried to trace the working of the Russian spirit in Russian philosophy and literature; for it is in these sources one should find the directive impulses to be freed from mediaevalism and the autocratic régime. Indeed, the dreams of Russian philosophers, poets, dramatists, and novelists are not the products of a vacuum: they are rooted in the unconscious mind of the nation. Their writings open "the windows to eternal things" and reveal the spiritual life of Russia nourishing within herself the idea of universal salvation.

Immediately after the Revolution of 1917 there appeared a group of "peasant poets" who had been heretofore almost inarticulate. I have included a number of excerpts from their writings which may interest the reader.

The dominant ideology of Soviet Russia, however, finds its confirmation in the rich contents of pre-revolutionary classical literature. The rise of bourgeois liberalism, the growth of peasant unrest, the ever-increasing forces of social conflicts—all these realities of Russian life are described with that clarity of expression which gives Russian literature a dynamic character. Notwithstanding the denial of freedom that is so necessary for the creative spirit, Russian authors under the Tsar portrayed the facts of serfdom, gruesome poverty, ignorance and illiteracy of the masses with realism and humaneness—the two striking characteristics of Russian literary art. In the midst of slavery and tyranny they glorified freedom, and it was from them came the repeated warning that imperial autocracy was driving the empire on to the very edge of an abyss. Sensitive to the appalling conditions of the people, some of the outstanding men in the domain of literature raised the sound of a revolutionary tocsin.

> "Now tremble, despots of the world!
> And you, unawakened slaves,—
> Listen, take heart, and revolt."

Thus wrote the great Russian poet Pushkin.

In the writings of Gogol, Dostoevsky, Turgenev, Tolstoy, Gorky, Chekhov, we discover some of those aspirations which are the precursors of the achievements of the Union of Soviet Socialist Republics. These men had the vision of a new synthesis of thought and life, and since they gave expression to the genuine Russian spirit, no political changes could impair the veritable source of spiritual energy of the nation. On the contrary, Soviet Russia has devoted herself with much zeal to the analysis and interpretation of the literary heritage of Russia. "Tolstoy is great," writes Lenin, "as one who gave expression to the ideas and sentiments which had formed among the millions of the Russian peasants by the time of the bourgeois revolution in Russia.... In order to make his great writings really accessible to all, it is necessary to fight and fight against such a social system which condemned millions and scores of millions to darkness, ignorance, hard labour and poverty—a socialist upheaval is necessary." Indeed, as Berdyaev says, "Russian thought became original and creative only in the nineteenth century." The literary giants of the epoch did not sow seeds of freedom in the desert.

But they did more: they became the allies of the oppressed humanity of the world. The hope that the Russian thought shall renew humanity is one of the main themes, for example, of Dostoevsky's novels.

"No one who looks steadily upon the nineteenth century," writes J. Middleton Murry, "can deny that the Russian spirit alone in modern times has taken mankind a great stride nearer to its inevitable goal. In Russian literature alone can be heard the trumpet-note of a new world: other writers of other nations do no more than play about the feet of the giants who are Tolstoy and Dostoevsky, for even though the world knows it not, an epoch of the human mind came to an end in them. In them humanity stood on the brink of the revelation of a great secret."

Since a great deal of emphasis is laid on the divergence of political and social systems between the Union of Soviet Socialist Republics and her present allies, I have considered it necessary to devote a chapter on *The Ideological Basis of Soviet Russia*. Here the reader may find a few selections, chiefly from the writings of Karl Marx, Engels, Lenin, and Stalin. The internal government of the Union of Soviet Socialist Republics functions within the framework of a system based upon the inviolable alliance of workers and peasants. And only within such a system can the aspirations of the October Revolution come to fruition.

"Why was it that capitalism smashed and defeated feudalism?" asks Stalin at a Conference of Stakhanovites. "Because it created higher standards of labour productivity, which enabled society to procure an incomparably greater quantity of products than was the case under the feudal system. Because it made society richer. Why is it that socialism can, should, and certainly will defeat the capitalist system of economy? Because it can furnish superior models of labour, a higher productivity of labour, than the capitalist system of economy. Because it can give society more products and can make society richer than the capitalist system of economy can."

In the chapter entitled *The Road to Fulfilment* I have quoted a few authoritative remarks about the achievements of the Union of Soviet Socialist Republics which, to a receptive mind free from preconceived ideas and prejudiced views, cannot but evoke unstinted praise. After the October Revolution, the Russian people engaged themselves in discovering and conquering the country in which they live. Of course, Russia, like my own country (India), is too vast for accurate generalities. The task of converting Russia from a purely agricultural into an industrial country was not easy. Perhaps the single factor which contributed much to its phenomenal success was the willingness of the people to make voluntary sacrifices enabling the Government to build up factories, tractor plants, power stations, etc. One of the greatest engineering undertakings of the modern world is the construction of the Dnieper Dam.

Imbued with the idea of creating a new Russia, the Soviets accomplished the miracle of transforming deserts into orchards, developed the Arctic territory, raised the social status of the workers and peasants, built schools and universities, and safeguarded their country against invasion by the formation of the Workers' and Peasants' Red Army. The Army stands to-day as a formidable fighting force.

The Anglo-Soviet Alliance has revived the question of religion in the Union of Soviet Socialist Republics, although it is known that its constitution has made adequate provision for religious freedom. To the vast majority of the peoples of the West, Soviet Russia appears as a Godless state repudiating Christian religion and traditions. But a distinguished English writer, Maurice Baring, observes:

"The Russian soul is filled with a human Christian charity which is warmer in kind and intenser in degree than I have met with in any other people anywhere else; and it is this quality being behind everything else which gives charm to Russian life, however squalid the circumstances of it may be, which gives poignancy to its music, sincerity and simplicity to its religion, manners, intercourse, music, singing, verse, art, acting—in a word, to its art, its life and its faith." [1]

The fact is that in pre-revolutionary days, under the Tsarist régime, institutional religion had become a strong ally of superstition and cant. The Orthodox Church was a corrupt, wealthy, and reactionary body which opposed every measure of social justice and education of the masses. Soviet Russia changed all that by confiscating properties from which churches exacted a rich harvest of revenue, and separated Church from State. But freedom of worship is maintained and churches are crowded. There are now over 30,000 independent religious communities, over 8000 churches and about 60,000 priests and ministers of religion in the Soviet Union. Some four and a quarter million copies of religious and devotional books were circulated during the last five years.

As regards the charge of anti-religious bias, I believe that the underlying spirit of the Union of Soviet Socialist Republics, a multi-national state comprising varieties of culture and beliefs, is to lay emphasis on the human values implied by the integral freedom of MAN. After all, humanity is the test of a true religion. In his essay entitled "Man," Gorky defines religious feeling as: "a happy and proud awareness of a harmonious link that joins man to the universe. This feeling is born of an aspiration for synthesis, inherent in every individual; it is nourished by experience . . . and is gradually transformed into pathos through the joyous sensation of inner freedom, which has awakened in man." [2]

It is from this vision of a new type of man who would not conform to the idea of "the subordination of man to forces

---

[1] *Mainsprings of Russia*, Maurice Baring.
[2] Gorky, in the *Mercure de France*, 1907.

supposed to lie outside of himself," but would deliberately aim at a harmonious development of all his faculties, that Russia of to-day draws her inspiration. The former Archbishop of Canterbury (Dr. Lang), addressing a New Year pageant of Empire and Allies, said: "There is a beacon shining through the clouds of destiny. That is Russia, who is fighting as one man; not for any system or party but for the cause of freedom and for the soil which her people passionately love." Perhaps the source of this beacon lies in Russia's faith in the dignity of MAN.

In the chapter on *Soviet Foreign Policy* I have selected a few excerpts from speeches of Soviet leaders to show that the Union of Soviet Socialist Republics desired peace and that aggressive war formed no part of her policy. She has no need either of living space (*Lebensraum*) or of entering into external markets. Her Government is not subservient to any financial cliques or military castes. Peace she needed for the reconstruction of the country, and with that object in view both the Government and the Communist Party even compromised the concept of the World Revolution aimed at by the Third International. But the Soviet Union remained on guard to defend peace with the greatest vigour, and could not be taken unawares.

The chapter on *The Testament of Faith in Soviet Russia* contains a number of striking observations by some eminent persons of the world on the achievements of the Union of Soviet Socialist Republics within the first quarter-century of its existence. In his last public address, on his eightieth birthday, Rabindranath Tagore paid tribute to "the unstinted energy with which Soviet Russia was trying to fight disease and illiteracy . . . steadily liquidating ignorance and poverty and abject humiliation from the face of a vast continent," and to Russia's abolition of class distinctions. "I unreservedly admire," declared Heinrich Mann, "the firmness of the Soviet people, their courage, their unshakable determination, their devotion to a cause for which they are as willing to die the death of heroes as to live. . . . The Slav nation was the first to oppose to the invaders its noble will, predetermining their destruction. Who can doubt that all Slav peoples have a great future before them? Even more readily than my indignation and sympathy, I express my conviction that they will rise and fulfil their mission, and together with the Soviet Union show an example to humanity." These appreciations show that there is no need for the Soviet Union to engage in a crusade of ideals, and that the creation of a Socialist state is in itself a lesson in the making of a new civilisation. It emerged triumphant through the ordeals of revolutions and civil war, through trials of devastation and famine, and through many mistakes and miscalculations at the initial stage. To-day no contemporary state can ignore its achievements, its power and its prestige.

No anthology on Soviet Russia would now be complete without including some of the features of the Russo-German War. It is in this grim struggle against German Fascism that the real spirit of Russia is becoming manifest. The Archbishop of Canterbury (Dr. Temple), on the occasion of his enthronement, wrote to the Metropolitan Sergius of Moscow:

"I have watched with ever-growing admiration the heroic resistance of the peoples of the Union of Soviet Socialist Republics to the sudden and treacherous invasion of their motherland; I have learnt with sympathy and with sorrow of the bitter suffering which they have endured without flinching, and with indignation of the pitiless barbarities inflicted upon them; I have rejoiced at the memorable successes vouchsafed to the valiant constancy of the armed forces of the Union of Soviet Socialist Republics, to the steadfastness of its peoples and to the courage and wisdom of its leadership; and, whatever may happen in the nearer future, I look forward, in sure confidence that God's blessing will rest upon the comradeship in arms of the peoples of the Union of Soviet Socialist Republics with the peoples of the British Commonwealth, to the certain deliverance of all who are oppressed or are threatened by the Nazi and Fascist tyrannies and to the coming of the day of peace and of the brotherhood of all mankind."

In this grim struggle against Fascism the true self of Russia has emerged and the world has gained new insights into her creative achievements. Buttressed by the application of Marxist principles to means of production, the Soviet economy has shown much resilience, and the entire people are so imbued with their positive ideals of life and labour that they have so far withstood the German invasion with unexampled courage and fortitude.

In chapter 9 I have made a selection from various pronouncements relating to the Anglo-Soviet Alliance against Fascism. It is to be hoped that this Alliance will lead to mutual understanding between the Union of Soviet Socialist Republics, Britain and the United States; and that it will bear fruit not only in winning the war but also in laying the foundations of peace.

Finally, I have made an attempt to give an idea of the new spirit of Soviet Russia as is expressed in her literature. The new horizon, in the realities of life and labour, is becoming clear in her cultural development—the development which follows the path along which Russian literary art has long travelled in its visions and its hopes. From the point of view of the new world to be built, the Soviet authors are devoting themselves to the search for a new realism heralding the birth of a new epoch.

"The foundation of the Soviet Union is one of the biggest events in the history of the world," writes Mr. Baughan in an essay on "Politics in the Theatre," and he declares that "the French Revolution was a stage melodrama compared with it. The utopian ideas of government from Plato and his seventeenth-century disciple, Sir Thomas More, to the more modern socialistic sentimentalists, have been transformed into hard practical reality. Those ideas have crystallised into facts." Both ideas and facts of the Union of Soviet Socialist Republics are presented in this anthology as a guidance to those who desire close co-operation with her, not merely in the organisation of war-effort but in the establishment of a New World Order.

At a time when relations between Soviet Russia and the United Nations have reached a point of cordiality not achieved since its birth, I trust this anthology will serve a useful purpose in showing the nature and content of the historical process now manifest in the Russian Horizon.

N. GANGULEE.

LONDON.

Chapter One

GLIMPSES INTO TSARIST RUSSIA

> Poor and abundant,
> Down-trodden and almighty
> Art thou, our Mother Russia.
> NEKRASOV: *Who can be happy in Russia?*

That great invalid, our beloved Russia.
                                    DOSTOEVSKY.

> Wondrous the picture,
> How homelike to me!—
> Distant plain whitening,
> Full moon on the lea;
> Light—in the heavens high,
> And snow flashing bright,
> Sledge in the distance
> In its lonely flight.
>   SHENSHIN: *A Russian Scene.*

Behold it once again, the old familiar place,
Wherein my fathers passed their barren, vacant days!
In muddy revels ran their lives, in witless bragging,
The swarm of shivering serfs in their oppression found
An enviable thing the master's meanest hound;
And here to see the light of heaven I was fated,
And here I learned to hate, and bear the thing I hated;
But all my hate I hid within my soul for shame,
And I at seasons too a yokel squire became;
And here it was my soul, untimely spoilt and tainted,
With blessed rest and peace too soon was disacquainted;
Unchildish trouble then, and premature desires,
Lay heavy on my heart, and scorched it with their fires.
The days of a man's youth in memory, 'tis notorious,
Are like a sumptuous dream, are trumpeted as glorious;
—Those beauteous memories file in order before me,
Only to fill my breast with anger and ennui!

Here is the dark, dark close. See, where the branches thicken,
What figure glimpses down the pathway, sad and stricken?
Too well the cause I know, my mother, of thy tears;
Too well I know who marred and wasted all thy years.
For ever doomed to serve a sullen churl untender,
Unto no hopeless hope thy spirit would surrender;
To no rebellious dream thy timorous heart was stirred;
Thy lot, like any serf's, was borne without a word.
No frigid soul was thine, I know, or void of passion,
But resolute, and framed in proud and lovely fashion;
And all the wrongs that still thy ebbing strength could bear
Thy last faint words forgave thy slayer, watching there!
And thou, too, with that sad mute sufferer partaking
Her dreadful lot, and all the outrage and the aching,
Thou also art no more, my heart's own sister, mine!
Out of those doors by cur and servile concubine
Infested, thou must flee from shame unto disaster,
Commit thy lot unto a strange, an unloved master,
Aye, and rehearse afar the doom that fell on her,
Thy mother. Even he, thy executioner,
Shuddered before thy bier, was once betrayed to weeping,
To see thee with that smile so cold and rigid sleeping. . . .

      NEKRASOV: *The Birthplace*
       (*Contemporary Review*, 1876).

In our village there's cold and there's hunger,
Through the mist the sad morn rises chill;
Tolls the bell—the parishioners calling
From afar to the church on the hill.

Austere and severe and commanding
Pealed that dull tone thro' the air.
I tarried in church that wet morning,
I can never forget the scene there.

For there knelt the village hamlet,
Young and old in a weeping crowd,
To be saved from the grievous famine
The people prayed aloud.

Such woe I had never witnessed,
Such agony of prayer,
And with lips compelled I murmured,
"O God, the people spare!"

. . . .

"Spare their friends, too, in Thy mercy!
Oh, hear our heartfelt cry!
For those who strove to free the serf
We lift the prayer on high.

For those who bore the battle's brunt
And lived to win the day,
For those who've heard the serf's last song,
To Thee, O God, we pray."

NEKRASOV: Te Deum.

    Life, our bark, has stranded
      On a shoal profound.
    High the shouts of labourers
      Far away resound.
    Over the blank river
      Drift alarms, and song.
    See, and Someone enters,
      Grey of coat, and strong,
    Shifts the timbered rudder,
      Lets the sail go free;
    Breasting at the boat-hook,
      Pushes off to sea.
    —Quietly the crimson
      Poop wears round at last;
    Look, the motley houses
      Now have flitted past!
    Far away they're floating
      Gaily; yet, think I,
    Us they ne'er shall carry
      With them as they fly!

ALEXANDER BLOK:
Life, our Bark, has stranded.

Why does our peasant go in bast shoes instead of leather boots? Why does such dense and widespread ignorance prevail throughout the land? Why does the *mooshik* seldom or never eat meat, butter, or even animal fat? How does it come to pass that you rarely meet a peasant who knows what a bed is? Why is it that we discern in all the movements of the Russian *mooshik* a fatalistic vein, devoid of the impress of conscience? Why, in a word, do the peasants come into the world like insects and die like summer flies? The common Russian man not only suffers, but consciousness of his pain is singularly blunted, deadened. He looks upon his misery as a species of original sin to be borne instead of grappled with, as long as his staying powers hold out.   SALTYKOV: *Provincial Sketches.*

There are many villages of twenty or thirty houses that have not a single man that can read; if any come to them with a ukase, or without a ukase, pretending to have one, they believe him, and suffer damages; for they are all blind—they see nothing and understand nothing. They are not able to dispute with the people that pretend having ukases, and they frequently pay unwarranted taxes to them.   POSOSHKOV.

Most of the peasant huts are eighteen by twenty-one feet. In such a hut are housed on the average about seven people, but there are huts—little cages—no larger than twelve feet square. The stove occupies about one-fifth of the total air space. It plays here a tremendous rôle in the life and the economy of the family. Not only do the peasants warm themselves by it, but they also sleep on it and use it for drying clothes, shoes, grain, hemp. Not only do they bake and cook with the stove, but they also depend upon it for steam baths. And under the stove chickens, calves, and sheep are often protected from the frosts of winter. Not infrequently the cow is also brought into the hut at the time of calving. Practically the only furniture is a table which serves both cooking and dining purposes. On this table, too, all kinds of housework are done, harness repaired, clothes are made and mended. A common saying among the peasants is: "We are so poor that we haven't even anything with which to feed the cockroaches."

Thus wrote a political leader at the beginning of the twentieth century, on Russia. Quoted by M. ILIN in *Moscow has a Plan.*

> To whom I like I mercy show,
> And whom I like I kill;
> My fist—my only constable,
> My only law—my will.
> A blow from which the sparkle flits,
> A blow that knocks the teeth to bits,
> A blow that breaks the jaw!
>
> NEKRASOV: *The Landlord.*

I hereby pledge myself:
1. I go out to work at sunrise and to work until sunset.
2. If I leave work without legitimate cause, I must pay a double forfeit, not asking for any pay for the time of my work.
3. I pledge myself to go to work the moment I am called.
4. If the steward summons me to any work on Sundays or holidays, I am not entitled to refuse.
5. If I go away anywhere on weekdays or holidays without the permission of the steward, I must work to make up for these days.
6. If I fall sick or die my family must do my work in my place.
7. Under no circumstances can I leave work before the time is up.

> Pledge that the women labourers of the landowner Count Pototsky had to sign.

The Russian state is now passing through the second stage of the feudal system, namely, the epoch of autocracy. Undoubtedly, it is tending directly towards freedom. In part this tendency is even more straightforward in Russia than in other countries. The unfailing signs of it are: (1) That people lose all esteem for the former objects of their veneration, e.g. for rank and honour. (2) The action of power is so weakened that no measure of government can be put into operation which calls only for moral and not also for physical constraint. The true reason of this is that at present public opinion is in entire contradiction to the form of government. (3) No partial reform is possible, because no law can exist if it may any day be overtaken by a gust of arbitrary power. (4) A general discontent is observed such as can only be explained by a complete change of ideas and by a repressed but strong desire for a new order of things. For all these reasons we may surely conclude that the actual form of government does not correspond to the state of popular feeling, and that the time has come to change this form and to found a new order of things.

SPERANSKY, in an Address to the Tsar, 1809.

The purpose of Speransky's plan was establishment of the Government's authority upon permanent principles aided by laws, and, thereby, communication to the working of that authority of a greater amount of dignity and true power.

First, the plan expounds an order of State's general bases. Such an order's authority, it says, comes exclusively of the people, and therefore, for a Government to be legal, that Government must be based upon the will of the people. Also, a Government can act only in accordance with given conditions, and act lawfully only if those conditions be fulfilled. Conditions of the sort are expressed in regulations called fundamental laws. A State's fundamental laws, therefore, flow solely from the will of the people. But inasmuch as the people, though the composers of the laws, cannot, as a single whole, superintend their working, a requisite for the purpose is an upper social class of a given degree of education and independence, as well as one whose interests are identical with the people's. And inasmuch as an upper class, a monarchical aristocracy, of the sort acts on commission from the people, the political position which it occupies rests upon a popular majority. A due State order, therefore, possesses three bases. Those three bases are: (1) a constitutional monarch, limited by fundamental laws; (2) a monarchical aristocracy, for superintendence of the working of those laws and all their authority; and (3) a free people, the link between whom and the monarchical aristocracy in question is unity of interests.

Russia's position of the day offers reasons in plenty for introduction of a new order of State, but, at the same time, few effective elements for such an order's creation. The reasons are as follows. It is manifest that from the period of Alexis onwards Russia's tendency has ever been towards freedom. And in view of the conditions governing her present position of affairs, she now needs freedom more than ever. Already existent in Russia there is a system of civil law, but, to guarantee that system, there is existent nothing—the system may at any moment be shattered upon the rock of absolutism. At present popular enlightenment would be to no purpose—it would even be harmful. For what avails it to give a slave enlightenment when enlightenment can but render him more than ever sensible of his grievous plight. In the prevailing universal dissatisfaction, in the prevailing universal tendency to criticise, we see expressed the fact that all are grown weary of the order in being. Manifestly that order corresponds with public opinion no longer. Unfortunately, that order does not as yet comprise the elements of a new one, of one correctly compounded. True, there are laws in existence, and there are institutions in existence, and there exist certain charters to define certain rights and duties; but none of these things have a durable basis, and, above all, Russia does not possess a monarchical system proper. The Russian community has for its two chief social classes the *dvoriané*, the landowners, and the *krestiané*, the landworkers. But the former are only Crown slaves, and the latter are only the former's slaves, and not a human being in Russia is really free save only Russia's mendicants and Russia's cultivators of Philosophy. Reform of the order in being, therefore, should begin with abolition of class relations as they at present subsist—with abolition, that is to say, of the position of the social classes as it at present subsists.

But how are the necessary elements for the foundation of a due, a legal State order in Russia to be created? Well, an aristocracy might, as the law's supervisor, be able to create those elements if to the composition of that aristocracy there be assigned the first three or four grades of the existing *dvorianin*-service hierarchy. True, such a category will, at the start, include many persons without significance or worth, but in time, within a few generations, these will disappear, owing to the influence of apportionment of serious work to the class. And as for the community in general, it must, if it is properly to carry on its affairs, and also to participate in its own administration, consist of free members exclusively. Wherefore social reform should begin with emancipation of the bonded *krestiané*. Any difficulties arising in this regard must simply be overcome. For serf-right is an institution so utterly opposed to all sound sense that it may be looked upon as a temporary evil bound eventually to disappear. And as regards the bonded *krestiané's* emancipation, it must be effected through two methods. First, there must be defined exactly the dues lawfully demandable of the bonded *krestianin* by the landowner. And, next, there must be instituted certain courts for adjudication of differences between the two parties concerned. Only in this manner can the bonded *krestianin* pass from a status of personal attachment to a status merely of soil-attachment. Next again, there must be re-established his, the *krestianin's*, right to change his landowner. And when that shall have been done the *krestianin* will stand emancipated outright. From this there will become created two social classes altogether new—a monarchical aristocracy, and a free *krestianstvo*, and the Russian community as a whole will be divided into three social classes, consisting of a *dvorianstvo*, of a middle class, and of a class of manual workers, with all three such classes enjoying civil rights, but only the first two political rights as well. The administrative system to be built upon this vertical social division will consist of Ministries, and of institutions elective and local of character. Which institutions, again, will consist of three parallel series—of a legislative, of a judicial, and of an executive.   KLUCHEVSKY: *A History of Russia.*

>Will serfdom be abolished at a ruler's nod?
>Shall I see the long-awaited dawn of freedom
>Rising above our fatherland?
>>PUSHKIN: *The Village.*

>Thus spake the Tsar:
>"O my people, listen! . . .
>In my imperial wisdom
>I have deemed it best
>To give all human rights to men."

>The little child
>Leaped joyously from bed. . . .
>"Hush," his mother said,
>"Close your eyes and go to sleep;
>You will play another time.
>That was only Papa Tsar
>Telling you a nursery rhyme."
>>PUSHKIN, from his poem *Noel*; reference is to liberal pretensions of Alexander.

Political enfranchisement was a corollary of emancipation from serfdom. The press had been forbidden to discuss it. The initiation of the peasants into the duties of citizenship, into collective work carried on under personal responsibility, was a preliminary condition of national progress, but even to moot such an innovation has been punished as treason. At the very least, freedom in the choice of means by which the emancipated millions might wish to satisfy their consciences and save their souls was a postulate of healthy, moral development, but not only was it persistently withheld from the *mooshik*, it was not accorded even to the intellectuals. The one was forced to remain in the State Church because without compulsion the State Church, now hardly more than a police department, might soon be devoid of a congregation, and the others were only permitted to choose between orthodoxy and atheism, and most of them chose atheism. E. J. DILLON: *The Eclipse of Russia.*

In economics no law was respected. There was no consideration for the peasantry on whom the dead weight of the Empire pressed. The masses were kept not only without political rights but in utter ignorance of the circumstance that they had any claim to them. And the embargo was issued with wanton cynicism. The peasantry was no more than a wealth-creating machine for the behoof of the ruling class, and the rulers took so little thought even of their own less pressing interests that they failed to keep the machine properly lubricated or in smoothly working condition. And everywhere the same piratical instincts of the autocracy and its instruments met the eye.
E. J. DILLON: *The Eclipse of Russia.*

As for the Church, it was a mere museum of liturgical antiquities. Vladimir Solovieff used to liken it to a casket for an orient pearl whose lustre was dimmed by a thick crust of Byzantine dust. Its function in the State was never much more than that of a police department for the control of the kind of thought that is least open to regulation from without—that which speculates on problems of religion. The clergy, with the exception of a few self-mortifying anchorites and ascetics, were a body of social parasites, poor, squalid, grasping, and ignorant, their lives challenging and receiving alternate pity and contempt from the benighted flock whose shepherds they set up to be.

From the very outset the Russian Church was the repository of petrified forms to which a magic virtue was ascribed. No life-giving spirit ever animated that rigid body, for Byzance was powerless to give what it did not possess. How completely the spiritual energies of which a church is supposed to be the source were superseded by mechanical devices may be gathered from the well-attested fact—one of many—that the second Tsar of the House of Romanoff, Alexis Mikhailovitch, being a "truly religious monarch," was wont to bow down reverently before the holy images, his forehead striking the cold stone floor one thousand five hundred times every morning. Saintly prince!

E. J. DILLON: *The Eclipse of Russia.*

Coercion in religious matters did more to spread political disaffection than the most enterprising revolutionary propagandists. It turned the best spirits of the nation against the tripartite system of God, Tsar, and fatherland, and convinced even average people not only that there was no life-giving principle in the State, but that no faculty of the individual or the nation had room left for unimpeded growth. Whithersoever one turned, progress was barred by artificial obstacles. Schools, universities, the bar, the law courts, the press, the church and the chapel, the peasants' reunions, the *zemstvo* assemblies were so many narrow cages in which thought as well as action were caught and confined. The bulk of the nation felt the economic pressure of this gigantic incubus most painfully, for except in the religious domain it was rare that curiosity of an intellectual character made itself felt among the peasants, and then it generally assumed grotesque shapes.

E. J. DILLON: *The Eclipse of Russia.*

Earth is Hell, and Hell bows down before the Tsar,
All its monstrous, murderous, lecherous births acclaim
Him whose Empire lives to match its fiery fame.
Nay, perchance at sight or sense of deeds here done,
Here where men may lift up eyes to greet the sun,
Hell recoils heart-stricken; horror worse than Hell
Darkens earth and sickens Heaven; Life knows the spell,

Shudders, quails and sinks—or, filled with fiercer breath,
Rises red in arms devised of darkling death.
Pity mad with passion, anguish mad with shame,
Call aloud on justice by her darker name. . . .
>   SWINBURNE, in *Fortnightly Review*, 1890.

The sun o'er the wide steppe is sinking,
And gilding the tall waving grass:
The chains of the convicts are clinking,
And raising the dust as they pass.

They march with slow footsteps, way-weary,
Their close-shaven heads hanging low,
With faces grown sullen and dreary,
And hearts that are burdened with woe.

They move, and their shadows grow with them,
While, drawn by a pair of old hacks,
Two light, creaking waggons keep with them,
The escort rides close at their back.

Now, brothers, we'll strike up a chorus,
And lose half our troubles in song!
Forget the hard fate that's before us,
And sing as we're marching along.

Their song sets the silence aquiver,
Their voices ring clear o'er the plain,
They sing of the broad Volga river,
Or freedom that ne'er comes again.

They sing of a freedom as boundless
As the steppes, ripple-marked by each gust.
The darkness has fallen—
Still faintly I hear their chains clink in the dust.
>   *The Convoy Song of the Sibiriak.*

Even in the deep Siberian mines
You keep your proud endurance.
Your work and your noble effort
Shall not have been in vain.
Hope, the faithful sister of misfortune,

Shall awaken courage once again;
Friendship and love will speak to you
As now my free voice reaches through stone.
The heavy chains from off your limbs will fall,
Destroyed will be th' encircling prison-wall.
Release will bring the welcome of sweet liberty,
Your swords by brothers' hands restored will be.
> PUSHKIN, in honour of the Martyrs of the Decembrists, 1827.

Our bitter toil shall not be lost,
The spark shall burst in burning flame;
Our loyal godly Russian host
Shall gather round our banner's name.

Our chains we shall forge into swords
Again to blaze with Freedom's fire,
Shall storm with them the Tsar's cohorts,
With joy the people shall respire.   ODOYEVSKY.

The moral level of society was lowered, its development interrupted—everything of progress, of energy, smitten out of life. The vast peasant world was silent and indifferent. A terrible state of things, is it not? But do not imagine that Russia is doomed. The Russia of the future was a few young men, scarcely more than children, so insignificant, so little noted, that they might with ease be held between the sole of the foot of the autocracy and the ground. In them was the heritage of the Fourteenth of December, the heritage of universal science and of a Russia wholly belonging to the people.
> HERZEN: *The Pole Star.*

Slavdom and Slav aspirations must arouse a whole host of enemies among Russian Liberals. When will these obsolete and retrograde dregs be washed away!—for a Russian Liberal can't be considered as anything but as obsolete and retrograde. The so-called "educated society" of old is a motley collection of everything that has separated itself from Russia, that has not understood Russia and has become Frenchified—that is what a Russian Liberal is, and that is why he is a reactionary.
> DOSTOEVSKY, in a letter to A. N. Maikov, 1868.

In a strange land there lived a dog in a thick forest. He deemed his citizens to be uncultured, so passed his days in the country of the wolves and bears. The dog no longer barked, but growled like a bear and sang the song of wolves. When he returned to the dogs, he out of reason adorned his native tongue. He mixed the growl of bears and howl of wolves into his bark, and began to speak unintelligibly to dogs. The dogs said: "We need not your newfangled music—you only spoil our language with it"; and they began to bite him, until they killed him.

I have read the tombstone of that dog: "Never disdain your native speech, and introduce into it nothing foreign, but adorn yourself with your own beauty."

SUMAROKOV: *The Corruptions of Languages.*

You ask me, my friend, what I would do: (1) if I were a small man and a small gentleman; (2) if I were a great man and a small gentleman; (3) if I were a great man and a great gentleman; (4) if I were a small man and a great gentleman. To the first question I answer: I should use all my endeavour to become acquainted in the houses of distinguished people and men of power; I would not allow a single holiday to pass without making the round of the city, in order to give the compliments of the season; I would walk on tiptoes in the antechambers of the mighty, and would treat their valets to tobacco; I would learn to play all kinds of games, for when you play cards you can sit down shoulder to shoulder with the most distinguished people, and then bend over to them and say in a low tone, "I have the honour to report to your Excellency such and such an affair," or again become bolder and exclaim, "You have thirteen and I fourteen." I would not dispute anything, but would only say, "Just so; certainly so; most certainly so; absolutely so." I would tell the whole world that such and such a distinguished gentleman had condescended to speak to me, and if I could not say so truthfully, I would lie about it, for nothing so adorns speech as a lie, to which poets are witnesses. Finally, I would obtain by humility and flattery a profitable place, but above all I would strive to become a governor, for that place is profitable, honourable and easy. It is profitable, because everybody brings gifts; it is honourable, because everybody bows before a governor; it is easy, because there is very little work to do, and that is done by a secretary or scribe, and, they being sworn people, one may entirely rely upon them. A scribe has been created by God by whom man has been created, and that opinion is foolish which assumes that a scribe's soul is devoid of virtue. I believe there is little difference between a man and a scribe, much less difference than between a scribe and any other creature.

If I were a great man and a small gentleman, I would, in my constant attempt to be useful to my country and the world at large, never become burdensome to anyone, and would put all my reliance upon my worth and my deserts to my country; and if I should find myself deceived in this, I should become insane from so much patience, and should be a man who not only does nothing, but even thinks nothing.

If I were a great man and a great gentleman, I would without cessation think of the welfare of my country, of incitements to virtue and dignity, the reward of merit, the suppression of vice and lawlessness, the increase of learning, the cheapening of the necessaries of life, the preservation of justice, the punishment for taking bribes, for grasping, robbery and theft, the diminution of lying, flattery, hypocrisy and drunkenness, the expulsion of superstition, the abatement of unnecessary luxury, the limitation of games at cards which rob people of their valuable time, the education, the founding and maintenance of schools, the maintenance of a well-organised army, the scorn of rudeness, and the eradication of parasitism.

But if I were a small man and a great gentleman, I would live in great magnificence, for such magnificence is rarely to be found in a great soul; but I will not say what else I would do.

SUMAROKOV.

By our general convictions, we are socialists and democrats. We are convinced that only on socialistic grounds humanity can become the embodiment of freedom, equality, fraternity, securing for itself the general prosperity and the full and harmonious development of man and social progress. We are convinced, moreover, that only the *Will of the Nation* should give sanction to any social institution, and the development of the nation may be called sound only when independent and free, and when every idea which is to receive practical application has previously passed the test of the national understanding and national will.

We think, therefore, that as socialists and democrats we must recognise, as our immediate purpose, the liberation of the nation from the oppression of the present state by making a political revolution with the object of transferring the supreme power into the hands of the nation.

We think that the *Will of the Nation* should be sufficiently clearly expressed and applied by a National Assembly, freely elected by the vote of all citizens, and provided with instruction from their electors. This we do not consider to be the ideal form of the manifestation of the will of the nation, but it is the only one practically realisable, and we feel bound, therefore, to accept it.

Submitting ourselves completely to the will of the nation, we, as a party, feel bound to appear before the country with our own programme, which we shall propagate before the revolution, recommending it to the electors during the electoral periods, and which we shall defend in the National Assembly.

This programme consists of the following heads:

(1) The permanent popular representative Assembly, elected by universal suffrage, to have the supreme control and direction in all general State questions.

(2) Large provincial self-government, and elective nomination to all offices.

(3) Independence of the village commune (*mir*) as an economic and administrative unit.

(4) Nationalisation of land.

(5) A series of measures tending to bring all the factories into the hands of the workers.

(6) Complete freedom of conscience, of speech, of the press, of meetings, of associations, and of electoral agitation.

(7) Extension of the right to vote to all citizens having attained full age, without any class or wealth distinctions.

(8) Substitution of a standing army by a territorial militia.

        The Programme of the party of the "Will of the People" (*Narodnaïa Volia*), 1879.[1]

---

[1] Taken from *The Russian Storm-cloud*, by Stepniak.

Property! I have never repudiated it. On the contrary, I dare lay claim to defend it, for I recognise that every one has a right to the property secured by his labour. Tell me, is it I who destroy property, or the manufacturer, who, leaving to the workman 1s. 3d. of the day's labour, takes the other 2s. 3d. for nothing? Or the speculator, who, gambling on the Stock Exchange, ruins thousands of families, and enriches himself at their expense, without himself producing anything?

Communism as compulsory, neither I nor any other of the propagandists preaches. We only claim the right of the labourer to all the product of his labour.

As to the family, I should like to ask what it is that undermines it? Is it the social regime that compels the woman to abandon her family and go into the factory to earn a meagre wage—the factory in which she and her children must become demoralised: is it this régime which forces the woman in her misery to become a prostitute? Or is it we who are undermining the family, we who are trying to root out this misery?

As to religion, I can only say that I have always remained faithful to its spirit, and to its fundamental principles as they were preached by the very founder of Christianity.

I am accused of exciting to revolt. But I have never urged people to direct revolt. . . . Massacres, as massacres, are hateful to me. . . . I admit only that the revolution by force, under certain given conditions, is a necessary evil. . . .

The Public Ministry says again that we wish to introduce an era of anarchy; but this word, in the sense in which the literature of to-day employs it, and as I myself understand it, does not mean disorder and despotism. It is not despotism, for it recognises that the liberty of one person ends where that of another begins. It is only the negation of that vexatious authority which stifles the free development of society. . . .

Gentlemen, I belong to that category of people who are known under the name of peaceful propagandists. Their problem consists in rousing the conscience of the masses to ideals of a better, juster social order, or to make clear those ideals which unconsciously have already taken root in them: to show them the faults of the present order, so that in the future the same faults may be avoided. But we do not determine when this future will arrive, nor is it possible for us to determine it, because its realisation is not dependent upon us. . . . I am convinced that the day will come when our sleepy and indolent society will awaken, and when it will feel ashamed for having allowed itself so long to be trodden down, to be deprived of brothers, sisters, and daughters, in order to be destroyed for the mere free confession of their convictions. And this society will avenge our ruin.

Persecute us, gentlemen, for material force is on your side; but we have with us the moral force, the force of historic progress, the force of the idea, and ideas cannot be destroyed by bayonets.

SOFIA BARDINA, a member of *Narodnaïa Volia*,
before the Procureur, 1879.

Our conditions for the cessation of hostilities are:

First, a general amnesty for all political offenders, since they have committed no crime, but have simply done their duty as citizens.

Second, the convocation of the representatives of the whole of the people, for the examination of the best forms of social and political life, according to the wants and desires of the people.

We consider it necessary to point out that the legalisation of power by the representation of the people can only be arrived at when the elections are perfectly free. The elections should, therefore, take place under the following conditions: that the deputies shall be chosen by all classes without distinction, in proportion to the number of inhabitants; that there shall be no restriction of any kind upon electors or deputies; and that the elections and the electoral campaign shall be perfectly free.

The Government will, therefore, grant, as provisional regulations, until the convocation of the popular assemblies (*a*) complete freedom of the press; (*b*) complete freedom of speech; (*c*) complete freedom of public meeting; and (*d*) complete freedom of electoral addresses.

These are the only means by which Russia can enter upon the path of peaceful and regular development. We solemnly declare, before the country, and before the whole world, that our party will submit unconditionally to the National Assembly which meets upon the basis of above conditions, and will offer no opposition to the Government which the National Assembly may sanction.

> From a letter of the Executive Committee of *Narodnaïa Volia* to Alexander III after his accession to the throne.

You have spoken your mind and your words will be known to all Russia, to all the civilised world. . . . January 29, 1895,[1] has dispelled that halo which surrounded your young, uncertain appearance in the eyes of many Russians. You yourself have raised your hands against your own popularity. But not your popularity alone is now at stake. If autocracy in word and deed proclaims itself identical with the omnipotence of bureaucracy, if it can exist only so long as society is voiceless, its cause is lost. It digs its own grave and soon or late—at any rate, in a future not very remote—it will fall beneath the pressure of living social forces. . . . You first opened the struggle, and the struggle will come.

> THE RUSSIAN LIBERALS, in an open letter to the Tsar, 1895.

We have become beggars, we have been oppressed; we are burdened by toil beyond our powers; we are scoffed at; we are not recognised as human beings; we are treated as slaves who must suffer their bitter fate and who must keep silence. We suffered, but we are pushed farther into the den of beggary, lawlessness, and ignorance. We are choked by despotism and irresponsibility, and we are breathless. We have no more power, Sire, the limit of patience has been reached. There has arrived for us that tremendous moment when death is better than the continuation of intolerable tortures. We have left off working, and we have declared to our masters that we will not begin to work until they comply with our demands. We beg but little; we desire only that without which life is not life, but only hard labour and eternal torture.

---

[1] When Nicholas II ascended the throne and the *zemstvos* timidly petitioned the young Tsar to lessen the rigidity of autocracy, he replied on the occasion of his wedding, January 29, 1895, by reading a statement: "I am aware that in certain meetings of the *zemstvos* voices have lately been raised by persons carried away by absurd illusions as to the participation of the *zemstvo* representatives in matters of internal government. Let all know that, in devoting all my strength to the welfare of the people, I intend to protect the principle of autocracy as firmly and unswervingly as did my late, never-to-be-forgotten father."

The first request which we made was that our masters should discuss our needs with us; but this they refused, on the ground that no right to make this request is recognised by law. They have also declared to be illegal our requests to diminish the working hours to eight hours daily, to agree with us about the prices of our work, to consider our misunderstandings with the inferior administration of the factories, to increase the wages for the labour of women and of general labourers, so that the minimum daily wage should be one rouble per day, to abolish overtime work, to give us medical attention without insulting us, to arrange the workshops so that it might be possible to work there and not find in them death from awful draughts and from rain and snow. All these requests appeared to be, in the opinion of our masters and of the factory and mill administrations, illegal. Every one of our requests was a crime, and the desire to improve our condition was regarded by them as impertinence, and as offensive to them.

Sire! here are many thousands of us, and all are human beings only in appearance. In reality, in us, as in all Russian people, there is not recognised any human right, not even the right of speaking, thinking, meeting, discussing our needs, taking measures for the improvement of our condition. We have been enslaved, and enslaved under the auspices of Thy officials, with their assistance, and with their co-operation. Every one of us who dares to raise a voice in defence of working-class and popular interests is thrown in jail or is sent into banishment. . . .

Sire! we, working-men, have no voice in the expenditure of the enormous amounts raised from us in taxes. We do not know even where and for what is spent the money collected from a beggared people. The people are deprived of the possibility of expressing their desires, and they now demand that they may be allowed to take part in the introduction of taxes and in the expenditure of them. The working-men are deprived of the possibility of organising themselves in unions for the defence of their interests. . . .

Sire! Do not refuse assistance to Thy people. Bring them from the grave of legal oppression, beggary, and ignorance. Give their destiny into their own hands. . . .

The Russian Workers' Petition to Nicholas II,
January 9, 1905.

Distress, deep affliction, overwhelm me at the sight of boys playing bare-footed in the street, of a beggar in rags, a drunken coachman. . . . Tossing a copeck to a beggar woman, I fly from her as if I had done evil. . . . Has a man, after all this, any right to forget himself in art, in knowledge?
BELINSKY: *Russian Literature in* 1844.

Dinner at the "Continental," to commemorate the anniversary of the great reform (the abolition of serfdom in Russia). Tedious and absurd. To dine, drink champagne, make a noise, deliver speeches about the national consciousness, the conscience of the people, freedom and such things, whilst slaves in tail-coats are running round your tables, veritable serfs, and your coachmen wait outside, in the street, in the bitter cold, that is lying to the Holy Spirit.
CHEKHOV: *Diary*.

I did not understand what these sixty-five thousand people in Rostov lived for and by. I knew that Kimry lived by boots, that Tula made samovars and guns, that Odessa was a sea-port, but what our town was, and what it did, I did not know. Great Dvoryansky Street and the two other smartest streets lived on the interest of capital, or on salaries received by officials from the public treasury; but what the other eight streets, which ran parallel for over two miles and vanished beyond the hills, lived upon, was always an insoluble riddle to me. And the way these people lived one is ashamed to describe! No garden, no theatre, no decent band: the public library and the club library were only visited by Jewish youths, so that the magazines and new books lay for months uncut; rich and well-educated people slept in close, stuffy bedrooms on wooden bedsteads infested with bugs; their children were kept in revoltingly dirty rooms called nurseries, and the servants, even the old and respected ones, slept on the floor in the kitchen, covered with rags. On ordinary days the houses smelt of beetroot soup, and on fast days of sturgeon cooked in sunflower oil. The food was not good, and the drinking water was unwholesome. In the town council, at the governor's, at the head priest's, on all sides in private houses, people had been saying for years and years that our town had not a good and cheap water-supply, and that it was necessary to obtain a loan of two hundred thousand from the Treasury for laying on water; very rich people, of whom three dozen could have been counted up in our town, and who at times lost whole estates at cards, drank the polluted water too, and talked all their lives with great excitement of a loan for the water-supply—and I did not understand that; it seemed to me it would have been simpler to take the two hundred thousand out of their own pockets and lay it out on that object.   CHEKHOV.

The Tsarist Government left to the Soviet power a terrible heritage of insanitary conditions. The exceptionally bad material conditions of the working masses of town and country, the police oppression which stifled all public activity, the merciless exploitation of the workers and poorer peasants, the low cultural level of the population and the consequent low sanitary culture, all combined to create a favourable soil for epidemic diseases among the population. The medical organisation was totally incapable of combating epidemic diseases: in 1913, 34 provinces with a rural population of some 80 million had only 2790 medical stations. The medical service was divided up among 11 departments (the departments of War, Means of Communication, Crown Domains, Education, Agriculture, Zemstvos, Municipalities, etc.). Impotent and primitive in quality, the medical service was also miserably inadequate in extent. Large territories (which now form the autonomous regions and republics of Kirghizia, Chuvashia, Uzbekistan, etc.) were almost totally destitute of medical aid. Sorcery and superstition were widespread. All this made a favourable ground for disease, especially for infectious diseases, which took an annual toll of millions of lives.
   N. A. SEMASHKO: *Health Protection in the U.S.S.R.*

There are a great many of us young girls in Russia, unprotected, working as apprentices in different enterprises. Everywhere we are overwhelmed with abuse and fined. . . . More than one girl has come to prostitution through the assistant manager of our factory. If a girl wants to remain decent she is sacked. Every year we have several cases of young girls committing suicide. The reasons? Enslavement, loss of honour, shame.
   Nevsky Star, 1912.

The number of children and juveniles of school age in Russia is over 20 per cent. of the population, but the number of pupils attending school is only 4·7 per cent., i.e. one-fifth of the total number of children! This means that nearly four-fifths of the children and juveniles of Russia are deprived of education! Russia is the only country left in Europe—the only savage country —in which the masses of the people are so robbed of education, enlightenment, and knowledge. LENIN, 1913.

We ought in Russia to give the teacher particularly good conditions, and it ought to be done as quickly as possible. We ought to realise that without a wide education of the people Russia will collapse like a house built of badly baked bricks. A teacher must be an artist, in love with his calling; but with us he is a journeyman, ill-educated, who goes to the village to teach children as though he were going to exile. He is starved, crushed, terrorised by the fear of losing his daily bread. But he ought to be the first man in the village; the peasants ought to recognise him as a paver, worthy of attention and respect; no one should dare to shout at him or humiliate him personally, as with us everyone does—the village constable, the rich shopkeeper, the priest, the rural police commissioner, the school guardian, the councillor, and that official who has won the title of school-inspector but who cares nothing for the improvement of education and only sees that the circulars of his chief are carried out. . . . It is ridiculous to pay in farthings the man who has to educate the people. It is intolerable that he should walk in rags, shiver with cold in damp and draughty schools, catch cold, and about the age of thirty get laryngitis, rheumatism, or tuberculosis. We ought to be ashamed of it. Our teacher, for eight or nine months in the year, lives like a hermit: he has no one to speak a word to; without company, books or amusements, he is growing stupid, and if he invites his colleagues to visit him, then he becomes politically suspect—a stupid word with which crafty men frighten fools. All this is disgusting; it is the mockery of a man who is doing a great and tremendously important work. . . .
CHEKHOV, to Gorky: From *Reminiscences of Tolstoy, Chekhov and Andrev*, by MAXIM GORKY.

It seems to me that we—worn out, stereotyped, banal people —have grown quite mouldy. While we intellectuals are rummaging among old rags and biting each other according to the dear

Russian custom, something is boiling around us. There is a life of which we know nothing. Great events will take us unaware, like sleeping fairies.   CHEKHOV: *Note-Books*.

I see a huge building, in the front wall a narrow door, which is wide open. Beyond it stretches a dismal darkness. Before the high threshold stands a girl—a Russian girl.

The impenetrable darkness is breathing frost, and with the icy breeze from the depth of the building a slow, hollow voice is coming.

"O you! wanting to cross this threshold, do you know what awaits you?"

"I know it," answers the girl.

"Cold, hunger, hatred, derision, contempt, insults, prison, suffering, even death?"

"I know it."

"Complete isolation, alienation from all?"

"I know it. I am ready. I will bear all sorrow and miseries."

"Not only if inflicted by enemies, but by kindred and friends?"

"Yes, even by them."

"Well, are you ready for self-sacrifice?"

"Yes."

"For an anonymous self-sacrifice? You shall die, and nobody, nobody shall know even whose memory is to be honoured."

"I want neither gratitude nor pity. I want no name."

"Are you ready—for a crime?"

The girl bent her head.

"I am ready even for a crime."

The voice paused awhile before renewing its questioning.

"Do you know," it said at last, "that you may lose your faith in what you believe now; that you might come to feel that you were mistaken, and have lost in vain your young life?"

"I know that also. And, nevertheless, I will enter."

"Enter, then!"

The girl crossed the threshold, and a heavy curtain fell behind her.

"A fool!" gnashed some one outside.

"A saint!" answered a voice from somewhere.

    TURGENEV: *The Threshold* (*Verses in Prose*.)[1]

---

[1] This is a poetical epitome of the tragic position of Russians under the Tsar devoted to their country.

Over dull grey wastes of water winds are massing darkening storm-clouds. There, 'twixt clouds and surging sea-waves, proudly soars the Stormy Petrel, darting sheer like jet-black lightning.

Now he skims the foam with wing-tip, now an arrow shooting cloudward, he cries out—and clouds hear gladness in that cry so fierce and daring.

In that crying—thirst for tempest! Might of anger, flame of passion, surety of final triumph hear the storm-clouds in that crying.

Sea-gulls moan in fear of tempest—moan and whirl above the waters, fain to bury deep their terror underneath the surging billows.

Divers also moan in panic, they, denied the joys of battle, fear the raucous blast of thunder.

Foolish penguins hide fat bodies timidly behind the cliff-crags. . . . And alone the Stormy Petrel soars in freedom, proud and dauntless, over surging dark grey sea-foam!

Ever darker, ever lower sink the clouds down to the sea-waves; billows wail, toss ever higher crests to meet the breaking thunder.

Thunder crashes. White with fury, waves are wrangling with the storm-wind. But the wind in hatred seizes herds of waves in ruthless clutches, crashes them against the cliff-crags, shatters solid emerald masses into foamy dust and spraylets.

Prouder cries the Stormy Petrel, darting sheer like jet-black lightning, pierces arrow-like the storm-clouds, razes sea-foam with his pinions.

Now he hovers, like a demon,—black and dauntless tempest-demon, he is mocking, he is sobbing. . . . He is mocking at the storm-clouds, from sheer gladness he is sobbing!

In the thunder—wary demon—he has long ago sensed tiredness, he is sure, no cloud will ever smother up the sun—no cloud!

Winds are whining. . . . Thunder crashing. . . .

Blue with flame the clouds are blazing over dark abysmal waters. Sea-waves catch swift darts of lightning, quench them in their deeps unfathomed. Just like writhing fiery serpents, swift reflections of those lightnings, disappear into the sea-depths.

"Storm! At last the storm is breaking!"

Cries the dauntless petrel soaring 'twixt the sea's roar and lightning; cries the harbinger of triumph.

"Let it break with greater fury!"

    GORKY: *The Song of the Stormy Petrel*[1] (Trans. by Herbert Marshall and R. Magidoff).

[1] This was first published in 1901 when the signs of revolt against the Tsarist régime were manifest. They heralded the Revolution of 1905.

Chapter Two

THE DREAM OF A NEW RUSSIA

RUSSIA, I see thee from my wondrously beautiful, distant abode, I see thee. . . . There is nothing in thee to fascinate, to allure the eye. . . . But what impenetrable, mysterious force draws one to thee? . . . Why does thy melancholy song, floating all over thy width and length from sea to sea, resound unceasingly in the ear? What is in it, in that song? What is it that calls and sobs and clutches at my heart? What are these strains that so poignantly greet me, that go straight to my soul, that throb about my heart? Is it not there, not in thee, that boundless thought should be born since thou art boundless thyself? What a marvellous, radiant expanse, unknown to the earth! Russia!

GOGOL: Dead Souls.

> The living steppe—nothing but rye!
> No castles, no mountains, no sea . . .
> I thank thee, my native land,
> For thy healing spaciousness.
> However fair these foreign lands,
> It is not for them to heal our sorrow
> And drive away a Russian grief.
> . . . A temple of sighs, a temple of mourning,
> This humble temple of my land.
> Go there!
> And Christ will lay His hands upon you
> And with His holy will remove
> The soul's chains, the heart's pain,
> The plague of a conscience ill-at-ease.
> . . . I listened; and like a child was moved,
> And long I sobbed and beat my brow
> Against the old flagstone, praying
> That He might forgive and He might defend me,
> And might bless me with the sign of the cross,
> This God of the oppressed and mournful,
> God of the generations standing
> Before this altar, bare and poor.   NEKRASOV.

Scanty nature of my native land, you are dear to my sad soul! Formerly, in the days of my fleeting spring, the distant shores of other countries enticed me.

And my glowing imagination painted brilliant pictures before me: I saw the transparently blue vault of the heavens, and the crenellated summits of mighty mountains.

Merged in the gold of midday beams, it seemed to me, the myrtle, the planes, and the olive trees called me into the shade of spreading branches, and roses beckoned silently to me.

Those were days when my spirit did not ponder, among the seductions of life, over the aims of existence, and, being frivolous, I only demanded enjoyment from it.

But that time speedily disappeared without a trace—and grief unexpectedly visited me, and much with which my soul was not familiar suddenly became dear to it.

I then abandoned my secret dream of a magic and distant land— and in my country I discovered beauties invisible to the world eye.

Furrowed fields, ears of yellow grain-fields, the speechless, majestic expanse of the steppes, the freshets of broad rivers in the spring, mysteriously rustling oak-forests;

Sacred silence of poor villages, where the labourer, oppressed by misery, prayed to heaven for a new, a better day—the great day of liberty—to rise over him;

I understood you then—and near to my heart suddenly grew the song of my native land, whether in that song was heard deep pining or unrestrained hilarity.

My country, nothing in thee captivates the stranger's eye; but thou art dear by thy stern beauty to him who himself has yearned for freedom and the wide expanse, and whose spirit has borne oppressive fetters.　　　　PLESHCHEEV: *My Country*.

A closer acquaintance with the simple life of the peasant has a healthy effect on the mind. I have long observed that the cultivated classes of society feel much sympathy with this primitive existence, and whether it be described in books or painted on canvas, it has always attracted and influenced men. But how can we explain the shock we feel when brought into actual contact with this primitive life and its labours? Is it rural life itself which is in fault, or did we in our ignorance of it, and our weariness of town life, imagine a completely idyllic existence, and having formed this image we could find it nowhere in the country, and thus disillusionment met us at the first contact?

Life in the open country accustoms us to look at things in a healthy, unexaggerated manner, and we then soon become reconciled to village life. We make allowances for its coarser side, when we consider the ignorance and the natural qualities of human nature; we remind ourselves that the village is still in a primitive state.

But, on the other hand, what a treasure of kindness and of poetry we find among the peasantry. Their blind trust in Providence surprises and touches us; this final idea of all philosophies, this last result of human wisdom and the efforts of the human intellect. This childish simplicity touches us, this giving up a search into the secrets of nature, this joyful, timid acceptance of her gifts with unbounded gratitude. Whose soul has not been stirred while watching this continual daily toil, begun with the sign of the cross, and carried on with such patient unmurmuring labour? When such a scene lies spread before you, and a vast expanse lies here showing the results of this primitive and patient labour, then your idyllic dream, the work of an idle fancy, seems to you to have vanished into nothingness. Look, and you will see that the poetry of real life and work far exceeds all that your idle imagination could picture.

GRIGOROVICH: *The Peasant.*

Away from the cities
I shall go to the fields, to the sun.
From the cup of thine azure skies
Give thy sacrament, O Earth.

There is nothing more prayerful
Than the hermit-huts in the ocean of rye,
When beyond the heated fields of purple
The incense is burnt by the pines.

Again I am a homeless pilgrim;
On the overflowed bank, beyond the river,
The radiant day I shall meet
With free songs of the village.

> Where the earth drinks from the quiet stream
> The fragrance of honey and rye,
> There in the crimson quiver of sunrise,
> My people, with thee I shall unite.
>
> FOMIN: *The Call of the Earth.*

ANYA. I used to think there was no spot on earth so beautiful as our garden.

TROFIMOV. All Russia is our garden.... Think only, Anya, your grandfather, and great-grandfather, and all your ancestors were slave-owners—the owners of living souls—and from every cherry in the orchard, from every leaf, from every trunk there are human creatures looking at you. Cannot you hear their voices? Oh, it is awful! Your orchard is a fearful thing, and when in the evening or at night one walks in the orchard, the old bark on the trees glimmers dimly in the dusk, and the old cherry-trees seem to be dreaming of centuries gone by and are tortured by fearful visions. Yes! We are at least two hundred years behind, we have really gained nothing yet, we have no definite attitude to the past, we do nothing but theorise or complain of depression or drink vodka. It is clear that to begin to live in the present we must first expiate our past, we must break with it; and we can expiate it only by suffering, by extraordinary unceasing labour....

ANYA. The house we live in has long ceased to be our own, and I shall leave it, I give you my word.

TROFIMOV. If you have the house keys, fling them into the well and go away. Be as free as the wind.... I have a foreboding of new life, Anya. I see glimpses of it already.

ANYA. The moon is rising....

TROFIMOV. Yes, the moon is rising. (*Pause.*) Here is the new life—here it comes! It is coming nearer and nearer; already I can hear its footsteps. And if we never see it—if we may never know it—what does it matter? Others will see it after us.   CHEKHOV: Trofimov in *The Cherry Orchard.*

You are crying, my dear mother, my beautiful mother ... you still have your wonderful, pure soul ... come with me, away from here, come. We will plant a new garden, finer than this. You

will see it, and you will understand . . . a deep joy will sink into your soul like the evening sun and you will smile, mother. Come, let's go. CHEKHOV: Anya comforting her mother,
in *The Cherry Orchard*.

A great renewal is about to descend on the whole world through Russian thought, and this will be achieved in less than a hundred years—this is my passionate belief. But in order that this great object may be achieved, it is essential that the *political* right and supremacy of the great Russian race over the whole Slav world should be definitively and incontestably consummated. (And our little Liberals preach the division of Russia into federal states.)
DOSTOEVSKY, in a letter to A. N. Maikov.

Reveal to the Russian the world of Russia; let him find the gold, the treasure hidden from him in the earth! Show him the whole of humanity, rising again and renewed by Russian thought alone, perhaps by the Russian God of Christ, and you will see into what a wise and truthful giant he will grow before the eyes of the astounded world—astounded and dismayed, because it expects of us nothing but the sword, nothing but the sword and violence, because, judging by themselves, the other peoples cannot picture us free from barbarism. . . .
DOSTOEVSKY: Prince Myshkin in *The Idiot*.

We are immoderate, we are an astonishing blend of good and evil; we are lovers of enlightenment and of Schiller, and at the same time we riot in taverns and pull out the beards of our drunken boon-companions . . . we are broad natures, Karamazov natures,—this is my point—capable of accommodating every possible contradiction and of contemplating simultaneously the two infinites, the infinite above us, the infinite of lofty ideals, and the infinite below, the infinite of the lowest and most repulsive degradation . . . we are broad like Mother Russia herself; we find room for everything, we reconcile ourselves to everything.
DOSTOEVSKY: The District Prosecutor in
The Brothers Karamazov.

Life is everywhere life, life in ourselves, not in what is outside us. There will be people near me (in prison), and to be a *man* among people and remain a man for ever, not to be downhearted nor to fall in whatever misfortunes may befall me—this is life; this is the task of life. I have realised this. This idea has entered into my flesh and into my blood. Yes, it's true! The head which was creating, living with the highest life of art, which had realised and grown used to the highest needs of the spirit, that head has already been cut off from my shoulders.

DOSTOEVSKY, in a letter to his brother.

My dear boy, I have never been able to imagine men as boorish and ungrateful. When they are deserted they will stand together more closely and more affectionately; they will hold each other's hands in the knowledge that henceforward they together represent the whole universe. For to fill the place of the lost great idea of immortality men will give to the world, to nature, to their neighbours, to every blade of grass, that overflowing love which they formerly consecrated to the vision of eternal life. So frenziedly will they cherish the earth and its life that gradually they will grow accustomed to seeing in it their beginning and end, and they will cherish it with a special affection, no longer the same as before. They will explore the phenomena of nature and discover unexpected secrets in her, for they will be looking at the world with new eyes, as a lover looks at his mistress. They will come to themselves and hasten to embrace one another, knowing that their days are numbered and that there is nothing else. They will work for one another, each giving his earnings to all and being only too glad to do so. Every child will know that he can find a father or mother in any human creature—for every man and woman will think as he watches the setting sun: To-morrow may be my last day; but what matter?—there will be others here when I am gone, and after them their children. So they will be supported, not by the hope of a meeting beyond the grave, but by the thought that others will replace them on earth who will always love and tremble for one another. They will turn quickly to love to stifle the sorrow that will be deep down in their hearts. They will be bold and fearless themselves but nervous for others, each fearful for the safety and happiness of his neighbour. They will be mutually affectionate without embarrassment and as endearing together as children; when they meet they will regard each other with a searching and meaningful look, a look filled with both love and kindness. DOSTOEVSKY: Versilov in *A Raw Youth*.

What have Russian boys been doing so far, some of them at least? Take this stinking pub, for example, where they meet and sit together in a corner. They have never met before, and when they go out of here they won't see each other again for the next forty years. But what do they talk about the moment that they are here? Nothing but universal problems: Is there a God? Does the immortal soul exist? Those who don't believe in God discuss socialism and anarchism and the reorganisation of mankind on a new pattern, which are the same questions, only tackled from the other way up.
    DOSTOEVSKY: Ivan in *The Brothers Karamazov.*

  The pure-hearted woman of Russia is prevailing over all hindrance and scorn. She is resolutely proclaiming her will to play her part in the affairs of the community and is giving herself to it unselfishly and with self-denial. Within the last decade the Russian man has given way terribly to cupidity, cynicism, materialism, while the woman has retained her faith in the pure idea and the service of it. Her struggle for higher education is revealing her earnestness and tenacity, and affording great examples of her courage.... Russian society will be saved and renewed chiefly by the women of Russia. After the late war, in which the Russian woman revealed herself in all her nobleness, serene and pure, there can be no more doubts about her great destiny. One day at last the age-old prejudice will vanish away and "barbarian" Russia will give due place to the Russian warrior's mother and sister, the self-denying martyr to the Russian man.... In the women of Russia we place all our hopes, from them will come the spiritual regeneration and the moral uplifting of our society.... The Russian woman has herself taken the place that is due to her, has herself climbed the steps as far as she has been allowed to go. She has proved what heights she can attain and what she can achieve.... In the land of Russia are many women with noble, generous hearts, swelling with eagerness for social work and self-sacrifice.
    DOSTOEVSKY: *Author's Diary,* 1877.

  In her (the heroine in Goncharov's novel *Oblomov*) we perceive the suggestion of a new Russian life; from her we may expect words that will scatter and burn up inertia and the sense of futility. Personal family cannot satisfy her . . . a tranquil and happy life frightens her . . . like a muddy abyss that threatens to suck you in and swallow you. DOBROLUBOV.

Not a single nation has ever been founded on principles of science or reason. . . .

Science and reason have from the beginning of time played a secondary and subordinate part in the life of nations; so will it be till the end of time. Nations are built up and moved by another force which sways and dominates them, the origin of which is unknown and inexplicable: that force is the force of an insatiable desire to go on to the end, though at the same time it denies that end. It is the force of the persistent assertion of one's own existence and a denial of death. It's the spirit of life, as the Scriptures call it, the "river of living water," the drying up of which is threatened in the Apocalypse. It's the aesthetic principle, as the philosophers call it, the ethical principle with which they identify it, "the seeking for God" as I call it more simply. The object of every national movement in every people and at every period of its existence is only the seeking for its god, who must be its own god, and the faith in Him as the only true one. God is the synthetic personality of the whole people, taken from its beginning to its end.

There never has been a nation without a religion, that is, without an idea of good and evil. Every people has its own conception of good and evil, and its own good and evil. ...

Reason has never had power to define good and evil, or even to distinguish between them even approximately; on the contrary, it has always mixed them up in a disgraceful and pitiful way; science has even given the solution by the fist. This is particularly characteristic of the half-truths of science, the most terrible scourge of humanity, unknown till this century and worse than plague, famine or war. A half-truth is a despot such as has never been in the world before. A despot that has its priests and slaves, a despot to whom all do homage with love and superstition hitherto inconceivable, before which science itself cringes and trembles in a shameful way.

DOSTOEVSKY: Shatov in *The Possessed*.

I reduce God to an attribute of nationality? . . . On the contrary,

I raise the people to God. And has it ever been otherwise? Every people is only a people so long as it has its own god and excludes all other gods on earth irreconcilably; so long as it believes that by its god it will conquer and drive out of the world all other gods. Such, from the beginning of time, has been the belief of all great nations, all anyway who have been specially remarkable, all who have been leaders of humanity. ... A really great people can never accept a secondary part in the history of Humanity, nor even one of the first, but will have the first part. A nation which loses this belief ceases to be a nation. But there is only one truth, and therefore only a single one out of the nations can have the true God, only one nation is "god-bearing," that's the Russian people. ...

DOSTOEVSKY: Shatov in *The Possessed*.

By God I understand one's untamable yearning for self-perfection, for truth and justice. Therefore even a bad man is better than a good book. It is so, isn't it? I deeply believe that there is nothing better than man on earth, the rest is a point of view. I have always been and shall be a man-worshipper, only I cannot express it with adequate force.

GORKY, to Count Leo Tolstoy.

> Go to the humiliated,
> Go to the hurt,
> Follow their steps.   NEKRASOV.

I see the Russian people as exceptionally fantastically gifted, original. Even fools in Russia are foolish in an original way, in a peculiar manner, and as to loafers—these are positively geniuses. I am sure that by their fancifulness, by the unexpectedness of their twists, by the significant form, so to speak, of their thoughts and feelings, the Russian people are the most grateful material for an artist.   GORKY: *On Russia*.

What fine people they are, Nilovna! I mean the young workers. How sturdy, how sensitive, what a passion for knowledge! You have only to look at them and you can't help feeling certain that Russia one day will be the foremost democracy in the world.

GORKY: *Mother*.

We venture to make the assertion, which to many at present may seem strange, but which will be in a few years only too evident: Western Europe is on the high road to ruin! We Russians, on the contrary, are young and fresh and have taken no part in the crimes of Europe. We have a great mission to fulfil. Our name is already inscribed on the tablets of victory; the victories of science, art and faith await us on the ruins of toftering Europe. ODOYEVSKY.

The idea of a social revolution is a European idea, but the conclusion should not be drawn from this that the Western peoples are the only ones called to realise it. . . . In fact, should socialism prove unable to re-establish decaying society and complete its destiny—Russia will complete it. . . . The revolutionary idea of socialism can become with us an idea of the people. Whereas in Europe socialism is taken for the phantom of disorder and terror, with us, on the contrary, it appears a prophetic vision of the future development of our people. HERZEN.

Our poor country will be the one which will give humanity a new word. Yes, the duty of the Russian is indubitably bound up with all Europe, with the whole world. To be truly *Russian* means to be the brother of all, a universal man. . . . To the true Russian the destiny of all Europe, of every foreign nation, is as near to his heart as the destiny of Russia.

The Russian soul, the genius of the Russian people, is probably better fitted than any other to shelter the idea of world-wide unity and brotherhood.

DOSTOEVSKY, at the Pushkin Celebrations.

Our people will shine forth in the world, and all men will say: "The stone which the builders rejected has become the head stone of the corner. . . ."

DOSTOEVSKY: Father Zossima in
The Brothers Karamazov.

Whosoever would be great in the Kingdom of God, let him be the servant of all. That is how I understand the Russian destiny in its *ideal*. DOSTOEVSKY: *The Journal.*

I believe in Russia, I believe in the body of Christ.... I believe that Christ will come again in Russia.
                    DOSTOEVSKY: Shatov in *The Possessed*.

The only task acceptable to Russia is to be a society based upon the highest moral principles.... All that has for basis self-denial and self-sacrifice is included in one word: *Christianity*. Only one task is possible for Russia: to become the most Christian of human societies. That is why she has always remained and will remain indifferent to all that is petty, conventional, and accidental.
                                                    KHOMYAKOV.

Have you not noticed that Russia does not see her salvation in mysticism or pietism but in the achievements of civilisation, of enlightenment, of humanitarianism?... The Orthodox Church has always been the supporter of despotism and the whip; but why did you bring Christ into all this? What have you found in common between Him and any other thing, and particularly the Orthodox Church? He was the first to proclaim to men the teaching of freedom, equality, and brotherhood, and in His martyrdom He sealed the truth of His doctrine.
                            BELINSKY, in a letter to Gogol.

When I hear that the Church is perishing, or going to perish, because of this, that, or the other, that is being done by men in power, it reminds me of the story of the boy and the eagle. A little boy rushed one day into the parlour to his father, crying excitedly, "Father, an eagle, an eagle in the kitchen! Come quickly and rescue it, for the woman cook will not let it go."

And the father said, "Peace, my boy. If it were really an eagle it would fly away, nor could a woman cook stand for a moment in its way. Believe me, it is only a hen."

When I hear that the Church of Christ, which, if it exists at all, is real, eternal, spiritual, and Divine, is going to perish because of what the Government is doing, I think of that eagle caged in the kitchen by the woman cook, and I say to myself, "Peace, peace. It is no eagle, it is only a hen."   TOLSTOY: *My Religion*.

All have sinned before all men in all things. Each of us bears the guilt of all and of everything on earth, not merely the general

world guilt, but each one individually for all and each on this earth.   DOSTOEVSKY: Father Zossima in
The Brothers Karamazov.

The Russian wanderer needs the happiness of all men wherein to find his own peace.   DOSTOEVSKY: *The Journal.*

. . . Tormented by slavery, sad and dejected,
In alien lands all unknown and rejected,
I live but to utter that name long neglected;
Across the wide seas and the countries that sever,
One word to my motherland calling for ever—
      "Liberty! Liberty!"

It came o'er the waves to the place of my wailing,
'Mid silence, at midnight—a rumour assailing
My senses, through darkness and tempest prevailing—
I hear it! my heart can abandon it never,
That voice from my country that sounds on for ever—
      "Liberty! Liberty!"

My heart, long accustomed to doubt in its yearning,
Sprang up as it throbbed with new ecstasy burning
Like a bird from its cage to the wide world returning.
It sings a farewell to its prison for ever,
While solemn and clear rings the note of endeavour—
      "Liberty! Liberty!"

In the dreams I behold, with the snows that surround him,
The peasant, long-bearded—the glad news has found him;
He shakes from his great limbs the fetters that bound him,
And speaks the glad word, the unchanging for ever
Eternal—the future can silence it never—
      "Liberty! Liberty!"

But if there should chance—if there came any reason—
To fear for that Liberty, let her in season
Cry out, and I fly to encounter the treason;
And if from that uttermost struggle I never
Return, I can call with the cry "Live for ever,
      "Liberty! Liberty!"

It may be I die with strangers around me,
Yet hope and belief in the future have found me.
O comrade! ere Death in his shackles has bound me,
That name do thou whisper, to last me for ever,
That name—of our love, of our faith and endeavour—
"Liberty! Liberty!"
OGAREV: *To Iskander.*[1]

Political freedom is needed by the Russian proletariat, as pure air is needed for healthy respiration . . . but the needed political liberty the Russian proletariat can conquer only for itself. The Russian proletariat will cast off the yoke of autocracy in order to continue, with still greater energy, its work against capitalism and the bourgeoisie up to the complete victory of socialism.
From a Manifesto.

An economic Revolution not only may, but *must* come in Russia.   TOLSTOY: *Diary.*

O, proud falcon! In battle with enemies you bled to death . . . but time will come and drops of your fiery blood will kindle like sparks in the darkness of life. Many hearts will be set afire with the mad thirst for freedom, for light. We sing a song to the madness of the brave.   GORKY: *The Song of the Falcon.*

National revolution must not be taken as having anything in common with, or to be in any way modelled on, the movement which is common to class-warfare in Western Europe. This movement always stops short when property, tradition, and so-called civilising, moral principles are in danger; and up to the present time its action has been confined to replacing one political system by another. The people's salvation must depend on setting in motion a revolution which will root out the State system in its entirety and completely destroy class and governmental traditions in Russia.   NETCHAYEV: *Catechism.*

. . . all ties with the past must be broken, and parents, friends, studies and social position forsaken: a man's whole life must be given up to the service of the masses. You say that, as a revolu-

---

[1] Pseudonym of Herzen.

tionary, you may be sentenced to hard labour? But have not the people to whom we are henceforth going to devote our lives been, in a sense, sentenced to hard labour? Have they not worked even harder than convicts for their miserable crusts of bread? You fear the prison-chains? But is the nation free, unfettered? No, it is enslaved by poverty just as we are enslaved by the most wretched of all tyrannies.

LAVROV: *Historical Letters*, an appeal to the Russian intellectuals to turn to the people.

The rôle of the proletariat in history is as revolutionary as the moujik's is conservative. For millions of years oriental despotism supported by the moujik has remained unshaken; in a relatively short space of time the proletariat has shaken the whole foundations of Western European society, and in Russia its development and political education is proceeding far more rapidly than was the case in the West. In Russia the proletariat, like the giant of the fairy-story, is literally growing larger and stronger every hour. In ten years or so it has been changed out of all recognition.

PLEKHANOV: *The Socialist's Aims in the Fight Against Famine in Russia.*

Forward, without fear of doubt, to the valiant deed, my friends! I have already seen the dawn of the holy redemption in the skies!

Courage! We will take each other's hands and boldly will move onward—and let our union grow and be strong under the banner of science!

We will chastise the priests of sin and falsehood with the word of truth—and we will awaken the sleeping from their sleep and will lead the host to battle.

We will not build an idol for ourselves, either upon earth or in heaven; we will not fall before it in the dust for all the gifts and benefits of the world.

We will proclaim the teaching of Love to the poor and to the rich—and for it we will endure persecution, forgiving our malevolent enemies.

Blessed is he who has exhausted his life in a sanguinary struggle, in heavy cares; he has not, like an indolent and tricky slave, buried his talent in the ground!

Let holy truth burn as a guiding star for us—and, believe me, a noble voice will not resound in vain in the world.

Hearken, then, O brothers, to the word of a brother, as long as we are full of youthful strength! Forward, forward—and without returning, whatever fate may have in store for us!

PLESHCHEEV: *Forward.*

The Russian people have been wedded to Liberty. Let us trust that out of this union new strong men will be born in our land, which is exhausted both physically and spiritually. Let us firmly believe that in the Russian man will flare up in a bright flame the forces of his reason and will, forces that have been extinguished and crushed by the age-long yoke of a police régime.

GORKY: *Thoughts out of Season.*

Brothers, the time has come for us to forswear this life that is full of greed, rancour, and darkness; this life where people are violated, where there is no place for us, where we are not considered as human beings.

GORKY: *Mother.*

If all of us who live in towns and villages, all of us without exception, agreed to divide among ourselves the labour spent by mankind for the satisfaction of physical needs, then each one of us would perhaps have to work not more than two or three hours a day. Imagine that we all, rich and poor, work only three hours a day, and the rest of our time is free ... all of us giving that leisure to the sciences and arts. Just as the peasants mend the road collectively, so all collectively, the whole community, would seek after truth and the meaning of life—and, I am certain of it, the truth would be found soon, man would rid himself of the continuous, tormenting, oppressive fear of death, and even of death itself.

CHEKHOV: *The House with the Mezzanine.*

A new age is dawning, the people are marching on us all. A powerful, health-giving storm is gathering; it is drawing near, soon it will be upon us, and it will drive out laziness, indifference, prejudice against work, and rotten dullness from our society.

CHEKHOV: Baron Tuzenbach in
The Three Sisters.

Autocracy is an obsolete form of government which may suit the demands of people cut off from the world somewhere in Central Africa but not the demands of the Russian people, who are growing ever more and more enlightened ... and therefore that form of government and the Orthodoxy bound up with it can only be upheld (as is now being done) by violence. Measures of coercion make it possible to oppress, but not to govern, a people. To be able to do that, it is necessary first of all to let them express their wishes and needs and, having heard them, to fulfil those which respond to the demands not of one class or section but of the majority—the mass of the working people.

Those demands are: the abolition of special laws making pariahs of the peasants; freedom to migrate; freedom of education; freedom of conscience; and above all, the whole 100 million people will say with one voice that they desire freedom to use the land—that is to say, the abolition of private property in land.

TOLSTOY.

Sire, no conspiracy has been formed by any party, revolutionary or otherwise; no plot has been laid against your person or against autocratic rule by any group whatsoever in the Socialist Party: it is Russian society as a whole which is conspiring to destroy the entire existing régime.

TOLSTOY, to the Emperor Nicholas II.

Property to-day is the root of all evil: of the sufferings of those who possess it or are deprived of it, the reproaches of conscience of those who misuse it, and the danger of collision between those who have a superfluity and those who are in need.

States and Governments intrigue and go to war for property: the banks of the Rhine, land in Africa, China, or the Balkan Peninsula. Bankers, traders, manufacturers, and landowners work, scheme, and torment themselves and others for property; officials and artisans struggle, cheat, oppress, and suffer for the sake of property; our Law Courts and police defend property; and our penal settlements and prisons, and all the horrors of our so-called repression of crime, exist on account of property.

TOLSTOY.

So I came to the conclusion that our wealth is the cause of the misery of the poor.

I see that the life of the working people demands strain and labour (as all natural life necessarily does), and that many working folk, especially the old men, the women, and the children, simply perish from intense work while the life of the non-workers reaches a degree of security which in olden times people only dreamed of in fairy-tales. We have reached the condition of the owner of the purse with the inexhaustible rouble: that is to say, a position in which a man is not merely freed from the law of labour for the maintenance of life, but is able without labour to use all life's bounties and hand on to his children, or to whom he likes, that purse with the inexhaustible rouble. . . . I see that the ideal of an industrious life has been replaced by the ideal of an inexhaustible purse. . . . I sit on a man's neck, weighing him down and making him carry me, and yet assure myself and others that I pity him greatly and wish to ease his lot by all possible means—except by getting off his back! . . .

And I came to feel that in money itself, in the very possession of money, there is something evil and immoral; and that money itself, and the fact that I possess it, is one of the chief causes of the evils I saw around me—and I asked myself, What is money?
TOLSTOY.

I understand that man, besides living for his personal welfare, must serve the welfare of others, as bees do . . . and that man's unhappiness comes from the slavery in which some men hold others. I understand that the slavery of our times is caused by violence; by the army-system, the monopolisation of land, and the exaction of money. And having understood the meaning of these three instruments of the new slavery, I could not but wish to free myself from using them. TOLSTOY.

I put the question to him [Tolstoy], "Suppose the Emperor were to ask you what he should do; what would you say?"

He was silent for a time, then he said, "I am praying to God to give me wisdom to make the right answer."

Then, after another pause, he said, "If you ask me to imagine such an incredible thing, then I would say:

Nationalise the land.

Declare absolute liberty of conscience.

And establish the liberty of the Press.

If these three things are done, all the rest would come right.'" WILLIAM T. STEAD, to Tolstoy.

These millions of Russians, able to read, stand before us like hungry jackdaws with open mouths and say to us: "Gentlemen writers of our native land, throw into these mouths literary food worthy of yourselves and of us; write for us, who hunger for words, and free us from those penny-dreadfuls and the rubbish of the market." The simple honest Russian folk deserve that we should respond to their call. I have thought much about this, and to the best of my ability have decided to make an effort in that direction. TOLSTOY, to Danilevsky.

"You will agree with me," the stranger says, "that the duty of literature is to aid man in understanding himself, to raise his faith in himself, to develop his longing for truth; to combat what is bad in men; to find what is good in them, and to wake up in their souls shame, anger, courage; to do everything, in short, to render men strong in a noble sense of the word, and capable of inspiring their lives with the holy spirit of beauty. . . . It seems to me, we need once more to have dreams, pretty creations of our fancy and visions, because the life we have built up is poor in colour, is dim and dull. . . . Well, let us try; maybe imagination will help man to rise for a moment above the earth and find on it his true place, which he has lost."

GORKY: *The Reader.*

If man were completely deprived of the ability to dream, if he could never look ahead and mentally conceive in an entire and completed picture the results of the work he is only just commencing, then I cannot imagine what stimulus there would be to induce man to undertake and complete extensive and fatiguing tasks in the sphere of art, science and practical work. . . . If there is some connection between dreams and life, then all is well.

PISAREV.

"Can you," the *Reader* goes on to ask, "create for men ever so small an illusion that has the power to raise them? No! All of you teachers of the day take more than you give, because you speak only about faults—you see only those. But there must also be good qualities in men: you possess some, don't you? ... Don't you notice that, owing to your continual efforts to define and to classify them, the virtues and the vices have been entangled like two balls of black and white thread which have become grey by taking colour from each other? ... I doubt whether God has sent you on earth. If He had sent messengers, He would have chosen stronger men than you are. He would have lighted in them the fire of a passionate love of life, of truth, of men.

"Nothing but everyday life, everyday life, only everyday people, everyday thoughts and events!" the same pitiless *Reader* continues. "When will you, then, speak of 'the rebel spirit,' of the necessity of a new birth of the spirit? Where is, then, the calling to the creation of a new life? Where the lessons of courage? Where the words which would give wings to the soul?

"Confess, you don't know how to represent life so that your pictures of it shall provoke in a man a redemptive spirit of shame and a burning desire of creating new forms of life. ... Can you accelerate the pulsation of life? Can you inspire it with energy, as others have done?

"I see many intelligent men round about me, but few noble ones among them, and these few are broken and suffering souls. I don't know why it should be so, but so it is: the better the man, the cleaner and the more honest his soul; the less energy he has, the more he suffers and the harder is his life. ... But although they suffer so much from feeling the want of something better, they have not the force to create it.

"One thing more," said my strange interlocutor after an interval. "Can you awake in man a laughter full of the joy of life and at the same time elevating to the soul? Look, men have quite forgotten good wholesome laughter!

"The sense of life is not in self-satisfaction. After all, man is better than that. The sense of life is in the beauty and the force of striving towards some aim; every moment of one's being ought to have its higher aim. Wrath, hatred, shame, loathing, and finally a grim despair—these are the levers by means of which you may destroy everything on earth. What can you do to awake a thirst for life when you only whine, sigh, moan, or coolly point out to man that he is nothing but dust?

"Oh, for a man, firm and loving, with a burning heart and a powerful all-embracing mind. In the stuffy atmosphere of shameful silence his prophetic words would resound like an alarm-bell, and perhaps the mean souls of the living dead would shiver!"

GORKY: *The Reader.*

We are marching in a compact group along a precipitous and difficult path, firmly holding each other by the hand. We are surrounded on all sides by enemies, and are under their almost constant fire. We have combined voluntarily, precisely for the purpose of fighting the enemy, and not to retreat into the adjacent marsh, whose inhabitants, from the very outset, have reproached us for having chosen the path of struggle and not the path of conciliation. LENIN: *What is to be done.*

They [the working people] saw it possible that even under a free Government, if it fell into the hands of other social classes, they might still continue to starve.... The Russian workman is revolutionary, but he is neither violent, dogmatic, nor unintelligent. He is ready for barricades, but he has studied them, and alone of the workers of the world he has learned about them from actual experience. He is ready and willing to fight his oppressor, the capitalist class, to a finish. But he does not ignore the existence of other classes. He merely asks that the other classes take one side or the other in the bitter conflict that draws near.... WILLIAM WALLING: *Russia's Message.*

1. The Russian revolutionary movement, which was faced with carrying out tasks of a bourgeois and democratic order, found the bourgeoisie incapable of taking the lead. This bourgeois revolution, which from its inception had been forsaken by the bourgeoisie, would be enabled to attain its object, thanks to the proletariat, which would assume the leadership of the peasants in revolt against the feudal system.

2. The main problem was the agrarian question.

3. The peasant revolution, carried out under proletarian leadership, was to sweep away the remnants of feudalism and prepare the way for the class-struggle of the proletariat and peasantry

against the bourgeoisie. What was required, therefore, was a *revolutionary, democratic dictatorship of the proletariat and peasantry* in order to root out completely all vestiges of feudal bondage.

LENIN, at a Congress of the Bolsheviks in London, 1905.

The peculiarity of the Russian Revolution consisted in the fact that while from a social standpoint it was middle-class and democratic, it was proletarian in its choice of weapons. It was middle-class and democratic because the democratic Republic was its immediate aim, which it sought to achieve with its own strength. It sought to achieve the eight-hour day, the confiscation of the vast estates of the nobility—in a word, all that the middle-class Revolution in France in 1792-3 had in great part accomplished. At the same time, the Russian Revolution was proletarian not only in the sense that the proletariat formed the advance-guard of the Revolution and gave it its leaders, but also because that specially proletarian weapon—the strike—was the chief means used to stir up the masses and was the outstanding characteristic of the wave-like progression of the decisive events.

LENIN, 1905.

> Trust not the days of calm, of pause and silence,
> Colourless, wearisome and bitter as deceit!
> While the open wounds still bleed
> The past will not die, no indeed. . . .
> But through death-like fog it will lure into the distance.
> Oh, hast thou guessed
> How in the stifled peace of homeless poverty,
> In the iron gnashing of wakeful factory,
> And in the crowd, hiding old dreams and distress,
> The anger and might of the enslaved people had ripened?
> Oh, hast thou heard
> From disastrous conflagrations, from desolate fields,
> From cemeteries overgrown with hungry crosses,
> From heavens o'ercast with the sadness of brothers' tears,
> The approaching breath of threatening storms?
> Trust not the days of calm, of pause and silence;
> They are deceitful, like a dream at twilight.

> Under the sacrificial ashes the past did not die. . . .
> The people is not conquered;
> In prisons it sharpens the sacred swords. . . .
>
> BOGDANOV: *The Past*.[1]

Is the emotion of national pride foreign to the Greater Russian class-conscious proletariat? Certainly not. We love our language and our native land. It is we who strive most strenuously to uplift her [Greater Russia's] workers, i.e. nine-tenths of her population, to living the class-conscious existence of class-conscious Socialists. It is we who are most distressed by beholding our native country subjected to the violence and oppression of Tsarist hangmen, landowners, and capitalists. We are proud that this violation should have met with resistance in our midst in the heart of Greater Russia . . . that the large Russian working class has organised a powerful revolutionary Party out of the masses, and that the peasant in Greater Russia has at the same time begun to become democratic and to free himself from the priests and the landowners.

We are filled with national pride, and it is for that reason especially that we regard with a peculiar hatred our past of serfdom . . . our present serfdom. . . . A nation cannot itself be free whilst it oppresses other peoples—such was the teaching of the great representatives of logical Democracy in the nineteenth century, Marx and Engels, who have become the teachers of the revolutionary proletariat. And we Greater Russian workmen, because we are filled with national pride, want to see a free and independent, a democratic and republican and proud Greater Russia whose relations with its neighbours shall be inspired by the humanitarian principle of equality and not by the servile principle of prior or exclusive rights degrading to every great nation.

LENIN, 1914.

It seems to me that a new era is approaching. Having passed beyond the psychological dialectic of Dostoevsky and absorbed from it its finest essence, its passion, its enthusiasm, the man of to-day begins to feel himself set on a new road. He begins to see the one-sidedness of the individualistic cult, he begins to

---

[1] Here the poet reminds his countrymen of the reaction resulting from the revolution of 1905.

gravitate towards the social ideal, to perceive the bond which unites him with humanity. He is no longer inclined to call it commonplace; he fixes his eyes, not on its banality but on its sufferings, on its aspiration towards the truth, its indefeasible right to the perfecting of its earthly life and to the free poetry of heaven. A new man is being born whose new and single will is bent towards life, but who acts under the impulse of a conscious, individual religion. And this new man, for the clothing with flesh of his lofty ideas, takes again into his hand that ancient but trusty instrument—solidarity with society and with humanity. And he, this new man, will cause a new wave of energy to flow through literature, not a one-sided analytical creation in the province of personal psychology, but a synthetic creation in which personality, with all the riches of its psychological and philosophical constitution and its manifold needs, shall appear as the living tabernacle of a mighty organism.

A. VOLYNSKY, 1916.

> I believe, I do believe: there is happiness.
> The sun has not yet set.
> Like a red prayer-book are the skies
> Which predict the glad tidings.
> I believe, I do believe: there is happiness.
>
> Ring and peal, thou golden Rus!
> Blow, thou turbulent wind!
> Blest is he who looked with cheer
> Upon thy pastoral sadness.
> Ring and peal, thou golden Rus!
>
> I love the rumble of stormy seas
> And the glitter of stars on the waves.
> The blessed suffering,
> And the blessing people . . .
> I love the rumble of stormy seas.

ESSENIN: *I Believe.*

Chapter Three

THE BIRTH OF SOVIET RUSSIA

It must be understood that the structure of the Russian soul is all its own and completely different from that of Westerners. The more penetrating minds of the West realise this well enough, and are attracted by the puzzle it presents. The Russian East is a huge world, as big as western Europe and all its peoples put together. It is a plain of vast extent, with no strongly marked outline or landmarks; there is neither the confused mass of mountains and valleys nor anything defining the particular shape of any region. And the life of Russia flows along the infinitude of her plains. The geography of the land coincides with the geography of her soul, a symbolic expression of its spirit. The evenness, the unending distances, the indefiniteness of the features of the Russian earth embody the nature of the Russian man and typify similar qualities in his soul. It is not a matter of chance that such-and-such a people lives in such-and-such a land, amid such-and-such natural surroundings: there is an inward bond between them; the nature of a countryside is determined by the people who live in it. Everywhere on the face of the earth can be felt the difficulty man has had to conquer it, to give it form, to bring it under cultivation. In Russia man is dominated by the land and its elements, and indiscipline is common to both. The soul is drawn to infinite flat distances and is lost in them; it cannot bear to live within the clearly marked frontiers of a differentiated culture and submit to an order which it does not find in its physical surroundings. The soul of the European is a castle fortified by a religious and cultural discipline; that of the Russian is apocalyptic and fluid by "build" and inclination, ever gliding towards the beckoning horizon, especially to that far one which seems to hide the end of the world.

Nicholas Berdyaev.

The war has created such an immense crisis, has so strained the material and moral forces of the people, has dealt such blows at the modern social organisation, that humanity finds itself faced by an alternative: either it perishes, or it entrusts its fate to the most revolutionary class for the swiftest and most radical transition to a superior method of production.

Owing to a number of historical causes—the greater backwardness of Russia, the unusual hardships incurred by her because of the war, the utter rottenness of Tsardom and the extreme tenacity of the traditions of 1905—the revolution broke out in Russia earlier than in other countries. The result of the revolution has been that the political system of Russia has in a few months caught up with that of the advanced countries.

But that is not enough. The war is inexorable, it puts the alternative with ruthless severity: either perish, or overtake and outstrip the advanced countries economically as well.

LENIN, before the October Revolution.

Three external circumstances made the victory of the proletarian revolution possible. First, the fact that it opened in the middle of a desperate conflict between the two great imperialistic groups consisting of England and France on the one hand and Germany and Austria on the other. Preoccupied by this war to the death, these groups could not pay any attention to the October Revolution. Secondly, owing to the fact that the October Revolution occurred in a country waging an imperialist war, the working masses were forced to a proletarian revolution as providing the only means of escape. Thirdly, the fact that the war had created a revolutionary spirit in Europe. These are the three external circumstances. But in addition various internal circumstances combined to promote the Revolution. First, the fact that it was supported by the working classes. Secondly, that it was supported by the war-weary soldiers. Thirdly, that it was led by a Party, the Bolsheviks, which owed its strength not only to its experience and discipline but also to its connection with the working masses. Fourthly, because the opponents of the October Revolution could be easily identified, consisting as they did of more or less feeble Russian bourgeoisie, landowners utterly demoralised by peasant risings, and Mensheviks and Social-Revolutionaries rendered completely bankrupt by their support of the war. Fifthly, the leaders of the October Revolution had at their disposal huge districts of a young State, where they could manœuvre as they chose. Sixthly, in their fight with the enemy the leaders of the October Revolution had at their disposal adequate supplies of raw material, foodstuffs, etc.

STALIN: *The Way to the October Revolution.*

A decisive victory of the revolution over Tsardom is the revolutionary-democratic dictatorship of the proletariat and the peasantry. . . . And such a victory will be precisely a dictatorship, i.e. it must inevitably rely on military force, on the arming of the masses, on an uprising, and not on institutions of one kind or another, established in a "lawful" or "peaceful" way. It can be only a dictatorship, for the realisation of the changes which are urgently and absolutely indispensable for the proletariat and the peasantry will call forth the desperate resistance of the landlords, of the big bourgeoisie, and of Tsardom. Without a dictatorship it is impossible to break down that resistance and to repel the counter-revolutionary attempts. But of course it will be a democratic, not a Socialist dictatorship. It will not be able (without a series of intermediary stages of revolutionary development) to affect the foundations of capitalism. At best it may bring about a radical redistribution of landed property in favour of the peasantry, establish consistent and full democracy, including the formation of a republic, eradicate all the oppressive features of Asiatic bondage, not only in village but also in factory life, lay the foundation for a thorough improvement in the position of the workers and for a rise in their standard of living, and—last but not least—carry the revolutionary conflagration into Europe. Such a victory will by no means as yet transform our bourgeois revolution into a Socialist revolution; the democratic revolution will not directly overstep the bounds of bourgeois social and economic relationships; nevertheless, the significance of such a victory for the future development of Russia and of the whole world will be immense. Nothing will raise the revolutionary energy of the world proletariat so much, nothing will shorten the path leading to its complete victory to such an extent, as this decisive victory of the revolution that has now started in Russia.

LENIN: *Problems of the Revolution.*

The capitalists . . . seeing that the position of the Government was untenable, resorted to a method which since 1848 has been for decades practised by the capitalists in order to befog, divide, and finally overpower the working class. This method is the so-called "Coalition Ministry" composed of bourgeois and of renegades from the Socialist camp.

In those countries where political freedom and democracy have existed side by side with the revolutionary movement of the workers—for example, in England and France—the capitalists make use of this subterfuge, and very successfully too. The "Socialist" leaders, upon entering the Ministries, invariably prove mere figure-heads, puppets, simply a shield for the capitalists, a tool with which to defraud the workers. The "democratic" and "republican" capitalists in Russia set in motion this very same scheme. The Socialist Revolutionaries and Mensheviki fell victim to it, and on June 1st a "Coalition" Ministry, with the participation of Tchernov, Tseretelli, Skobeliev, Avksentiev, Savinkov, Zarundy, and Nikitin, became an accomplished fact. . . .

LENIN: *Problems of the Revolution.*

By the Grace of God, We, Nicholas II, Emperor of all the Russias, Tsar of Poland, Grand Duke of Finland, etc. . . . to all our faithful subjects, be it known:

At this time when a vast struggle is taking place against a foreign enemy, who for the past three years has endeavoured to enslave our country, God has seen good to subject Russia to a new and terrible trial. Internal troubles threaten to have a fatal repercussion on the progress of this war. The destiny of Russia, the honour of our heroic army, the happiness of the people, the whole future of our dear country requires that the war be carried through at all cost to a victorious end.

Our cruel enemy is making his final effort and the day approaches when our valiant army, acting in concert with our glorious allies, will finally overthrow him.

In these times, when Russia's very existence is being decided, our conscience bids us to facilitate the close union of our people and the organisation of all its forces in order to bring about the rapid realisation of victory.

That is why, in common with the Duma, we think that we are right to abdicate from the throne of the Russian State and lay down the supreme power.

Unwilling to part from our well-loved son, we bequeath our heritage to our brother, Michael Alexandrovitch, and will give him our benediction when the time arrives for him to ascend the throne. We beseech him to rule in close union with the Nation's representatives who sit in the legislative assemblies, and to take an inviolable oath before them in the name of this beloved country.

We appeal to all the loyal sons of Russia, we beg them to carry out their holy, patriotic duty by obeying the Tsar, and, together with the country's representatives, to lead the Russian State along the paths of prosperity and glory.

May God help Russia! NICHOLAS.
NICHOLAS II: Proclamation, 1917.

The poison of insult and the bile of torment
Oppressed our souls like lead.
Raising our arms toward the skies
Our grievous bondage we cursed.

We have waited. There will rise the dawn,
And disperse the darkness of our native land.
And we shall be happier and warm
In the rainbow-tinted glitter of spring.

We waited, too long we waited
Under the yoke of darkness and dread;
We prayed, complained, and wept
And froze in winter's cold.

And then what? Of a sudden, like a magic dream,
A dream of May flowers,
Came to us with healing power
Dazzlingly beautiful Freedom.

Young, clad in gold,
With a wreath of lilies and roses;
With love, ineffable caresses,
And with a palm of peace in her hand.

Darkness is gone, the distance shines,
And boundless space is open;
Sadness and grief are forgotten,
And hearts and souls rejoice.

NECHAYEV: *Freedom.*

My knowledge of Lenin's revolutionary activities since the end of the 'nineties, and especially after 1901, after the appearance of *Iskra*, had convinced me that in Lenin we had a man of extraordinary calibre. I did not regard him as a mere leader of the Party, but as its actual founder, for he alone understood the inner essence and urgent needs of our Party. When I compared him with the other leaders of our Party, it always seemed to me that he was head and shoulders above his colleagues—Plekhanov, Martov, Axelrod and the others: that, compared with them, Lenin was not just one of the leaders, but a leader of the highest rank, a mountain eagle, who knew no fear in the struggle, and who boldly led the Party forward along the unexplored paths of the Russian revolutionary movement. . . .

I first became acquainted with Lenin in 1903. True, it was not a personal acquaintance; it was maintained by correspondence. But it made an indelible impression upon me, one which has never left me throughout all my work in the Party. . . .

STALIN, on Lenin.

For me personally Lenin is not only the marvellously perfect incarnation of a will directed toward a goal which no one before him has dared to face practically. For me he is one of the "just" men, one of the monstrous, fairy-like, and unexpected men in Russian history, men of will and talent, such as Peter the Great, Mikhail Lomonosov, Leo Tolstoy, and others of that calibre. I think that such men are possible only in Russia, whose life and history always remind me of Sodom and Gomorrah. . . .

Robust and thick-set, with the cranium of Socrates and the all-seeing eyes of a past-master in ingenious shrewdness, he often assumed an odd and somewhat comical pose; he threw his head back, and bending it toward one shoulder, he thrust his fingers somewhere under his armpits, behind his vest. There was something marvellously dear and funny in that pose, something of a triumphant rooster, and at such a moment he radiated all joy, a great child of this damned world, a fine man who found it necessary to bring himself as a sacrifice to enmity and hatred, for the sake of attaining the goal of love and beauty.

His movements were light and agile, and a spare but strong gesture harmonised perfectly with his speech, also spare of words and surcharged with ideas. On his Mongolian face burned and played the keen eyes of an indefatigable hunter after falsehood and sorrow in life; they burned, contracting, winking, smiling ironically, flashing with anger. The flash of those eyes made his speech even more torrid and terribly clear. At times it seemed that it was the indomitable energy of his mind which spurted from his eyes as sparks, and the words, saturated with it, seemed to scintillate in the air. His speech always produced the physical sensation of irrefutable truth, and although this truth was often unacceptable to me, I still could not help feeling its power. . . .

I have never met a man who could laugh so infectiously as Vladimar Ilyitch. It was strange to see such a stern realist, a man who saw so well and felt so deeply the inevitability of great social catastrophes, a man irreconcilable, relentless in his hatred towards the capitalist world, laughing like a child, till the tears came, till he choked with laughter. To laugh like that one must have the soundest and healthiest of minds.   GORKY, on Lenin.

Throughout the journey we did not say a word to a single German; outside Berlin some German Social-Democrats got into a neighbouring compartment, but none of us engaged them in conversation. . . . [In Finland] the platforms of the stations we went through were thronged with soldiers. Yussevitch leant out of the window. "Long live world revolution," he cried. The bewildered soldiery began to stare at the travellers. A pale-faced lieutenant passed several times up and down near us, and as Ilyitch and I were in an almost empty compartment further up, he sat down beside my companion and opened the conversation. The lieutenant was a die-hard, and said so; Ilyitch defended his point of view and was, like the German, very pale. The coach became gradually full of soldiers, who climbed on the seats to get a better view of what was going on and to get a clearer hearing of the man who was speaking against the war in language so easy to understand. Their attention became more and more rapt, and their expressions graver and graver. . . .

We arrived at Petrograd. The working masses, soldiers and sailors, flocked to meet their chief. How did they recognise him? I do not know. All around us was a seething mass of human beings.

. . . Red flags, a naval guard-of-honour from Cronstadt, the searchlights from the fortress of Peter and Paul lighting up the

way from the Finland station to the Kechinskaya Palace; armoured cars, the road lined with workmen and workwomen. Ilyitch was hoisted on to the top of an armoured car. He began to speak. He was surrounded by all those he held most dear in the world —the masses.
> KRUPSKAYA, describing Lenin's Return to Russia.

The Soviets are the new State apparatus. . . . This apparatus represents a connection with the masses, with the majority of the people, that is so intimate, so indissoluble, so readily verifiable and renewable, that nothing like it was even approached in the previous State. This apparatus, because it is elective and its personnel is subject to recall in accordance with the will of the people without any bureaucratic formalities, is far more democratic than were the former ones. It represents a firm connection with the most diverse occupations, thus facilitating all sorts of radical reforms without resort to bureaucracy. . . . It makes it possible to combine the advantages of parliamentarism with the advantages of immediate and direct democracy, i.e. to unite, in persons of elected representatives of the people, both legislative and executive functions. Compared with bourgeois parliamentarism, this is a step forward in the development of democracy which has a historical world significance.
> LENIN, November 1917.

Russia is declared a republic of soviets of workers, soldiers, and peasants' deputies. All central and local authority is invested in these soviets.

The Russian Soviet Republic is established on the basis of a free union of free nations, as a federation of national soviet republics.

Within the fundamental aim of suppressing all exploitation of man by man, of abolishing for ever the division of society into classes, of ruthlessly suppressing all exploiters, of bringing about the socialist organisation of society and the triumph of socialism in all countries, the Third All-Russian Congress of Soviets of workers, soldiers and peasants' deputies further decrees:

In order to establish the socialisation of land, private ownership of land is abolished; all land is declared national property and is handed over to the labouring masses, without compensation, on the basis of an equitable division giving the right of use only.

All forests, underground mineral wealth, and waters of national importance, all livestock and appurtenances together with all model farms and agricultural enterprises are proclaimed national property.

As the first step towards the complete transfer of factories, works, shops, mines, railways, and other means of production and of transport to the ownership of the workers' and peasants' Soviet Republic, and in order to ensure the supremacy of the labouring masses over the exploiters, the Congress ratifies the soviet law on the workers' control of industry, and that on the Supreme Economic Council.

LENIN: Preamble to the Fundamental Law of July 10, 1918.

Lenin made the Soviets the basis of the new Republic, and the word "Soviet" itself has now entered all languages as symbolic of the Government of the workers and the rule of emancipated labour.

The Soviets mean war on the oppressors.

The Soviets mean the end of the landlords, capitalists, kulaks, merchants, and profiteers.

The Soviets mean the alliance of the workers and peasants.

The Soviets mean Socialism. *Pravda*.

The October Revolution of the workers and peasants began under the common banner of Emancipation.

The peasants are being emancipated from the power of the landowners, for there is no longer the landowners' property right in the land—it has been abolished. The soldiers and sailors are being emancipated from the power of autocratic generals, for generals will henceforth be elective and subject to recall. The working-men are being emancipated from the whims and arbitrary will of the capitalists, for henceforth there will be established the control of the workers over mills and factories. Everything living and capable of life is being emancipated from the hateful shackles.

There remain only the peoples of Russia, who have suffered and are suffering oppression and arbitrariness, and whose emancipation must immediately begin, whose liberation must be effected resolutely and definitely.

During the period of Tsarism the peoples of Russia were systematically incited one against another, the results of such a policy are known; massacres and *pogroms* on the one hand, slavery of peoples on the other.

There can be and there must be no return to this disgraceful policy. Henceforth the policy of a voluntary and honest union of the peoples of Russia must be substituted.

From Preamble to Declaration of the Rights
of the Peoples of Russia.

Masters!—this is no slip of the tongue—I address myself to you Masters, you men and women workers, you peasants, Red soldiers and sailors! You are now the masters, the real masters of our glorious new country. I salute you, my comrades, in the name of science, which is there to serve your present and future happiness. There are not many men of science here among us to-day; yet I have my thoughts, my memories . . . yes, memory! I am getting old. . . . But there are many scientists who forget . . . yes, who have forgotten that they were brought up by the poor and hungry and who are now repaying the people with ingratitude and with treason. I once had such a pupil who had forgotten—his name was Vorobieff, Vikenti Michailivich Vorobieff. . . .

Comrades! my ear, like the pendulum of an old clock, is measuring time, and there is precious little of it left to me. I want to tell you that our beloved work demands the lifetime of a man to fulfil. At my age every second is precious, but you who are young, you have the years; but your problem is also greater. And so I make this appeal to you: go straight ahead to the goal without pausing. Your achievements will be for those who come after you, but you must struggle forward.

I wish you Godspeed, comrades. I am over seventy but my thoughts are with you. So long as my hands can wield a pen, so long as my eyes can read, I will defend the Revolution. Guard it with your lives, do not hand over our beloved Petrograd to the Whites, even as I did not surrender my manuscript to them.

Au revoir, Red soldiers and sailors. The Red is unconquerable.

It is not only the colour of blood: it is the colour of creation,—the sole life-bringing colour in nature, filling the young plants with sap and warmth.

Au revoir, whether there be few or many in this hall, I am now speaking to the whole world. And I want to say that, since the postal service has been restored I have received many letters from colleagues abroad, from the dons of Universities in France, England and Switzerland and from their Governments. They are all offering me money, houses, laboratories, and country villas so that I may leave my "barbarian country" and go to them. I want you all to know that the Soviet Mail can bring me curses from my learned revolutionary colleagues, but I shall remain here with my people, my Government and my University, which happens to be unheated and cold, because I shall never reject the honour of doing my share in the Revolution in exchange for anything the world can offer me. That is why I came here ... so short a time remains to me ... and time flies. ... Au revoir.

RACHMANOV: Professor Polejaev in
The Deputy from the Baltic.

DECLARATION OF THE RIGHTS OF THE PEOPLES OF RUSSIA

... The first Congress of Soviets, in June of this year, proclaimed the rights of the peoples of Russia to self-determination.

The second Congress of Soviets, in November last, confirmed this inalienable right of the peoples of Russia more decisively and definitely.

Executing the will of these Congresses, the Council of People's Commissars has resolved to establish, as a basis for its activity in the question of Nationalities, the following principles:

(1) The equality and sovereignty of the peoples of Russia.

(2) The right of the peoples of Russia to free self-determination, even to the point of separation and the formation of an independent state.

(3) The abolition of any and all national and national-religious privileges and disabilities.

(4) The free development of national minorities and ethnographic groups inhabiting the territory of Russia.

Decrees will be prepared immediately upon the formation of a Commission on Nationalities.

In the name of the Russian Republic,
People's Commissar for Nationalities,
DJUGASHVILI-STALIN.
President of the Council of People's Commissars,
V. ULIANOV (LENIN).

The policy of national oppression, inherited from the autocracy and monarchy, is supported by the landlords, capitalists, and petty bourgeoisie in order to protect their class privileges and to cause disunity among the workers of the various nationalities. Modern imperialism, which increases the striving to subjugate weak nations, is a new factor intensifying national oppression.

To the extent that the elimination of national oppression is achievable at all in capitalist society, it is possible only under a consistently democratic republican system and State administration that guarantee complete equality for all nations and languages.

The right of all the nations forming part of Russia freely to secede and form independent states must be recognised. To deny them this right, or to fail to take measures guaranteeing its practical realisation, is equivalent to supporting a policy of seizure and annexation. It is only the recognition by the proletariat of the right of nations to secede that can ensure complete solidarity among the workers of the various nations and help to bring the nations closer together on truly democratic lines. . . .

The right of nations freely to secede must not be confused with the expediency of secession of a given nation at a given moment. The party of the proletariat must decide the latter question quite independently in each particular case from the standpoint of the interests of the social development as a whole and of the interests of the class struggle of the proletariat for Socialism.

The Party demands broad regional autonomy, the abolition of supervision from above, the abolition of a compulsory State language, and the determination of the boundaries of the self-governing and autonomous regions by the local population itself in accordance with the economic and social conditions, the national composition of the population, and so forth.

The party of the proletariat resolutely rejects what is known as "national cultural autonomy," under which education, etc., is removed from the competence of the State and placed within the competence of some kind of national diets. National cultural autonomy artificially divides the workers living in one locality, and even working in the same industrial enterprise, according to their various "national cultures"; in other words, it strengthens the ties between the workers and the bourgeois culture of individual nations, whereas the aim of the Social-Democrats is to develop the international culture of the world proletariat.

The Party demands that a fundamental law shall be embodied in the constitution annulling all privileges enjoyed by any nation whatever and all infringements of the rights of national minorities.

The interests of the working class demand that the workers of all the nationalities of Russia should have common proletarian organisations: political, trade union, educational institutions of the co-operatives, and so forth. Only such common organisations of the workers of the various nationalities will make it possible for the proletariat to wage a successful struggle against international capital and bourgeois nationalism.

> The Resolution on the National Question adopted by the April Conference, 1917.

> Come out from the small, untidy huts
> Into the open, ye sons of the people!
> See how bright the fire is burning. . . .
> Russia calls upon us to build a new life,
> To fight for the peasant's cause. . . .
> Enough of weariness and laziness.
> Awake from the age-long sleep,
> Ye ploughmen, my brothers.   KUZMICHEV.

The ownership of the land in Russia is the basis for immense oppression, and the confiscation of the land by the peasants is the most important step of our Revolution. But it cannot be separated from the other steps, as is clearly manifested by the stages through which the Revolution has had to pass. The first stage was the crushing of autocracy and the crushing of the power of the industrial capitalists and landowners, whose interests are closely related. The second stage was the strengthening of the Soviets and the political compromise with the bourgeoisie. The mistake of the Left Socialist Revolutionaries lies in the fact that at that time they did not oppose the policy of compromise, because they held the theory that the consciousness of the masses was not yet fully developed. . . .

If Socialism can only be realised when the intellectual development of all the people permits it, then we shall not see Socialism for at least five hundred years. . . . The Socialist political party—this is the vanguard of the working class; it must not allow itself to be halted by the lack of education of the mass average, but it must lead the masses, using the Soviets as organs of revolutionary initiative. . . .

LENIN, at Peasants' Congress, November 1918.

The Land question can only be permanently settled by the general Constituent Assembly.

The most equitable solution of the Land question should be as follows:

(1) The right of private ownership of land abolished for ever; land cannot be sold, nor leased, nor mortgaged, nor alienated in any way. All dominical lands, lands attached to titles, lands belonging to the Emperor's cabinet, to monasteries, churches, possession lands, entailed lands, private estates, communal lands, peasant freeholds, and others, are confiscated without compensation, and become national property, and are placed at the disposition of the workers who cultivate them.

Those who are damaged because of this social transformation of the rights of property are entitled to public aid during the time necessary for them to adapt themselves to the new conditions of existence.

(2) All the riches beneath the earth—ores, oil, coal, salt, etc.—as well as forest and waters having a national importance, become the exclusive property of the State. All minor streams, lakes, and forests are placed in the hands of the communities, on condition of being managed by the local organs of government.

(3) All plots of land scientifically cultivated—gardens, plantations, nurseries, seed-plots, green-houses, and others—shall not be divided, but transformed into model farms, and pass into the hands of the State or of the community, according to their size and importance.

Buildings, communal lands and villages with their private gardens and their orchards remain in the hands of their present owners; the dimensions of these plots and the rates of taxes for their use shall be fixed by law.

(4) All studs, governmental and private cattle-breeding and bird-breeding establishments, and others, are confiscated and become national property, and are transferred either to the State or to the community, according to their size and importance.

All questions of compensation for the above are within the competence of the Constituent Assembly.

(5) All inventoried agricultural property of the confiscated lands, machinery, and livestock are transferred without compensation to the State or the community, according to their quality and importance.

The confiscation of such machinery or livestock shall not apply to the small properties of peasants.

(6) The right to use the land is granted to all citizens, without distinction of sex, who wish to work the land themselves, with the help of their families, or in partnership, and only so long as they are able to work. No hired labour is permitted.

In the event of the incapacity for work of a member of the commune for a period of two years, the commune shall be bound to render him assistance during this time by working the land in common.

Farmers who through old age or sickness have permanently lost the capacity to work the land themselves shall surrender their land and receive instead a Government pension.

(7) The use of land shall be equalised—that is to say, the land shall be divided among the workers according to local conditions, the unit of labour, and the needs of the individual.

The way in which land is to be used may be individually determined upon: as homesteads, as farms, by communes, by partnerships, as will be decided by the villages and settlements.

(8) All land upon its confiscation is pooled in the general People's Land Fund. Its distribution among the workers is carried out by the local and central organs of administration, beginning with the village democratic organisations and ending with the central provincial institutions—with the exception of urban and rural societies.

The Land Fund is subject to periodical redistribution according to the increase of population and the development of productivity and rural economy.

In case of modification of the boundaries of allotments, the original centre of the allotment remains intact.

The lands of persons retiring from the community return to the Land Fund; providing that near relations of the persons retiring, or friends designated by them, shall have preference in the redistribution of those lands.

When lands are returned to the Land Fund the money expended for manuring or improving the land, which has not been exhausted, shall be reimbursed.

If in some localities the Land Fund is insufficient to satisfy the local population, the surplus population should emigrate.

The organisation of the emigration, also the costs thereof, and the providing of emigrants with the necessary machinery and livestock, shall be the business of the State.

Land-Decree—Peasants' "Nakaz" (Instructions),
November 1918.

The indispensable conditions of the victory of the Socialist Revolution, which alone will secure the lasting success and the complete realisation of the Land-Decree, is the close union of the peasant workers with the industrial working class, with the proletariat of all advanced countries. From now on, in the Russian Republic, all the organisation and administration of the State, from top to bottom, must rest on that union. That union, crushing all attempts, direct or indirect, open or dissimulated, to return to the policy of conciliation with the bourgeoisie—conciliation, damned by experience, with the chiefs of bourgeois politics—can alone ensure the victory of Socialism throughout the world.

From a Resolution at Peasants' Congress,
November 1918.

CITIZENS OF RUSSIA!

With the insurrection of November 7th the working masses have won for the first time the real power.

The All-Russian Congress of Soviets has temporarily transferred this power both to its Executive Committee and the Council of People's Commissars.

The General Line of Educational Activity: Every genuinely democratic power must, in the domain of education, in a country where illiteracy and ignorance reign supreme, make its first aim in the struggle against this darkness. It must acquire in the shortest time universal literacy, by organising a network of schools answering to the demands of modern pedagogics; it must introduce universal, obligatory, and free tuition for all, and establish at the same time a series of such teachers' institutes and seminaries as will in the shortest time furnish a powerful army of people's teachers so necessary for the universal instruction of the population of our boundless Russia. . . .

But a real democracy cannot stop at mere literacy, at universal elementary instruction. It must endeavour to organise a uniform secular school of several grades. The ideal is, equal and if possible higher education for all citizens. So long as this idea has not been realised for all, the natural transition through all the schooling grades up to the university—a transition to a higher stage—must depend entirely upon the pupil's aptitude, and not upon the resources of his family. . . .

Instruction and Education: One must emphasise the difference between instruction and education.

Instruction is the transmission of ready knowledge by the teacher to his pupil. Education is a creative process. The personality of the individual is being "educated" throughout life, is being formed, grows richer in content, stronger and more perfect.

The toiling masses of the people—the workmen, the peasants, the soldiers—are thirsting for elementary and advanced instruction. But they are also thirsting for education. Neither the Government nor the intellectuals nor any other power outside of themselves can give it to them. The school, the book, the theatre, the museum, etc., may here be only aids. They have their own ideas, formed by their social position, so different from the position of those ruling classes and intellectuals who have hitherto created culture. They have their own ideas, their own emotions, their own ways of approaching the problems of personality and society. The city labourer according to his own fashion, the rural toiler according to his, will each build his clear world-conception permeated with the class-idea of the workers. There is no more superb or beautiful phenomenon than the one of which our nearest descendants will be both witnesses and participants; the building by collective Labour of its own general, rich, and free soul.

Instruction will surely be an important but not a decisive element. What is more important here is the criticism, the creativeness of the masses themselves; for science and art have only in some of their parts a general human importance. They suffer radical changes with every far-reaching class upheaval.

Throughout Russia, particularly among the city labourers but also among the peasants, a powerful wave of cultural educational movement has arisen; workers' and soldiers' organisations of this kind are multiplying rapidly. To meet them, to lend them support, to clear the road before them, is the first task of a revolutionary and popular Government in the domain of democratic education.   From a Manifesto, November 1918.

There are certain fundamental types of sick individualists of this talented world of people who have turned their backs on society. No! What was necessary was not to turn one's back on society, but to find within it the granite, the electrified metal, capable of bringing about a revolution in its very organism. And Gorky gradually, but early, began to understand the revolutionary and constructive rôle of the proletariat. It was a revelation for him. And he sings a hymn to his discovery, a hymn to the mighty camp of Revolution, a magnificent hymn, in his *Mother*.

And then there is his *Confession*, which is often attacked for its fundamental theme, which is that of a talented young peasant who goes in search of God, and becomes convinced that there is no God and cannot be one. But the world did not grow dim for him because he found no God; life did not appear sombre; for in place of God he had found man, and FACTORY man in particular. The factory lights the country with its dawn, the factory offers that which will lead man out of his blind-alley.

In one of his latest excellent articles, Comrade Bucharin, borrowing a term from Kirilov, one of the oldest Proletarian writers, talks of the Iron Messiah.

It is this Iron Messiah, with its massiveness, its collectivity, its organisation, with its revolutionary temperament and the force of its national, penetrating, and healthy energy, which roused Gorky's enthusiasm, and compelled him, the last of those prophets who only foretold the Revolution and the first great writer to go over to the Proletarian movement, to say, "You are come into the world to save it!"

LUNACHARSKY, on Gorky, 1923.

The collective might, the beautiful ecstasy of collective life, the miracle-working power of the collective—that is what the author believes in, that is what he calls on us to believe in. But has he not said himself that the people are at present disunited and subdued? Has he not told us that one must look for collectivism only among the newly born people, in factories and foundries? Yes, only there, only in the agglomeration of a class-minded collective, in the slow building up of an all-proletarian organisation, is one to find the real work of transforming men into mankind, if only the preliminary work. . . . So Gorky presents his miracle as a symbol of the future, as a pale specimen—pale in comparison with the future, but brilliant in comparison with the surrounding present.

LUNACHARSKY, on Gorky's *The Confession*.

. . . The tremendous task of organisation that lay on our shoulders was to transform the whole State economic mechanism into one huge machine, into an economic organism working in such a way that hundreds of millions of people should be guided by a single plan. LENIN.

Lenin is dead, but he lives on in the soul of each member of the Party. Each member of the Party is a particle of Lenin. Our entire Communist family is the collective incarnation of him.

From a Proclamation issued by the Communist Party.

In departing from us, Comrade Lenin bequeathed to us the duty of holding aloft and guarding the purity of the great title-member of the Party. We vow to you, Comrade Lenin, that we will fulfil your behest with honour.

In departing from us, Comrade Lenin bequeathed to us the duty of guarding the unity of our Party like the apple of our eye. We vow to you, Comrade Lenin, that we will fulfil this behest of yours also with honour.

In departing from us, Comrade Lenin bequeathed to us the duty of guarding and strengthening the dictatorship of the proletariat. We vow to you, Comrade Lenin, that we will spare no effort also to fulfil this behest of yours with honour.

In departing from us, Comrade Lenin bequeathed to us the duty of strengthening the alliance between the workers and the peasants. We vow to you, Comrade Lenin, that we will also fulfil this behest of yours.
> From the Funeral Speech delivered by STALIN.

Citizens, the old masters are gone, leaving behind them an enormous inheritance. It now belongs to the whole nation.

Citizens, guard this inheritance, guard the palaces, they will become palaces of your national art, guard the pictures, statues, buildings—these are the embodiment of your spiritual power and of that of your ancestors.

Art consists of those fine things which gifted men have created even under the oppression of despotism, and which testify to the power and beauty of the human mind.

Citizens, do not touch a single stone, guard your monuments, buildings, old objects, documents—all these are your history, your pride. Remember that this is the soil from which your new national art will grow forth.
> GORKY: Text of his appeal for the preservation of the Nation's art-treasures, circulated by the Soviet's Executive Committee.

Comrades, this day marks a turning-point in the history of the Soviet system. It places a landmark between the old period, now past, when the Soviet Republics, although they acted in common, yet each followed its own path and was concerned primarily with its own preservation, and the new period, already begun, when an end is being put to the isolated existence of each of the Soviet Republics, when the Republics are amalgamating into a single confederate state in order successfully to cope with economic disruption, and when the Soviet Government is concerned not only with its preservation, but with developing into an important international power, capable of influencing the international situation and of modifying it in the interests of the toilers.

> STALIN, on December 30, 1922, at the First All-Union Congress of Soviets.

Su, Fratelli, su, compagne . . .

Rise, ye brothers; rise, ye sisters!
To the ranks, ye steel-tempered fighters!
The light of the Future's sun
Already shines on the banner of crimson.

Degraded and imprisoned,
We have boldly sworn to fight
For our cause; in our ranks
There's no room for treason.

Has Labour been freed from its bitter fate
By the Children of Toil
That the shackles of bondage
May bind us again? Never, never!

Mines, factories, foundries
Have maimed us and bent—
By the nobility, like beasts of burden,
We were hitched to a plough.

In unity is our strength;
While single—each one is a pariah!
The world's heart—the proletariat—
We are the levers of the universe!

If the faith in equality and fraternity
Is not a lie, or a wicked jest,
If the rebellion is not a blasphemy,
Then the struggle is not madness.

Strengthen ye, brothers and sisters,
The power of Labour over capital.
To give way to the foe in the least
Is the wretched slave's cowardice.

Has Labour been freed from its bitter fate
By the Children of Toil
That the shackles of bondage
May bind us again? Never!
No, never! No, never, never!
        BEDNY (Pseudonym): *The Workmen's Hymn.*

In October 1917, when the great proletarian Revolution began in our country, when we overthrew the Tsar, the landlords and capitalists, the great Lenin our teacher, our father and tutor, said that henceforth there must be neither ruling nor subject peoples, that the peoples must be equal and free. In this way he buried the old Tsarist, bourgeois policy and proclaimed a new policy, a Bolshevik policy—a policy of friendship, a policy of brotherhood between the peoples of our country.
        STALIN, at a Conference of Collective Farmers.

To convert our country from an agrarian into an industrial country able to produce the machinery it needs by its own efforts —that is the essence, the basis of our general line.
        STALIN, at the Fourteenth Party Congress, 1925.

My wish to the workers of the Dynamo Plant and to the workers of all Russia is that industry should forge ahead, that the number of proletarians in Russia should increase in the near future to twenty or thirty million; that collective farming in the countryside should develop fully and predominate over individual farming; that advanced industry and collective farming in the countryside should finally weld the proletarians of the factories and the labourers of the soil into a single Socialist army; that the victory in Russia should culminate in victory throughout the world.
        STALIN: *The Foundations of Leninism.*

While the confiscation of the landlords' estates was the first step of the October Revolution in the countryside, the introduction of collective farming is the second and, moreover, the decisive step, which marks a most important stage in the process of laying the foundations of Socialist society in the U.S.S.R.
        Resolution of the Sixteenth Party Congress.

We are not responsible for the technical and economic backwardness of our country. It has existed for centuries and has come down to us as an inheritance from our entire history. This backwardness was also felt to be an evil in pre-Revolutionary days, and it continued to be so after the Revolution. Peter the Great's attempt, after his experience of developed Western States, feverishly to build factories and other works to supply the army and to increase the defensive strength of the country, was a unique attempt to burst the bonds of this backwardness. It is only natural that neither of the old classes—feudal aristocracy or middle class—was able to solve the problem provided by the backwardness of our country. Indeed, these classes were not only incapable of solving this problem but even of visualising it properly. The centuries-old backwardness of our country can only be overcome by successful Socialisation, and only the proletariat, which had established its dictatorship and directs the destinies of the country, is able to accomplish it.

STALIN, at the Central Committee of the Russian Communist Party, 1928.

The history of old Russia is the history of defeats due to backwardness. She was beaten by the Mongol khans, by the Turkish beys, by the Swedish feudal barons, by the Polish-Lithuanian squires, by the Anglo-French capitalists, by the Japanese barons. *All* beat her for her backwardness—for military backwardness, for cultural backwardness, for governmental backwardness, for industrial backwardness, for agricultural backwardness. She was beaten because to beat her was profitable and could be done with impunity.

Do you remember the words of the pre-revolutionary poet [Nikolai Nekrasov]: "You are both poor and abundant, you are both powerful and helpless, Mother Russia"? These words of the old poet were well known to those gentlemen. They beat her, saying, "You are abundant, so we can enrich ourselves at your expense." They beat her, saying, "You are poor and helpless, so you can be beaten and plundered with impunity." Such is the law of capitalism—to beat the backward and weak. The jungle law of capitalism. You are backward, you are weak, so you are wrong, hence you can be beaten and enslaved. You are mighty, so you are right, hence we must be wary of you. That is why we must no longer be backward. . . . Do you want our Socialist Fatherland to be beaten and to lose its independence? If you do not want this you must put an end to this backwardness as speedily as possible and develop genuine Bolshevik speed in building up the Socialist system of economy. There are no other ways. That is what Lenin said during the October Revolution: "Either death, or we must overtake and surpass the advanced capitalist countries." We are fifty to a hundred years behind the advanced countries. We must cover this distance in ten years. Either we do this or they will crush us.

    STALIN, at an Industrial Conference, 1931.

 . . . The masses are on the square. The festival, the tumult,
   the joy!
The beloved brothers and sisters in their meeting rejoice,
Forgetting factories, hammers, and chisels, and their torment,
Boldly they have taken one another's hands,
Knowing well that they all are friends:
They closely encircle the tribune,
Proclaiming brotherhood, the Commune,
As their indissoluble, reciprocal union;
And, with the ringing tocsin,
The summoning brass, they celebrate;
Turbulently, joyfully they await
Lenin, dearer to them than a brother,
With the sun of their eyes they smile;
From the tribune he will tell them,
In the words of the Messiah,
Of Communism in Soviet Russia
And of the universal victory of the proletariat.

    The band plays. The drums beat,
    The trumpets triumphantly blare,
    The boisterous tocsin is raging—
    Its brass is inviting
    And calling.
    The band plays. The drums beat,
    The trumpets triumphantly blare.

        MALASHKIN.

Spread out, O eagle's wings,
Toll, tocsin, and ye the thunders rumble,—
The fetters of oppression are but broken links
And the prison of life doth crumble!
Vast are the Black Sea plains,
Turbulent is Volga, and rich with gold is Ural.
Go, vanish into air, the bloody block and chains,
The prison and iniquitous tribunal!

> For land and freedom, for earned bread
> We march in arms to meet our foes!
> Upon us enough they did tread!
> Rush on to fight, to blows!

Over Russia there passed a fiery pheasant,
Kindling vehement wrath in the heart. . . .
Virgin-Mother,—our little earth Thou art—
Bear Thou the free bread for the peasant!
The rumours of old and the dreams came true,
Svyatogor [1] is the people, and now wide awake,
Honey is on the loaves of a rustic cake,
And the tablecloth shows a bright pattern too.

> For land and freedom, for earned bread
> We march in arms to meet our foes!
> Upon us enough they did tread!
> Rush on to fight, to blows!

KLUYEV.

Sovietland, so dear to every toiler,
Peace and progress build their hopes on thee,
There's no other land the whole world over
Where man walks the earth so proud and free.

Chorus.

Fatherland of mine, so vast and spacious,
Filled with forests, plains and rivers fair.

---

[1] A giant of Russian folklore; the reference to his awakening is taken from a popular ballad.

I know not of any other country
Where man's freedom can with ours compare.
> Popular song in U.S.S.R. (English text by
> Nancy Head.)

The voice of the city is sleepless,
The factories thunder and beat.
How bitter the wind, and relentless,
That echoes our shuffling feet.

Chorus.

Yet, comrades, face the wind, salute
The rising sun!
Our country turns towards the dawn.
New life's begun.

Triumphant and singing in triumph,
Advances the army of Youth,
And this is the new generation
Reborn in the battle for truth.

Chorus.

The universe envies us, comrades,
Our hearts are made strong in the strife,
Salute to the struggle for freedom.
Salute to the morning of life!

Chorus.

> Popular song in U.S.S.R. (English text by
> Nancy Head.)

We live badly. We change nature, but as yet we have not changed our own selves. And this is the most essential thing. Why have we begun this tremendous task which will take not five, but fifteen, twenty, and perhaps more years? Why do we mine millions of tons of coal and ore? Why do we build millions of machines? Do we do these things merely in order to change nature?

No, we change nature in order that people may live better. We need machines in order that we may work less and accomplish more. By the end of the Five-Year Plan the working day in a factory will be reduced by 50 minutes. If we assume that the working year consists of 273 days (not counting rest days and holidays), the worker will labour 227 hours a year less than he did at the beginning of the Plan. And 227 hours is almost 73 seven-hour working days.

He will work less and yet accomplish more. During seven hours in the factory he will do what now requires eleven and a half hours.

And if this is so, his wages will be raised by fifty per cent.

In comparison with conditions before the Revolution, every worker will labour three hours less a day and yet will receive twice as much pay.

But this is not all. Work will be made easier. No longer will there be bent backs, strained muscles, swollen veins on the forehead. Loads will travel, not on people's backs, but over conveyers. The heavy crowbar and hoe will give place to the pneumatic hammer and compressed air.

Instead of dark, gloomy shops with dim, yellow lamps there will be light, clean halls with great windows and beautiful tile floors. Not the lungs of men, but powerful ventilators will suck in and swallow the dirt, dust, and shavings of the factories. Workers will be less fatigued after a day's labour. There will be fewer "occupational" diseases. Think of all the people who die now of these illnesses! Every metal-worker has lungs eaten up by metal dust. You can always tell a blacksmith by his pale face, a stoker by his red inflamed eyes.

After we build Socialism, all will have equally healthy faces. Men will cease to regard work as a punishment, a heavy obligation. They will labour easily and cheerfully.

But if work will be a joy, rest will be a double joy.

Can one rest now in a crowded and noisy home amid the hissing of oil-burners, the smoke of the kitchen, the drying of wet cloths, the filth of dim windows, dirty furniture, spittle-spattered floors, and with unwashed dishes on the table!

After all, man is not just muscles with which to work. He is not a machine. He has a mind that wants to know, eyes that want to see, ears that want to hear, a voice that wants to sing, feet that want to run, to jump, to dance, hands that want to row, to swim, to throw, to catch. And we must organise life so that not merely certain lucky ones, but all, may be able to feel the joy of living.

After Socialism is built there will no longer be dwarfs—people with exhausted, pale faces, people reared in basements without sunshine or air. Healthy strong giants, red-cheeked and happy —such will be the new people.
M. ILIN: Moscow has a Plan.

The Soviet Fatherland! How immense and endless, abundant and mighty, happy and joyous! Yes, we workers in the Soviet Union love our Fatherland. We are patriots. We love its blooming lands, the golden fields of its collective farms, its smoking coal-mines, its green forests, its orchards, its teeming cities. Dear to us is the happy sky of our Fatherland; its very air is sacred to us. Pravda, 1936.

> When I am threatened—
> "The old world will return,"
> I fall to the ground
> And freeze in fear.
> Give me a gun, Comrade,
> Give me some bullets,
> I'll go to battle;
> I shall defend my land—
> My Soviet land.
> A Song of a Tajik Farmer.

Comrades, our sweet spring has come,
And fresh strength runs in man and sun,
The world's awakened, May's begun,
With our great festival.[1]
   Greetings!

We all are ready for the strife,
For we ourselves have mastered life,
In happy crowds that dance and laugh
I honour Soviet youth.
   Greetings!

[1] First of May.

> Our Soviet power rules bright-eyed,
> Life's garden it has opened wide
> And enter now those once denied,
> Our happy unveiled girls.
> > Greetings!
>
> Then flow still faster, water-wheels,
> Faster still for Soviet mills,
> Till every grindstone overfills,
> With our mighty harvests.
> > Greetings!
>
> Suleyman weaves glad songs together
> Now such a time has come, brother,
> Now such a time is won, brother,
> For our glorious Soviet youth.
> > Greetings!
>
> > SULEYMAN STALSKY, a peasant poet from Daghestan. (Trans. by Herbert Marshall.)

Tsarist Russia struck upon the path of capitalist development much later than other European countries. The working class was still numerically small. The spontaneous outbreaks of the 'seventies and 'eighties of the last century still bore an elemental, unorganised character. It was the hard school of experience which taught the workers just how essential was organisation, if they were to attain even their most elementary demands.

In the 'nineties of the last century Lenin had already fully appraised the power of the working class and the historical rôle which it was to play in the future. In his book *What the "Friends of the People" Are* (1894) he proved, with characteristic conviction and iron logic, that Russia had already taken the road of capitalist development, that the working class would play a revolutionary rôle in social development, and that in collaboration with the peasantry it would bring into being that active guiding force which must clear away the despotic Tsarist régime which was barring the road to bourgeois democracy and, subsequently, to Socialist democracy.

Lenin was able to gauge the sentiments of the working people with surprising accuracy. He knew their hopes and tribulations, their principal needs, and the slogans which they would best understand, and which would lead them to victory. "With the people at the head of the people!" was his motto.

His organisational talents enabled him to gather, organise, and rally the best elements of the working-class movement. In 1895 he succeeded in uniting the various motley groupings and illegal political circles into a single League of Struggle for the Emancipation of the Working Class.

This accomplished, he threw himself into the job of strengthening his connections with the masses of the people, addressing large audiences of workers on the burning problems of the day. This task was all the more vital because during the 'nineties there was a boost in Russian industry, bringing a corresponding increase in the Russian working class and an extension of its movement. This was expressed in the mounting number of strikes. Lenin's leaflets of that period revealed with amazing simplicity the root of the evils which fell to the lot of the industrial workers, and formulated their economic and political demands.

Lenin's implacable ideological struggle led to the creation of the new Party of Bolsheviks, and enabled this Party to meet the first Russian revolution of 1905 with a well-planned programme of action, and to play a leading rôle in the economic and political struggle of the time—the political and general strikes of October, and armed uprising in December, the mass movement among the peasantry and the movement in the army and navy.

After the suppression of the 1905 uprising, the revolutionary wave receded and the evil period of black Tsarist reaction set in. In those years Lenin determinedly opposed all who displayed weakness of spirit or panic, who proposed the disbanding of illegal organisations, as well as those who objected to availing themselves of legal means to continue the struggle. Lenin called for intensified activity within the trade unions which had survived the debacle, within medical associations for the workers, co-operative societies, clubs and cultural societies, and evolved a plan for social insurance.

The importance which Lenin attached to the trade unions is clearly reflected in the number of articles he wrote and speeches he made on their rôle as mass fighting organisations of the working class, and on their importance in the general system of the working-class movement.

When the period of untrammelled reaction drew to a close and the working-class movement could again emerge (1912-1914), Lenin was tirelessly occupied with the organisation of a legal workers' press and with the guidance of the workers' group in the Fourth State Duma. He was preparing the working class for new battles.

Lenin determinedly opposed the imperialist world war of 1914 and all working-class leaders who advocated that it should be supported. He attempted to muster the international forces of the working class against the war. Day by day he intensified his activities to enlighten and strengthen the forces of the Russian and international working-class movements.

The creative and organisational genius of Lenin was particularly evident between February and October 1917, when with his closest collaborator, Joseph Stalin, he was preparing the Russian working class for the decisive battles of the great Socialist Revolution and the final struggle for power. Under Lenin's guidance, the working class established Soviet power and a workers' and peasants' State, and then proceeded to construct the new Socialist society.

It was thanks to the far-sightedness of Lenin, his singleness of pupose and his ability to organise the masses that the country was able to overcome the most harrowing difficulties and move forward towards Socialism. Lenin led the working class and the young Soviet Republic through the hazards and suffering of the German occupation of the Ukraine, Byelo-Russia, the Donbas, and other regions of the country in 1918, then through the grave years of intervention and civil war, to the restoration of industry and agriculture.

Lenin was the author of the giant project to electrify and industrialise the country and to collectivise agriculture. He guided the cultural revolution and placed the country firmly on the path of Socialist democracy.

Lenin worked out the doctrines of trade unionism in the new conditions of a Soviet State, determined its position in the Soviet system and its part in the job of re-creating all phases of Soviet life and guiding Soviet labour along the path of Socialist construction.

Lenin attributed enormous importance to the work of trade unions under Soviet power, regarding them as working-class mass organisations to serve as schools for the working people, educators of the new Soviet man, schools which would lead the people into active participation in the moulding of industry, agriculture, and transport along Socialist lines.

Lenin pointed out that it was the trade union's function to combine every possible solicitude for the material welfare and living standard of the masses with the work of guiding them in all spheres of Soviet construction, particularly in the construction of Socialist industry.

Every time a new difficulty faced the country, Lenin would invariably apply his favourite key to all problems, no matter how complex: *he was certain* that the creative energy and initiative of the people could overcome all obstacles.

J. JUSEFOVICH, in *Soviet War News*, 1943.

It fell to Lenin's lot to see the gigantic work of a lifetime crowned with success. He witnessed the victory of the Russian people, marching in the vanguard of all the peoples of our country in their struggle for liberty. All the riches of the earth, all aspects of human knowledge, every possible development of human talent and the whole range of military art were made available to the people, and thus to the country, by the Revolution which Lenin led.

Then the people stood up to their full height. They became the masters of their land, and the land flourished. Lenin's joy knew no bounds when the sanguinary battles were ended and peaceful construction began.

Lenin knew the Russian man in the street and his day-by-day labour. There was no aspect of Russian life which escaped his eager interest, no phase of the people's daily life in which he did not help. In talking with people he was always pleased when someone from another town or country village spoke about his life there. Lenin sought to help every person with whom he spoke, to learn general principles from his experiences in a way that would later help that person along life's path.

NIKOLAI TIKHONOV, in *Soviet War News*, 1943.

Chapter Four

THE IDEOLOGICAL BASIS OF SOVIET RUSSIA

IF there ever should exist a country where all wealth will be owned in common and where what is known as property will be abolished for ever, that country will at any rate be a happy one.
PLATO: Republic.

It is quite possible that in the eyes of vicious people the only stimulus to work is selfishness; but in the communal state, where people are trained in a public spirit and when all labour is equally honourable, the stimulus to work is love of society.
TOMMASO CAMPANELLA.

We have spent ages discussing the Rights of Man, but we have completely overlooked the most elementary of all rights—the Right to Labour—without which all else is valueless.
FOURIER.

The exploitation of man by man was the state of human relations in the past. The exploitation of nature by man in partnership with other men is the picture of the future.
SAINT-SIMON.

Nature has made all wealth the common property of all. At any rate, society is the sole owner of all wealth.
ROUSSEAU.

Communism is the best basis for individual development and freedom; not that individualism which drives man to the war of each against all, but that which is an opportunity for a full expansion of man's faculties, the superior development of whatever is original in him, the greatest fruitfulness of intelligence, feeling, and will.... Communist principles and institutions are of absolute necessity for society, not only to solve economic difficulties, but also to maintain and develop social customs that bring men in contact with one another. They must be looked to for establishing such relations between men that the interest of each should be the interest of all; and this alone can unite men instead of dividing them.

Such being our *ideal*, what does it matter to us that it cannot be realised at once! KROPOTKIN.

In place of the old bourgeois society, with its classes and class antagonisms, we shall have an association in which the free development of each is the condition of the free development of all. *The Communist Manifesto.*

The proletariat will use its political supremacy to wrest, by degrees, all capital from the bourgeoisie, to centralise all instruments of production in the hands of the State, i.e. of the proletariat organised as the ruling class; and to increase the total of productive forces as rapidly as possible. Of course, in the beginning, this cannot be effected except by means of despotic inroads on the rights of property, and on the conditions of bourgeois production; by means of measures, therefore, which appear economically insufficient and untenable, but which, in the course of the movement, outstrip themselves, necessitate further inroads upon the old social order, and are unavoidable as a means of entirely revolutionising the mode of production.

The Communist Manifesto.

Communists know very well that all kinds of conspiracies are not only useless but harmful. They know very well that revolutions are not made arbitrarily and by order, but that they everywhere appear as a necessary consequence of circumstances which do not at all depend on the will and direction of separate parties and whole classes. Nevertheless they see that the development of the proletariat in almost all civilised countries is suppressed by force, and by this the antagonists of the communists try to call forth revolutions. If for these reasons the oppressed proletariat is finally compelled to turn to revolution, communists will know how to defend the interests of the proletariat by action as they now do in words.

ENGELS: *Principles of Communism.*

My dialectic method is not only different from the Hegelian, but is its direct opposite. To Hegel, the life process of the human brain, i.e. the process of thinking, which, under the name of "the Idea," he even transforms into an independent subject, is the demiurgos of the real world, and the real world is only the external, phenomenal form of "the Idea." With me, on the contrary, the ideal is nothing else than the material world reflected by the human mind, and translated into forms of thought. . . . With him (Hegel) it (dialectics) is standing on its head. It must be turned right side up again, if you would discover the rational kernel within the mystical shell. MARX: *Capital.*

Dialectics comes from the Greek *dialego*, to discourse, to debate. In ancient times dialectics was the art of arriving at the truth by disclosing the contradictions in the argument of an opponent and overcoming these contradictions. There were philosophers in ancient times who believed that the disclosure of contradictions in thought and the clash of opposite opinions was the best method of arriving at the truth. This dialectical method of thought, later extended to the phenomena of nature, developed into the dialectical method of apprehending nature, which regards the phenomena of nature as being in constant movement and undergoing constant change, and the development of nature as the result of the development of the contradictions in nature, as the result of the interaction of opposed forces in nature.

In its essence, dialectics is the direct opposite of metaphysics.

(1) The principal features of the Marxist dialectical method are as follows:

(*a*) Contrary to metaphysics, dialectics does not regard nature as an accidental agglomeration of things, of phenomena, unconnected with, isolated from, and independent of, each other, but as a connected and integral whole, in which things, phenomena, are organically connected with, dependent on, and determined by, each other.

The dialectical method therefore holds that no phenomenon in nature can be understood if taken by itself, isolated from surrounding phenomena, inasmuch as any phenomenon in any realm of nature may become meaningless to us if it is not considered in connection with the surrounding conditions, but divorced from them; and that, vice versa, any phenomenon can be understood and explained if considered in its inseparable connection with surrounding phenomena, as one conditioned by surrounding phenomena.

(b) Contrary to metaphysics, dialectics holds that nature is not a state of rest and immobility, stagnation and immutability, but a state of continuous movement and change, of continuous renewal and development, where something is always arising and developing, and something always disintegrating and dying away.

The dialectical method therefore requires that phenomena should be considered not only from the standpoint of their interconnection and interdependence, but also from the standpoint of their movement, their change, their development, their coming into being and going out of being.

The dialectical method regards as important primarily not that which at the given moment seems to be durable and yet is already beginning to die away, but that which is arising and developing, even though at the given moment it may appear to be not durable, for the dialectical method considers invincible only that which is arising and developing.

(c) Contrary to metaphysics, dialectics does not regard the process of development as a simple process of growth, where quantitative changes do not lead to qualitative changes, but as a development which passes from insignificant and imperceptible quantitative changes to open, fundamental changes, to qualitative changes; a development in which the qualitative changes occur not gradually, but rapidly and abruptly, taking the form of a leap from one state to another; they occur not accidentally but as the natural result of an accumulation of imperceptible and gradual quantitative changes.

The dialectical method therefore holds that the process of development should be understood not as movement in a circle, not as a simple repetition of what has already occurred, but as an onward and upward movement, as a transition from an old qualitative state to a new qualitative state, as a development from the simple to the complex, from the lower to the higher.

(d) Contrary to metaphysics, dialectics holds that internal contradictions are inherent in all things and phenomena of nature, for they all have their negative and positive sides, a past and a future, something dying away and something developing; and that the struggle between these opposites, the struggle between the old and the new, between that which is dying away and that which is being born, between that which is disappearing and that which is developing, constitutes the internal content of the process of development, the internal content of the transformation of quantitative changes into qualitative changes.

The dialectical method therefore holds that the process of development from the lower to the higher takes place not as a harmonious unfolding of phenomena, but as a disclosure of the contradictions inherent in things and phenomena, as a "struggle" of opposite tendencies which operate on the basis of these contradictions.

Such, in brief, are the principal features of the Marxist dialectical method.

History of the Communist Party of the Soviet Union, Moscow, 1939.

The capitalist method of production and appropriation, and therefore also capitalist private property, is the first negation of individual private property based upon personal toil. The negation of capitalist production is accomplished by itself with a necessity which characterises the natural process. This is the negation of negation. Now not the individually producing worker is to be expropriated, but the capitalist who exploits many workers. This expropriation is accomplished by the action of immanent laws of capitalist production itself, i.e. it is due to the concentration of capital. One capitalist exterminates many others, and in hand with this concentration and expropriation of many capitalists by the few there develops in an ever larger degree the co-operative form of the producing process, the conscious technical application of science, the rational exploitation of land, the transformation of the implements of labour in such a manner that they can only be used collectively, an economy in the means of production, by means of their collective use in joint socialised work, the absorption of all peoples into the system of world markets and hence the international character of the capitalist order. Together with the progressive decreases in the number of magnates of capital who seize and monopolise all the advantages of this process of transformation, there is increasing poverty, oppression, enslavement, degeneration, exploitation; but simultaneously there is also the indignation of the working class which constantly increases numerically and is continually disciplined, united, and organised by the very mechanism of the capitalist process of production. The monopoly of capital becomes the fetters for that method of production which developed with it and under its influences. The concentration of the means of production and the socialisation of production reach such a degree that they become incompatible with their capitalist shell. The shell breaks. The expropriators are expropriated.

MARX: *Capital*.

It is under the form of these combinations that the first attempts at association among themselves have always been made by the workers. The great industry masses together in a single place a crowd of people unknown to each other. Competition divides their interests. But the maintenance of their wages, this common interest which they have against their employer, unites them in the same idea of resistance-combination. (Combination here means workers' combination.) Thus combination has always a double end, that of eliminating competition among themselves while enabling them to make a general competition against the capitalist. If the first object of resistance has been merely to maintain wages, in proportion as the capitalists in their turn have combined with the idea of repression, the combinations, at first isolated, have formed in groups, and, in face of constantly united capital, the maintenance of the association became more important and necessary for them than the maintenance of wages. This is so true that the English economists are all astonished at seeing the workers sacrifice a good part of their wages on behalf of the associations which, in the eyes of these economists, were only established in support of wages. In this struggle—a veritable civil war—are united and established all the elements necessary for a future battle. Once arrived at that point, association takes on a political character.

The economic conditions have in the first place transformed the mass of people of the country into wage workers. The domination of capital has created for this mass of people a common situation with common interests. Thus this mass is already a class, as opposed to capital, but not yet for itself. In the struggle, of which we have only noted some phases, this mass unites, it is constituted as a class for itself. The interests which it defends are the interests of its class.

MARX: *The Poverty of Philosophy*.

Social relations are closely bound up with productive forces. In acquiring new productive forces men change their mode of production; and in changing their mode of production, in changing the way of earning their living, they change all their social relations. The hand-mill gives you society with the feudal lord; the steam-mill, society with the industrial capitalist.

There is a continual movement of growth in productive forces, of destruction in social relations, of formation in ideas; the only immutable thing is the abstraction of movement.

MARX: *The Poverty of Philosophy*.

In the social production which men carry on they enter into definite relations that are indispensable and independent of their will; these relations of production correspond to a definite stage of development of their material forces of production. The sum total of these relations of production constitutes the economic structure of society—the real foundation, on which rises a legal and political superstructure and to which correspond definite forms of social consciousness. The mode of production in material life determines the social, political, and intellectual life-process in general. It is not the consciousness of men that determines their being, but, on the contrary, their social being that determines their consciousness. At a certain stage of their development, the material forces of production in society come in conflict with the existing relations of production, or—what is but a legal expression for the same thing—with the property relations within which they have been at work before. From forms of development of the forces of production these relations turn into their fetters. Then begins an epoch of social revolution. With the change of the economic foundation, the entire immense superstructure is more or less rapidly transformed. In considering such transformations a distinction should always be made between the material transformations of the economic conditions of production which can be determined with the precision of natural science, and the legal, political, religious, aesthetic or philosophic—in short, ideological forms in which men become conscious of this conflict and fight it out. Just as our opinion of an individual is not based on what he thinks of himself, so can we not judge of such a period of transformation by its own consciousness; on the contrary, this consciousness must be explained rather from the contradictions of material life, from the existing conflict between the social forces of production and the relations of production. No social order ever disappears before all the productive forces for which there is room in it have been developed; and new higher relations of production never appear before the material conditions of their existence have matured in the womb of the old society itself. Therefore, mankind always sets itself only such tasks as it can solve; since, looking at the matter more closely, we will always find that the task itself arises only when the material conditions necessary for its solution already exist or are at least in the process of formation.

MARX: *Preface to Critique of Political Economy*.

Labour is, in the first place, a process in which both Man and Nature participate, and in which Man of his own accord starts, regulates, and controls the material reactions between himself and Nature. He opposes himself to Nature as one of her own forces, setting in motion arms and legs, head and hands, the natural forces of his body, in order to appropriate Nature's productions in a form adapted to his own wants. By thus acting on the external world and changing it, he at the same time changes his own nature.

In the process of labour, Man adapts himself to external nature, yet he does so not passively, but actively, placing between himself and Nature, if necessary, the tools of labour, the tools of production. An instrument of labour is a thing, or a complex of things, which the labourer interposes between himself and the subject of his labour, and which serves as the conductor of his activity. MARX: *Capital*.

Our teaching is not a dogma, but a guide to action, Marx and

Engels always used to say, rightly ridiculing the learning and repetition by rote of "formulas" which at best are only capable of outlining general tasks that are necessarily liable to be modified by the concrete economic and political conditions of each separate phase of the historical process. . . . It is essential to realise the incontestable truth that a Marxist must take cognisance of real life, of the concrete realities, and must not continue to cling to a theory of yesterday. . . .   LENIN: *Collected Works.*

The masses of politically conscious workers and peasants must be won over by drawing up a vast programme for ten or twenty years ahead, by giving the plans a scientific basis and making them clear and definite. . . .

The unity of the proletariat in the epoch of social revolution can be achieved only by the extreme revolutionary party of Marxism, and only by a relentless struggle against all other parties.   LENIN: *Collected Works.*

At the basis of communist morality lies the struggle for strengthening and completing communism. . . . Communist morality is that which serves this struggle, which unites the toilers against every exploitation, against every petty property interest . . . the old society was based upon such principles that either you rob the other or the other robs you, either you work for another or another works for you . . . it is clear that people educated in such societies imbibe, so to speak, with their mother's milk the psychology, the habit, the concept of either the slave-owner or the slave or the petty property holder . . . such a psychology and such a mood cannot be in a communist . . . for a communist morality lies in this compact discipline of solidarity and the conscious mass struggle against exploiters.
  LENIN: *Collected Works.*

The dictatorship of the proletariat, if we translate this Latin, scientific, historico-philosophical expression into more simple language, means just this: that only a definite class, namely the urban and in general the factory, industrial workers, are capable of leading the entire mass of the working people and exploited in the struggle to overthrow the yoke of capital, in the process of the overthrow itself, in the struggle to retain and consolidate the victory, in the work of establishing a new Socialist public order, in the entire struggle for the complete abolition of classes.

LENIN: *The Great Initiative.*

There is a saying of the great Russian revolutionary Chernishevsky: "Political activity is not so smooth as the pavement on the Nevsky Prospect." He is no revolutionary who recognises the revolution of the proletariat only under the condition that it proceeds smoothly and easily; that the proletarians of the various countries immediately come into action; that right from the outset there is a guarantee against defeats; that the revolution will advance along the broad, free, and straight path to victory; that one will not here and there—on the way to victory—have to bear heavy sacrifices, to hold out in a beleaguered fortress and to climb up to the narrowest, most inaccessible winding and dangerous mountain paths. He is no revolutionary—he has not freed himself from the pedantry of the bourgeois intelligentsia—he will in fact again and again slide down into the camp of the counter-revolutionary bourgeoisie.

LENIN: Letter to the American Workers, 1918.

All agitation and propaganda and the entire work of the Communist Parties must be animated by the consciousness that no lasting improvement in the condition of the masses of the proletariat is possible within the capitalist order of society, and that only the overthrow of the middle class and the destruction of the capitalist states affords the possibility of commencing the work of improving the state of the working classes and of rebuilding the economic system destroyed by capitalism. This consciousness must not, however, find expression in an abandonment of the struggle for the daily necessities of life required by the proletariat before it is capable of securing them for itself by establishing its own dictatorship. . . . All objections to making such partial demands, all complaints on the part of Reformists against participation in this semi-warfare, are symptoms of the same incapacity to comprehend the essential nature of revolutionary action that manifested itself in the opposition of individual Communist groups to participation in the trade unions and in parliamentary life. It is not enough to proclaim to the proletariat the aim to be striven for without intensifying the everyday struggle that is alone capable of leading the proletariat towards the battle for the final objective.

Resolution of the Third World Congress of the Communist International, 1921.

The attitude of a political party towards its own mistakes is one of the most important and surest ways of judging how earnest the party is and how it in practice fulfils its obligations towards its class and the toiling masses. Frankly admitting a mistake, ascertaining the reasons for it, analysing the conditions which led to it, and thoroughly discussing the means of correcting it—that is the earmark of a serious party; that is the way it should perform its duties, that is the way it should educate and train the class, and then the masses. . . . All revolutionary parties which have hitherto perished did so because they grew conceited, failed to see where their strength lay, and feared to speak of their weaknesses. But we shall not perish, for we do not fear to speak of our weaknesses and will learn to overcome them.

LENIN: *Collected Works.*

In the mythology of the ancient Greeks there was a celebrated hero, Antaeus, who, so the legend goes, was the son of Poseidon, god of the seas, and Gaea, goddess of the earth. Antaeus was very much attached to the mother who had given birth to him, suckled him and reared him. There was not a hero whom this Antaeus did not vanquish. He was regarded as an invincible hero. Wherein lay his strength? It lay in the fact that every time he was hard pressed in a fight with an adversary he would touch the earth, the mother who had given birth to him and suckled him, and that gave him new strength. Yet he had a vulnerable spot—the danger of being detached from the earth in some way or other. His enemies were aware of this weakness and watched for him. One day an enemy appeared who took advantage of this vulnerable spot and vanquished Antaeus. This was Hercules. How did Hercules vanquish Antaeus? He lifted him from the earth, kept him suspended in the air, prevented him from touching the earth, and throttled him.

I think that the Bolsheviks remind us of the hero of Greek mythology, Antaeus. They, like Antaeus, are strong because they maintain connection with their mother, the masses, who gave birth to them, suckled them and reared them. And as long as they maintain connection with their mother, with the people, they have every chance of remaining invincible.

That is the cue to the invincibility of Bolshevik leadership.

STALIN: *Defects in Party Work.*

The art of leadership is a serious matter. One must not lag behind the movement, because to do so is to become isolated from the masses. But neither must one rush ahead, for to rush ahead is to lose contact with the masses. He who wants to lead a movement and at the same time keep in touch with the vast masses must wage a fight on two fronts—against those who lag behind and against those who rush on ahead.

STALIN, 1930.

... A simple way of stating the antithesis between the Socialist State and the Fascist States is to say that the politics of the one are based on hope, the politics of the others on fear. The success of Socialism makes for trust in the common man. The failure of capitalism, of which Fascism is the expression, means the need for his repression. The more complete the triumph of Soviet Socialism, the wider will be the liberties it confers. But the more complete the victory of the Fascist Powers, the more determined will be their assault upon the dignity of human personality. ...

The emphasis of Soviet democracy is on economic freedom; and it argues that the more profound the victory social ownership wins over the traditions of capitalist mentality, the more effective is the political freedom that inherently results. The weakness of capitalist democracy is the fact that it depends upon its ability to maintain the privileged position of those who own the instruments of production; its delicate equilibrium is only secure to the degree that it is capable of continuous economic expansion. It is a régime, not of social justice, but of concessions made possible by that expansion without jeopardy to the need of profit. But in its history a stage arrives when either the democracy must overcome the capitalism or capitalism will overcome the democracy. For since the making of profit is capitalism's law of life it must necessarily, as in Germany and Italy, transform political institutions to the logic of its needs. That is why all political democracy in an individualist system of ownership is in a dangerous condition. It has reached that crisis Marx and Engels foretold when its relations of production are in final contradiction with the forces of production. In that crisis, it cannot long maintain its earlier habit of political freedom.

Soviet democracy, on the other hand, has brought the relations into harmony with the forces of production. By establishing the common ownership of the means of production, it has abolished vested interest and the exploitation of man by man. As it is able more fully to utilise its resources, it is able increasingly to satisfy the wants it encounters; and that ability is the condition upon which political freedom grows.

HAROLD LASKI, in a Foreword on the
Soviet Constitution.

Having eliminated the remnants of the exploiting classes, we have established a society of two mutually friendly classes, the working class and the peasantry. This society has given rise to an intelligentsia of its own, which is no longer bourgeois or bourgeois-democratic, but is, in the main, a Socialist intelligentsia. This intelligentsia, linked with ties of blood to the working people and to Socialism, plays a great part in the work of directing the development and consolidation of the new society and state. The antagonism that used to exist between town and country has largely been uprooted, but a substantial difference between the above two classes still exists. This difference exists, primarily, because the workers are employed in establishments which are the possession of the whole people, are Socialist-state in character, while the peasants work on the collective farms, which are Socialist-co-operative in character. Both of these classes, the working class and the collective-farm peasantry, are already classes of Socialist society. And while the working class, as the more advanced class and the one better trained for the establishment of complete Communism, has retained its leading rôle, the peasantry in its turn does not maintain an attitude of passivity, but takes an active part in the building of the new society, in the building of Communism. This principle is embodied in the new Constitution of the U.S.S.R.

MOLOTOV: Report to the Eighteenth Congress
of the Communist Party, 1939.

Chapter Five

THE ROAD TO FULFILMENT

LOOK what the Soviets have done! They have taught the whole people to read and write, built up industry, created a new country.... Formerly science was divorced from life and alienated from the people, but now I see that science in the Soviet Union belongs to the people—the whole nation fully recognises the rôle of science (in its development). I therefore raise my glass and drink to the only Government in the world which could bring about such an achievement—to the Government of my country.

PAVLOV: Speech, 1935.

The question with Soviet Russia is not, What are the facts? —implying the facts of the moment, the static facts. What is the direction of motion, what are the dynamic facts? How is Soviet Russia developing, and what is she developing into?

This matter of the difference between static and dynamic facts seems to me to be of great importance in the problem of understanding Soviet Russia. The so-called impartial observer is apt to register the static facts only. He holds himself in and surveys the outside of things. Among recent philosophers, Bergson has been prominent as a critic of this surveying, snapshotting method of apprehending reality. He has shown that this cool impartial sort of method better apprehends the dead than the living part of reality. If the movement of a thing is to be understood, the observer must do more than watch its outside; he must project himself so that he apprehends the thing from the inside. By an effort of intuition he is to make contact with the thing to be understood, so there should be an interflow of spirit and a direct apprehension of the dynamic part of the thing's reality. I take it Bergson considers a thing cannot be fully understood unless there is some emotional contact between the observed and the observer, usually the observer's feeling of sympathy. If this is what Bergson is driving at, then it applies in the technique of apprehending the reality known as Soviet Russia. It is very difficult to learn this reality without having some sympathy with the Bolsheviks. If the observer has sympathy, he can apprehend the reality of the creative effort they are making.

Creativity in the social consciousness appears to me to be the most important fact to be observed in Soviet Russia. This spirit is capable of welding the Soviet nation into an irresistible unit; it works in the people and beneath the poverty, dilapidation, and disease, as the molten metal runs beneath the surface scum. . . .

J. G. CROWTHER: *Science in Soviet Russia.*

Scores and hundreds of times in the course of centuries have the toilers tried to throw their oppressors off their backs and become masters of their own conditions. But every time, defeated and disgraced, they were compelled to retreat, their hearts burning with a sense of wrong and humiliation, anger and despair, and they turned their eyes to the unknown heavens, where they hoped to find salvation.

The chains of slavery remained intact, or else the old chains were exchanged for new ones equally burdensome and humiliating.

Only in our country have the oppressed and suppressed masses of toilers succeeded in throwing off the rule of the landlords and capitalists and in putting in its place the rule of the workers and peasants.

You know, comrades, and now the whole world admits it, that this titanic struggle was led by Comrade Lenin and his party.

STALIN: Speech, 1935.

My joy and my pride is the new Russian man, builder of the new State.

To this small yet great man, who is to be found in all the remote nooks of the land, in factories and villages lost in the wide steppes and in the frozen marshes of Siberia, in the mountains of the Caucasus, and in the tundras of the north; to this often very lonely man working amidst people who as yet understand him with difficulty; to the shaper of his state, who modestly does his seemingly unimportant work which is of vast historical significance; to him I send my heartfelt greeting.

Comrade! Know and trust that you are the most needful man on earth. By doing your small work you have begun to create a really new world.

Learn and teach.
I firmly grip your hand, comrade!
>GORKY: *Greeting for the Tenth Anniversary
of the Russian Revolution.*

... Everything seems to have been rejuvenated from within. Gone are the Russian softness, the melancholy of the spirit, that specifically Russian gravitation toward sadness which used to be celebrated as our beauty. Yet what beauty was there in that? Rather was that our misfortune. We were squeezed hard, and naturally we squeaked. But now everybody talks here in a fine baritone. On this I congratulate you from the depth of my heart!
>GORKY : Speech, 1934.

As such a basis for the construction of a new world I regard the release of the enslaved will to live, that is, the will to act, for life is action. . . .

It seems to me that in the Soviet Union people are beginning to work, conscious of the significance of labour for the State, conscious of the fact that labour alone is the direct and the shortest road to liberty and culture. The Russian workman is earning for himself not a wretched niggardly subsistence, as used to be the case: he is earning for himself a State. He is aware of gradually becoming master of the whole country and leader of the peasantry on the road to freedom. . . .
>GORKY, on the occasion of the Tenth Anniversary
of the Russian Revolution.

The undoubted successes of Socialism in the U.S.S.R. on the front of construction have clearly shown that the proletariat can successfully govern the country without the bourgeoisie and against the bourgeoisie, that it can successfully build up industry without the bourgeoisie and against the bourgeoisie, that it can successfully guide the whole of the national economy without the bourgeoisie and against the bourgeoisie, that it can successfully build Socialism despite the encirclement of the capitalist States.
>STALIN, on the occasion of the Tenth Anniversary
of the Russian Revolution.

Your strength, comrades, is invincible. You have proved that in the civil war, and you are proving it again in your daily work. Your strength is truly unconquerable, and it is your pledge of victory over all obstacles. You must overcome everything—and you will. I cordially grasp your mighty hands.

GORKY: *To the Workers of Magnitogorsk and Others*, 1931.

Our proletarian revolution is the only revolution in the world which had the opportunity of showing the people not only political results but also material results. Of all workers' revolutions we know only one which managed to achieve power. That was the Paris Commune. But it did not last long. True, it endeavoured to smash the fetters of capitalism, but it did not have time enough to smash them, and still less to show the people the beneficial material results of revolution. Our Revolution is the only one which not only smashed the fetters of capitalism and brought the people freedom, but also succeeded in creating the material conditions of a prosperous life for the people. Therein lies the strength and invincibility of our Revolution.

STALIN, at the First All-Union Conference of Stakhanovites, 1935.

The October Revolution brought our country out of the system of world capitalism and opened a new chapter in world history. A country which under the rule of the Tsars had been transformed into "a prison of the peoples" has since the October days of 1917 become the pioneer of world history. . . .

The opponents of the Soviet system in the bourgeois press frequently say: No, the Soviet Union is not a Socialist country, but something entirely different. To console themselves they resort to the fable of "State capitalism"—a fable they themselves do not believe. And, indeed, who is going to believe that there is such a thing as capitalism without capitalists, capitalism without crises, capitalism without unemployed. . . .

Our State apparatus, which, despite all its defects, is enabling us to carry out the great plan of Socialist construction, is depicted by our enemies as a bureaucratic superstructure, incompatible with the development of individuals and individual talents. But this criticism of bureaucracy only serves to conceal the true aims of our enemies, namely, to undermine the apparatus of the Soviet system. . . . (But) we know very well that a real fight against bureaucracy is inseparable from the fight for the victory of Socialism, and that with the successful development of large-scale production in town and country, and with the rising cultural level of the masses, our ability to overcome bureaucracy increases immensely. We deem it one of our most important tasks to get the toilers to participate still more in the work of our organs, and, under the leadership of the Party, to make them still more active in the struggle against bureaucratic distortions in our apparatus, knowing that this is the surest way to hasten the advent of the complete victory of Socialism.

MOLOTOV, at the Seventh Congress of Soviets, 1935.

Crisis, unemployment, waste, and general poverty are incurable diseases of capitalism. Our system does not suffer from these diseases, because the Government is in our hands, in the hands of the working class, because we are conducting planned economy, are accumulating resources in a planned way and properly distributing them among the various branches of industry. . . .

The chief conclusion to be drawn is that the working class of our country, having abolished the exploitation of man by man and firmly established the Socialist system, has proved to the world the truth of its cause. That is the chief conclusion, for it strengthens our faith in the power of the working class and in the inevitability of its ultimate victory.

STALIN, at the Eighteenth Congress of the Communist Party, 1939.

Lenin created the Bolshevik Party and forged it in battle. He revealed new State forms—Soviet State, the power of the toilers. He was the father of the first Soviet State in the world, the founder of Socialist construction in our country. To his genius, to his untiring work and thought, we owe the Soviet order that has been created and strengthened in our country.

He created the indestructible union of workers and peasants. In his testament he charged the *Bolshevik Party with all its might* to strengthen this union. His genius, his labour and thought laid the foundation for the voluntary union of the peoples of our country.

By the genius of Lenin the Red Army was created. In the difficult years of civil war the armed power of the young Soviet State was forged. Lenin charged the Bolsheviks and all the Soviet people to spare no effort to strengthen our defences.

The Socialist order in our country flourished. Throughout the boundless extent of our motherland creative work went on. The Stalin Five-Year Plans created a powerful industry, the basis of our economy and military strength. New factories and workshops, mines and oil-wells, electric-power stations and shipyards were constructed in various parts of the country.

Every year spacious new schools for our children, hospitals, crèches, sanatoria, theatres, and clubs were built. The national culture of the peoples of the U.S.S.R. blossomed.

Socialist agriculture grew stronger. The number of well-equipped collective farms rapidly increased and the farmers became well-to-do. The number of cattle in the stock-breeding farms multiplied. On the initiative of collective farmers and workers, wonderful canals were built in Uzbekistan, Tadjikistan and Kirghizia in Central Asia. The bogs of Byelo-Russia were drained. Everywhere roads were built. . . .

As long as the Bolsheviks maintain their ties with the broad masses of the people they will be invincible.

Pravda, quoted in *Soviet War News*, 1942.

The road to the achievement of our national aims has always been an open and straightforward one. What is the truth of our progress, which follows from the country's historical development? The Russian people never subscribed to mad Tamerlane ideas of conquering the world. Its thoughts and efforts were centred on raising Russia to the level of world cultural, economic, and moral standards. Twenty-four years ago our young Soviet land was faced with the immeasurably difficult national task of overtaking European civilisation in the shortest period of time and, relying on our inexhaustible natural resources, of surpassing it. The task was one of life or death, for according to all the rules of logic our country, devastated by the world war, would have naturally ceased to exist as an independent State.

To execute this task we found those special forms which fully conformed to the specificity of Russia's historical development. These forms were deeply ingrained in the minds of the people in the shape of hopes and dreams about the rule of justice, goodness and peace. You will find the echo of the undying faith in this rule in our numerous heroic folk-tales and fairy-tales.

Our efforts were crowned with success. Soviet Russia arose like a phoenix from the poverty and gloom of the past centuries.

ALEXEY TOLSTOY, in *Soviet War News*, 1942.

The Soviet State this year celebrates the first quarter-century of its existence. It is unceasingly growing, developing, and becoming stronger, while during the same period many States of the old times have suffered defeat and decline and have disappeared.

The Soviet State system was created by the genius of Lenin and Stalin and by our people led by the Bolshevik Party.

In the year 1905, in the Soviet of Workers' Deputies which arose on the crest of the mighty revolutionary movement, Lenin opened the way for the future State power of the working people, for a united State of a new kind—the highest democracy.

The Soviet State came out of the fire of the greatest revolutions. This new form of State was fostered by the collective thought and will of the people, and it became the everlasting achievement of the people.

From the first day of its birth the Soviet State had the support of millions of workers and peasants whose sacred possession it became. It came through its first cruel trial during the years of civil war between 1918 and 1920. It came through trials of devastation and famine such as no contemporary State has ever experienced.

The Soviet State system is based on the inviolable alliance of workers and peasants. This system was created, forged, and strengthened by Lenin and grew into a gigantic force under the leadership of Stalin. No enemy force has ever succeeded in driving a wedge into this alliance of the two fraternal classes.

The peasants aided the workers in the difficult days of civil war, when famine threated to throttle the young Soviet Republic. They helped to build Socialist industry. The workers helped the peasants in the development of agriculture, in the conversion of a backward, poverty-stricken, individualistic farming system into a highly mechanised industry based on collectivism. They helped the farmers to establish a prosperous and cultured life.

This alliance between workers and peasants has withstood the German invasion. The Nazis failed to separate the Soviet rear from the Soviet front. They failed to pollute the Soviet waters with their quisling dung. They could not find such scoundrels within the Soviet State.

They failed, too, in their attempt to separate the great family of the Soviet peoples united in our State, and to create strife among them. As Stalin said, never before has the Soviet rear been so stable as it is now.

And the same foundations which give the Soviet State such stability make the armed forces of the Soviet people into a menacing army which produces heroes.

Pravda, quoted in *Soviet War News*, 1942.

The Soviet people are proud of their intelligentsia. Soviet intellectual workers are flesh of our flesh, blood of our blood. They are connected with the working class and peasantry by their very roots. They are in the same ranks as the workers and peasants, and they have the same rights as any other members of our Soviet society.

Their rôle in our country is very great. The basis of the wellbeing and development of Soviet society is firm unity between workers and peasants, strengthened by the alliance of those classes with the working intelligentsia. This is the guarantee of the stability and firmness of the Soviet régime.

For many years the Bolshevik Party and the Soviet people trained the cadres of the Soviet intelligentsia. As a result we now possess a numerous Socialist intelligentsia, springing from the people and differing fundamentally from the old bourgeois intelligentsia both in its composition and in its social and political character.

Its creative power emerges from a living, inexhaustible source. It is rich in talent. The Soviet people enter the ranks of the intelligentsia through a wide network of schools, universities, and other educational institutes. Stalin stipends for students, Stalin premiums for outstanding work in science, technology, literature and art, encourage fruitful and constant competition in study and creative work.

The Stakhanovite movement for greater efficiency is steadily growing among the intelligentsia. Their members combine initiative with lively thought, driving force, and inventiveness.

Our working intelligentsia is composed of many nationalities, as are the Soviet peoples. Since the coming into existence of the Soviet State, the culture of all the peoples in our country has constantly grown and developed. New schools, new universities, and scientific institutes have been built in all the national Soviet Republics.

Each one of our nationalities possesses a rich talent for creative work. But this talent can be completely utilised only when the people are free, when all paths are open to them. The Soviet intelligentsia is free—Socialist in content and national in form.

Soviet War News, 1942.

Russia is Russian in soul, and the traditions of Russian culture are alive in the U.S.S.R., as is evidenced by the achievements of literature, music, the stage, the ballet, and the films. In the first twenty years after the Revolution the publication of the works of Pushkin, Gogol, Turgenev, Tolstoy, and Chekhov reached a record figure of 75 million copies, or three times as many as in the period 1897-1916. Pushkin has been translated into 66 languages of the Soviet Union; Tolstoy into 54; Chekhov has now outstripped Dickens in the proportion of seven to one (14 million copies as against 2 million).

Russia has witnessed a democratisation of culture, in which the masses of people have come to participate. The importance and significance of this process should be fully realised. The culture of Russia is in the full tide of its youth. Under the *visible compulsions* the West should discern in Russia the traditional *invisible liberty*, just as the Russian Westernisers in the past perceived in the culture of the West the *invisible compulsions* under its *visible liberty*.

PROFESSOR KONOVALOV: Address at a Conference on "Britain and Russia in the New World Order," April 1942.

The whole of the Russian thought and literature of the nineteenth century was permeated by the search for wholeness and universality, and they constantly opposed themselves to the West-European spirit of division, of individualism and self-sufficiency. Russian culture of the nineteenth century was to a large extent inspired by an original form of Christian Socialism. It never knew the bourgeois mentality, and revolted passionately against all forms of "middle-class" psychology, in which it saw the fatal vice of Western civilisation. . . . Russian religious thought—in all its often contradictory trends—and the saints of the Russian Orthodox Church aspire to the consummation of all things, to the reunion and re-creation of the world and mankind. They are concerned with the here and now, with the paths and destinies of this world, perishing in sin and thirsting for salvation. It is striking how indifferent Russian thought is to *abstract* knowledge and *abstract* philosophy. Russian thought and the Russian spirit are *concrete*; it is not an accident that nearly all the Russian thinkers were artists. They are pragmatic and "projective": they search for real and creative action, for direct incarnation. . . . Consciously and unconsciously Russia's vision has always been the transfigured and reintegrated universe, the world of new social existence and new human relationships. There is no country in the world where the social character of Christianity has been so deeply realised as in Russia. The poet Tiutchev's image of Christ in the garb of a servant going across the Russian earth and coming to those in suffering and anguish will always remain a shining symbol of Russian Christianity.

> DR. EVGHENY LAMPERT: Address at a Conference on "Britain and Russia in the New World Order," April 1942.

For myself—as one accepting the religious view of life—if I find the Government of a country intensely concerned with feeding the hungry; ministering to the public health; developing education for the child, the youth and the adult; showing care for the cultural advance of the backward peoples; seeking for woman an equal status with man in all matters of public concern; giving to the Jews equal rights with their fellow-citizens—then I ask myself whether the term "godless" may not require closer scrutiny than heretofore; and whether—to put it directly—the teaching of our Lord recorded in St. Matthew 25, in which He identifies Himself

with the needy multitudes, may not require of us a new and juster appraisement of the life of Soviet Russia?
>REV. HENRY CARTER: Address at a Conference on "Britain and Russia in the New World Order," April 1942.

The Red Army is an army of working people and peasants, the army of the Soviet peoples. It was created in the face of the deadly danger of German invasion which hovered over the Soviet Republic in 1918. Lenin told the Soviet people then that they must learn to fight, that they must create an army that would not run away, but would be capable of braving hitherto unheard-of suffering. He warned them that unless they created such an army they would be pinned to the ground under the German heel.

The liberated peoples, led by Lenin and Stalin, created such an army. It routed and drove the German hordes from the Soviet Republic. Twenty-five years later the Red Army has proved itself worthy of its great organisers, Lenin and Stalin. By its devotion to the cause of the Soviet peoples, and its heroic defence of their interests, it has earned the love of all toilers.

In the U.S.S.R. the people and the Red Army are one whole, one family. Stalin has pointed out that it is an army of the brotherhood of the peoples of the U.S.S.R., an army for the defence of the liberty and independence of those peoples. That is why, at this crucial moment, it has the complete support of every nationality inhabiting the Soviet Union.

Mutual interests and common economic and political tasks unite all the nationalities of the U.S.S.R. in one historical destiny. Every Cossack and Uzbek, Georgian and Armenian, Ukrainian and Byelo-Russian, every Soviet citizen, regardless of his nationality, looks on the entire Soviet Union as his homeland. The prosperity and happiness of the Soviet Union means the prosperity and happiness of every national republic of each of the Soviet peoples.   ALEXANDER GORKIN, in *Soviet War News*, 1943.

A. CONSTITUTIONAL DEVELOPMENT

The Socialist character of Soviet democracy, that is, *proletarian* democracy, in its concrete, in its present application, consists, firstly, in the fact that the toilers and the exploited masses are the electors, while the bourgeoisie are excluded; secondly, in the fact that all bureaucratic formalities and restrictions of elections are eliminated and the masses themselves determine the manner and times of election and enjoy full freedom to recall their deputies; thirdly, in the fact that the best form of mass organisation of the vanguard of the toilers, the proletariat in large-scale industry, is created, which enables it to lead the largest number of exploited, to draw them into independent political life, educate them politically on the basis of their own experience, so that for the first time we have an approach to a state of affairs in which actually every member of the population learns to rule and begins to rule. LENIN: *Collected Works.*

Democracy under the capitalist system is *capitalist* democracy, the democracy of an exploiting minority based upon the restriction of the rights of the exploited majority and directed against this majority. Only under the dictatorship of the proletariat is real freedom for the exploited and real participation in the administration of the country by the proletarians and peasants possible. Under the dictatorship of the proletariat democracy is proletarian democracy—the democracy of the exploited majority based upon the restriction of the rights of the exploiting minority and directed against this minority.
STALIN: *Foundations of Leninism.*

ROY HOWARD: A new Constitution is being elaborated in the U.S.S.R. providing for a new system of elections. To what degree can this new system alter the situation in the U.S.S.R. since, as formerly, only one party will come forward at the elections?

STALIN: You are confused by the fact that only one party will come forward at these elections. You don't see how there can be an election struggle under these conditions. It is evident that the election lists will be put out not only by the Communist Party but by all kinds of public non-party organisations. And we have hundreds of such. We have no parties standing in opposition to each other, just as we have not a class of capitalists and a class of workers exploited by capitalists opposing each other.

Our society consists exclusively of free working people of

the cities and villages—workers, peasants, and the intelligentsia. Each of these layers may have its special interests and express them through numerous existing public organisations. But where there are no classes, where boundaries between classes are effaced, where only a few non-fundamental differences between the various layers of Socialist society remain, there can no longer exist a fertile ground for the formation of parties struggling among themselves. Where several classes don't exist there cannot be several parties, since a party is a part of a class.

Under National "Socialism" there is only one party. But nothing will come of this Fascist one-party system. In Germany capitalism remained, the classes and the class struggle remained, and it will break through to the surface just as it broke through in, let us say, Spain. In Italy, also, only one—Fascist—party exists, but for the same reasons there, too, nothing will come out of this. . . .

You think that there will be no election struggle, but there will be, and I foresee a very animated election struggle. Not a few organisations exist in our country which function poorly. Sometimes it happens that this or that local government organ does not know how to satisfy one or other of the many-sided and ever-increasing demands of the working population of the city and the countryside.

Have you or have you not built a good school? Have you improved living conditions? Are you a bureaucrat? Have you helped to make our labour more effective, our life more cultured? Such will be the criteria with which millions of voters will approach candidates, rejecting those unfit, striking them off the lists, advancing better ones, nominating them for elections.

Yes, the electoral struggle will be animated, it will be centred around numerous, very sharp questions, mainly practical questions, having first-rate significance for the people. Our new election system will keep a tight hand on all institutions and organisations and will force them to improve their work.

STALIN, at an interview with Roy Howard, 1936.

While for the peoples of capitalist countries the constitution of the U.S.S.R. will have the significance of a programme of action, for the peoples of the U.S.S.R. it is significant as the summary of their victories on the front of the emancipation of Mankind. After the path of struggle and privation that has been traversed, it is pleasant and joyful to have our Constitution, which deals with the fruits of our victories. It is pleasant and joyful to know what our people fought for and how they achieved this victory of world-wide historical importance. It is pleasant and joyful to know that the blood our people shed so plentifully was not shed in vain, that is, has produced results. This spiritually arms our working class, our peasantry, our working intelligentsia. It impels them forward and rouses a sense of legitimate pride. It increases confidence in our strength and mobilises us for fresh struggles for the new victories of Communism.

STALIN: *On the Draft Constitution of the U.S.S.R.*, 1936.

The Constitution was not the creation of Stalin, though no doubt he had a share in the original draft. That draft was first of all discussed, altered, and passed by the Supreme Soviet. It was then handed on to the people. It was published in full, with its 146 articles, in 10,000 newspapers. 60 million copies were circulated in pamphlet form in every language of the Union. 527,000 public meetings were held to expound and discuss, which, it is calculated, were attended by $36\frac{1}{2}$ millions of citizens. 150,000 suggestions and amendments were sent up to Moscow, which were all considered. The Supreme Soviet discussed all the more important amendments and adopted some of them. In this way the Constitution was indeed the act of the whole people. And can any say that a people which can take that share in the debate on a vital act of State has not shown the first and most vital quality of a democratic people?

SIR CHARLES TREVELYAN, on Soviet Democracy.

Of the laws that kept women in a dependent position not one stone remains standing in the Soviet Republic. I mean by that, the laws that exploited the weaker, often indeed the humiliating, position of women. . . . In democratic republics we see that equality of rights is indeed proclaimed, but at every step—in civil laws and the laws concerning women's position in the family and divorce—we find inequality and degradation of woman. . . . That is a violation of democracy. The Soviet has done more than any other country to realise the democratic idea by wiping out the last trace of the disabilities hitherto imposed upon women from its legislation.

> LENIN, at the Conference of Proletarian and Peasant Women, 1919.

Over 1700 women Deputies of the Supreme Soviet of the U.S.S.R. and of the Autonomous Republics, and over half a million women Deputies of local Soviets, are directly participating in the Government of our country. They are elected by the Soviet people.

Among the new intellectuals who have come from the people, and been nurtured by the Soviet Government, are about one million women—engineers, technicians, teachers, doctors, scientific workers, agronomists. Soviet women share actively in the building of our new life and enjoy equal standing with men, working in all branches of the national economy.

Under the Soviet Government the cultural level of women and the material welfare of the people have immensely improved. The Soviet Government displays exceptional solicitude for mothers, providing enormous funds for children's institutions and for allowances for mothers of large families.

> *Soviet War News*, 1942.

Every Soviet citizen is guaranteed in the new Constitution the right to work. Equally important he is given the right to adequate leisure, including holidays on full pay every year.

All Soviet citizens are guaranteed the right to material security in old age, sickness, and, in the event of loss of capacity, to work. All have the right to free education from the elementary school to the University. Soviet women have the same political, economic, and social status as men. All citizens have equal rights regardless of nationality or race. Freedom of conscience is assured by the separation of the Church from the State and the school from the Church. Freedom to practise all religions is accorded.

The Constitution guarantees: freedom of speech, the press,

assembly, and demonstration. The right of organisational self-expression and the inviolability of the home and person are guaranteed.

Asylum to working-class refugees, and those who have been persecuted for fighting for national liberation, is assured.

STALIN : Speech, 1936.

The Ukrainians are the second largest national group, being roughly 40 millions. All other national groups are considerably smaller. In the old days under the Tsars, the Central Government pursued a policy of suppression of all non-Russian nationalities. They wanted to Russianise by force all the national minorities. As a result, the "national" question under the Tsarist Empire was most acute and became a source of internal weakness in times of emergency.

But the Soviet Government completely reversed this policy and secured for all the national minorities full freedom for national existence and national development. To ensure this, there exist 47 Federated and Autonomous Republics, as well as Autonomous Regions inside the Soviet Union, of which 16 of the greater ones —the Federated Republics—in accordance with the Stalin Constitution of 1936, enjoy the right to secede from the Union.

M. MAISKY : Speech, 1942.

The Soviet regime has done one thing which we Mohammedans will never forget. It has accorded us religious liberty and civil equality.

It was different before the Revolution. Could a Mohammedan, for example, ever have dreamt of participating in conferences at the Kremlin in Moscow? Now Bashkirs, Tatars, Uzbeks, and Turkmens share in the sessions of the Supreme Soviet, in congresses and other assemblies held in the Kremlin Palace, on equal terms with their Russian, Ukrainian, and Byelo-Russian brothers.

That is why the Soviet Union has become our homeland. We cherish it. And when it is attacked we all rise up in its defence. Our people from Bashkiria, Crimea, Turkmenistan, Kirghizia and Kazakhstan are fighting so self-sacrificingly against Hitler's soldiers because they know that German Fascism would bring a régime a thousand times worse than that of Tsarist days. We know the Germans consider themselves a superior race privileged to govern the entire world. Their victory would mean the enslavement of millions of Mohammedans.

> THE MUFTI ABDUL RAHMAN RASSULAYEV, at an interview with Jean Richard Bloch, well-known French author, 1942.

From one end of the Union to the other in local assemblies up to the Supreme Soviet the people govern themselves. They have freedom of choice of their representatives. For the All-Union Supreme Soviet every man and woman from Minsk to Vladisvostok, and from Archangel to Samarkand, has a vote which is cast by ballot. There is one Deputy for every 300,000 inhabitants. No exceptions are made. Excluded categories in earlier Soviets, such as Tsarist policemen, priests, and former landlords and profit-makers, are now included.

But a deep new principle has come to full fruition in the new Constitution of the U.S.S.R. There are many races in the Union, speaking many tongues, in various stages of development. There are many peoples in the deserts, in the mountains, in the remote Arctic, whom we British should call inferior, whom we should claim to rule for their good and hope to lead on to a higher civilisation. In the U.S.S.R. they are all equal, they are all citizens, their rights are equal. No man may taunt another with his race. The S.S. man who struck a Jew, the innkeeper who excluded a Negro from his hotel, the sahib who kicked an Indian, would in the U.S.S.R. be liable to spend the next year or two in prison. Racial equality is for the first time a reality. Britain, America, South Africa have something yet to learn in that direction from Soviet democracy. In that respect also Russian modes of thought are most bitterly antagonistic to the arrogant racial doctrines of Nazi Germany.

> SIR CHARLES TREVELYAN, on Soviet Democracy.

B. AGRICULTURE AND INDUSTRY

Private ownership of land is abolished and the whole land fund is declared common property and transferred to the labourers without compensation on the basis of equalised use of the soil.

All forests, minerals, and waters of State-wide importance, as well as the whole inventory of animate and inanimate objects, all estates and agricultural enterprises, are national property. . . .

The transfer of all banks into the ownership of the Workers' and Peasants' State is confirmed, it being one of the conditions of the emancipation of the labouring masses from the yoke of capital. From the Decrees passed by the Bolshevik Government, November 7, 1917.

Article 7. Public enterprises of collective farms and co-operative organisations, with their livestock and implements, products raised and manufactured by the collective farms and co-operative organisations, as well as their public structures, constitute the public, Socialist property of the collective farms and co-operative organisations.

Every collective farm household, in addition to its basic income from the public collective farm enterprise, has in personal use a plot of land attached to the house and, in personal ownership, an auxiliary establishment on the plot, the house, produce animals and poultry, and minor agricultural implements—in accordance with the statutes of the agricultural artel.

Article 8. The land occupied by collective farms is secured to them for use without time limit, that is, in perpetuity.

Article 9. Alongside the Socialist system of economy, which is the dominant form of economy in the U.S.S.R., the law allows small private economy of individual peasants and handicraftsmen based on individual labour and excluding the exploitation of the labour of others.

Article 10. The personal ownership by citizens of their income from work and savings, home and auxiliary household economy, of objects of domestic and household economy as well as objects of personal use and comfort, are protected by law.

Article 11. The economic life of the U.S.S.R. is determined and directed by the national economic State plan for the purposes of increasing public wealth, of a steady rise in the material and cultural level of the toilers, of strengthening the independence of the U.S.S.R. and its defence capacity.

From the New Soviet Constitution, 1936.

There is no escape from poverty for the small farm. . . .

If we continue as of old on our small farms, even as free citizens on free land, we shall still be faced with inevitable ruin. . . .

If peasant farming is to develop further, we must firmly assure also its transition to the next stage, and this next stage must inevitably be one in which the small, isolated peasant farms, the least profitable and most backward, will by a process of gradual amalgamation form large-scale collective farms. . . .

Only if we succeed in proving to the peasants in practice the advantages of common, collective, co-operative, artel cultivation of the soil, only if we succeed in helping the peasant by means of co-operative or artel farming, will the working class, which holds the State power, be really able to convince the peasant of the correctness of its policy and to secure the real and durable following of the millions of peasants. LENIN: *Collected Works.*

Guided by Lenin's formulations on the necessity of a transition from small peasant farming to large-scale, co-operative-collective farming, and taking Lenin's co-operative plan as his basis, Stalin theoretically elaborated and put into practice the teaching on the collectivisation of agriculture. In so doing he contributed certain new elements:

(1) He made a thorough analysis of the question of the collective farm form of Socialist economy in the countryside.

(2) He showed that the main link in collective farm development at the present stage is the agricultural artel as the form most rational and most comprehensible to the peasants, making it possible to combine the personal interests of the collective farmers with their collective interests, and to make the collective farmers conform to the public interests.

(3) He proved the necessity for the change from the policy of restricting and squeezing out the kulaks to the policy of eliminating them as a class, on the basis of solid collectivisation.

(4) He revealed the significance of the machine and tractor stations as bases for the Socialist reorganisation of agriculture and as channels through which the Socialist State could render assistance to agriculture and the peasantry.

From a short biography of STALIN
by The Marx–Engels–Lenin Institute.

This solution is to be found in the transformation of the tiny scattered peasant farms into a vast and centralised industry on the basis of co-operative farming and in the adoption of collective farming based on a new and higher technical knowledge. The solution consists in the incorporation through example and as the result of conviction, but not of force, of the smaller and smallest farms in a great industrial organisation for communal, collective, and co-operative farming, employing agricultural machinery and tractors, and making use of scientific methods to intensify agricultural production. There is no other solution. Our agriculture will in no other way be able to catch up with and surpass the agricultural methods of the most highly developed capitalist countries (Canada, etc.).

STALIN, at the Fifteenth Congress of the Communist Party, 1927.

Under the old system the peasants each worked in isolation, following the ancient methods of their forefathers and using antiquated implements of labour; they worked for the landlords and capitalists, the kulaks and profiteers; they lived in penury while they enriched others. Under the new, collective farm system, the peasants work in common, co-operatively, with the help of modern implements—tractors and agricultural machinery; they work for themselves and their collective farms; they live without capitalists and landlords, without kulaks and profiteers; they work with the object of raising their standard of welfare and culture from day to day.

Only one thing is now needed for the collective farmers to become prosperous, and that is for them to work in the collective farms conscientiously, to make efficient use of the tractors and machines, to make efficient use of the draught cattle, to cultivate the land efficiently, and to cherish collective farm property. . . .

A combination of the private interests of the collective farmers with the collective interests of the collective farms—that is the key to the consolidation of the collective farms. . . .

STALIN, at the Congress of Collective Farm-workers, 1935.

Ussuri, the large Soviet forest region on the shores of the Sea of Japan, has become the granary of the Soviet Far East. Local hunters and fishermen have learned to raise rich crops of wheat, barley, and oats.

A few years ago, when the first collective farm settlers arrived in the Taiga from the Ukraine, they planted a few acres of sugar beet. The local farmers were quick to learn from the Ukrainians, and by last year the area under sugar beet had grown to some 13,000 acres.

The Ussuri region grows many other crops, such as soya bean, which yields a rich harvest. This year the area under soya bean will reach 170,000 acres; combine-harvesters will be used for the first time to gather the crop. Local agricultural specialists have adapted 600 machines for this purpose.

Rice is successfully grown in this region. Industrial crops are processed on the spot.

In recent years a large sugar refinery and vegetable oil plant have been operating in Voroshilov-Ussuriik, the centre of the region. The refinery is already satisfying much of the demand for sugar in the Soviet Far East. The oil plant produces large quantities of vegetable oil, soya bean fat and soap.

Between 1913 and 1941 the sown area in Western Siberia alone was doubled, an increase of 18 million acres. The grain yield of Western Siberia and Northern Kazakhstan in 1938 was already four times that of pre-revolutionary days. During the last three years the sown area and crop yield have been greatly increased.

The basis of the great development of agriculture in the east was the Socialist and technical reconstruction of agriculture. This involved the establishment of 1700 machine tractor stations with over 150,000 motor tractors, 53,000 harvester combines and hundreds of thousands of ploughs and other machines.

Soviet War News, 1942.

The collectivisation of agriculture was necessary for the consolidation of the Soviet economic system. Farming had to be transformed into a great industry by the introduction of modern machines and collective labour. There are over 140,000 collective farms in Soviet Russia, which involve at least some 120 million peasants. The farms are community-centres managed by their own organisations. Each Kolkhoz elects its own Executive Committee, and these Committees give direction to all economic activities of the community.

As a result of the collectivisation of agriculture, the Soviet Union has developed the largest agricultural industry in the world. Between 1913 and 1941 the sown area in Western Siberia alone was doubled and the grain yield in 1938 was about four times that of pre-revolutionary days.

From Various Sources.

In the half-century following the emancipation of the peasants the consumption of iron in Russia has increased five-fold; yet Russia remains an incredibly and unprecedentedly backward country, poverty-stricken and semi-barbaric, equipped with modern implements of production to one-fourth the extent of England, one-fifth the extent of Germany, and one-tenth the extent of America. LENIN: *Collected Works.*

Before the war of 1914-1918 Russia occupied fifth place in the world and fourth in Europe for volume of gross industrial output. The rich natural resources of the country remained undeveloped and the distribution of industry was extremely haphazard. During the years of the first Five-Year Plans, the Soviet Union built up a powerful iron and steel industry producing high-quality steel, ferro-alloys, and other material necessary for an extensive engineering industry. In 1928 engineering represented only 11 per cent. of the U.S.S.R.'s gross industrial output. By 1936 this figure rose to nearly 30 per cent.

As regards chemical industry, its gross output of chemicals increased eighteen-fold during the same period. In planning industries, the Soviet Union brought about great changes in the geographical distribution of industry. Engineering plants have been set up in the Urals, Western and Eastern Siberia, the Far East, and Central Asian Republics.

From Various Sources.

The peoples of the Central Asian Soviet Republics on the borders of India and China, who before the Revolution led a backward colonial existence, are playing an increasingly large part in the cultural and economic life of the Soviet Union.

The 1937 output of the heavy industry of Kirghizia, formerly a nomad country, was 95 times that of 1917. Since 1937 there has been a further considerable expansion of the industries of the Republic.

The number of students and school children in Uzbekistan in 1937 was 50 times greater than in 1914.

Soviet War News, 1942.

Over an infinite expanse of oil-fields crouch iron pumps with clanking chains; the great watch-towers of the past are disappearing; everywhere swing the clumsy "pilgrims." [1] Almost noiselessly they pump the oil from the depths of the earth. A little wooden shed contains a junction of oil pipes, that reach out like a spider's web in all directions. . . . Nowhere can one see workers smeared with black oil. . . . Nowhere can one hear the shouting and yelling of foremen, only the clinking and clanking of iron upon iron, as the "pilgrims" bow to the earth.

GORKY.

THE CAPTAIN. . . . Comrade Gromov never expected that his fate would be interwoven with thousands of people who have built the White Sea–Baltic Canal.

(*They all stand up and applaud Gromov.*)

GROMOV. . . . Yes, comrades, it's true, our destinies have become intermingled, and in this intermingling of thousands of lives there is much that is touching, much of the highest and best in humanity. Why will the White Sea Canal be famous? Because here the forces that have drawn people like Sadovsky and Dorokhov to participate in Socialist work are operating with unheard-of daring, with true Bolshevik austerity, and on the broad scale Comrade Stalin has taught us. These people, once rejected by society, outcasts, lost, and even enemies, are to-day recognised and highly valued by their country. Perhaps no one can understand this quite so well and feel so deeply about it as we do, who have trodden the glorious path of the White Sea Canal. For all of you with whom I have quarrelled and worked and won through to victory and united in firm friendship, for all of you I have the warmest regard, and I shake your hands now one and all!

[1] Pilgrims : Pumps, in use in the oil-fields, bought from abroad, are called Pilgrims.

THE CAPTAIN. Quiet, comrades! The first steamer is passing through, from the Baltic to the White Sea. And its name, for posterity to know, is *The Chekist*. Only let's not shout "Hurrah." Instead, let's just listen to the water singing in the locks!   NIKOLAI POGODIN: From his comedy
Aristocrats.

On the night of August 30, 1935, in the Donbas, an event took place which aroused the deepest response throughout our country and awoke the interest of the whole world. That night an ordinary miner, Alexei Stakhanov, achieved a record output in coal extraction with a miner's pick.

This spark kindled the flames of the Stakhanovite movement throughout the country—the movement of workers and peasants to attain an unprecedented level of Socialist Labour productivity. Before long this movement became universal in the U.S.S.R. New masses of men and women workers and collective farmers flocked to the ranks of this vanguard of production. Mighty national talents came to the fore.

The Stakhanovites were reared under Stalin. They became the bearers of technical progress and boldly overthrew the old standards, opening the way for a gigantic growth of our industry and our entire national economy.

Pravda, quoted in *Soviet War News*, 1941.

The Stakhanov movement is the expression of a new wave of Socialist emulation, a new and higher stage of Socialist emulation. . . . The significance of the Stakhanov movement lies in the fact that it is a movement which is smashing the old technical standards, because they are inadequate, which in a number of cases is surpassing the productivity of labour of the foremost capitalist countries, and is thus creating the practical possibility of further consolidating Socialism in our country, the possibility of converting our country into the most prosperous of all countries.

STALIN, at the First All-Union Conference
of Stakhanovites, 1935.

Stakhanovites are people who turn out several times more products than the standard calls for; they are people who know how to get the maximum out of modern machinery; they are people for whom labour is not a humdrum job, but creative endeavour. . . .

The ranks of the Stakhanovites are multiplying. The women who are going down into the mines to take the places of husbands called to the front are winning honours in the Stakhanovite watch. They have undertaken to work with the maximum efficiency, to do everything they can to surpass output standards and turn out as much coal and ore as the country needs.

ALEXEI STAKHANOV: *In Defence of Civilization against Fascist Barbarism.*

The elimination of the distinction between mental labour and manual labour can be achieved only by raising the cultural and technical level of the working class to the level of engineers and technicians. It would be absurd to think that this is unfeasible. It is entirely feasible under the Soviet system, where the productive forces of the country are freed from the fetters of capitalism, where labour is freed from the yoke of exploitation, where the working class is in power, and where the younger generation of the working class has every opportunity of obtaining an adequate technical education. There is no reason whatever to doubt that only such a rise in the cultural and technical level of the working class can undermine the basis of the distinction between mental labour and manual labour, that it alone can ensure the high level of productivity of labour and the abundance of articles of consumption which are necessary in order to begin the transition from Socialism to Communism.

In this connection, the Stakhanov movement is significant for the fact that it contains the first beginnings—still feeble, it is true, but nevertheless the beginnings—of precisely such a rise in the cultural and technical level of the working class of our country.

STALIN, at the Conference of Stakhanovites, 1938.

We have outstripped the principal capitalist countries as regards technique of production and rate of industrial development. That is very good, but it is not enough. We must outstrip them economically as well. We can do it, and we must do it. Only if we outstrip the principal capitalist countries economically can we reckon upon our country being fully saturated with consumers' goods, on having an abundance of products, and on being able to make the transition from the first phase of Communism to its second phase.

STALIN, at the Eighteenth Congress of the Communist Party, 1939.

The national economy of the U.S.S.R. is developing systematically in accordance with the laws of extended Socialist reproduction, which implies, first and foremost, a steady growth of production in all branches of the national economy.

In the first three years of the Third Five-Year Plan, the industrial output of the U.S.S.R. increased from 95,500 million roubles in 1937 to 137,500 million roubles in 1940, or by 44 per cent. This includes an increase in the output of the machine-building and metal-working industry by 76 per cent. ...

The increase of production in the Soviet Union was accompanied by a reconstruction of industry, especially of the machine-building industry, for the purpose of producing the most advanced and up-to-date equipment needed by the national economy and for the defence of the country.

N. VOZNESENSKY: Report at the Eighteenth All-Union Conference of the C.P.S.U., 1941.

C. SOCIAL WELFARE

The citizens of the U.S.S.R. have the right to education. This right is ensured by compulsory universal elementary education, by the fact that education, including higher education, is free, by a system of payment of State stipends to the overwhelming majority of students in higher education establishments, by instruction in schools being given in the native language, by the organisation in factories, State farms, machine and tractor stations and collective farms, of free, vocational, technical, and agricultural instruction for the working people.

Article 121 of the Soviet Constitution.

In 1914 there were 1950 secondary schools with 635,000 pupils and 42,000 teachers throughout the whole of Russia. In 1939 the U.S.S.R. had 15,800 secondary schools with 10,935,000 pupils and 377,000 teachers.

The number of higher educational institutions shows a similar increase. The industrialisation of the country and the large-scale mechanisation of agriculture demanded a tremendous number of specialists, of whom pre-revolutionary Russia had very few. The number of higher educational institutions increased from 91 in 1914 to 700 in 1936, of which 90 were agricultural colleges. The total enrolment at primary, secondary, and higher schools increased from 8,127,000 in 1913 to 38,335,000 in 1937.

A special feature is the growth of urban and rural clubs, which were an important influence in raising the cultural level of the people. Here there is scarcely any standard of comparison with the pre-revolutionary situation, as before November 1917 the number of clubs throughout the whole enormous territory of Russia was negligible. In 1939 there were 111,000 of them in the U.S.S.R.

The growth of literacy, the general improvement in the cultural level of the population, and the enormous increase in the number of intellectuals is reflected in the increased number of books and periodicals, and in newspaper circulations.

In 1913 there were in Russia 859 newspapers with a total circulation of 2,700,000. In 1938 there were 8500 newspapers with a daily circulation of 37,500,000 copies—a fourteen-fold increase.

In the 25 years' existence of the Soviet State over 9,000,000,000 copies of books and pamphlets have been published. The annual output of books during this period was multiplied by eight. In 1938, 693,000,000 separate volumes were printed.

Books are printed in more than 100 languages, including 40 languages of peoples who before the Socialist Revolution had no written language of their own. Works by Marx, Engels, Lenin, and Stalin have been issued in 727,000,000 copies. Works by Stalin have been published in 100 languages, with a total print of 420,000,000 copies. Maxim Gorky's works have been published in 65 languages with a print of 41,000,000 copies. Tolstoy's and Chekhov's works have been published in 60 languages.

Soviet War News, 1942.

Moslems of the U.S.S.R. are playing a considerable part in the defence of the Soviet Union. Men from Azerbaijan, Turkmenia, Uzbekistan, Kazakhstan, Kirghizia, Tataria, Bashkiria, Daghestan, and other Soviet Republics in the east are to be found on all sectors of the front. . . .

Under Article 123 of the Constitution of the U.S.S.R., all national inequality and disabilities have been abolished by law. All the languages of the peoples of the Union enjoy equal status. In the national Republics, the official languages are Russian and the language of the people who form the bulk of the inhabitants. . . .

In Tsarist Russia national minorities were not allowed to receive tuition in their own language. Even in schools and higher educational establishments where the language taught was Russian, Moslems were accepted only in limited numbers. . . .

The cultural life of the Moslem peoples of the U.S.S.R. has developed at an unprecedented pace. . . . The languages of the Moslem peoples and their old literature are being revived. Classical works of Russian, Ukrainian, and foreign literature are being translated into the languages of the Turko-Tatar people. . . .

The number of illiterates in the Moslem Republics is continually decreasing. In 1926 the percentage of literates among the people of the Turkmen Republic was 16·5 among men and 7·7 among women. In 1936 the figures were 73·3 for men and 60·6 for women. According to the 1939 census, in the Azerbaijan Republic there were 25,000 persons with higher education out of a total population of 3,200,000; in the Turkmen Republic, 4000 persons out of a total of 1,254,000; in the Kazakh Republic about 28,000 out of a total of 6,100,000. Many new higher educational establishments have been opened in these Moslem regions. . . . *Soviet War News*, 1942.

Citizens of the U.S.S.R. have the right to material security in old age as well as in the event of sickness and loss of capacity to work.

This right is ensured by the wide development of social insurance of workers and employees at the expense of the State, free medical aid, and the provision of a wide network of health resorts for the use of the toilers.

Article 120 of the Soviet Constitution.

The *social economic* and political relations in the U.S.S.R. created by the Revolution of November 1917 became the foundation of the Soviet system of medicine. The basic principles on which the Soviet State was built up were reflected in the organisation of its medical service.

The organisation of prophylactic and medical aid for the population of the U.S.S.R. is regarded as one of the basic duties of the State. Medical care is not left, as it was before the Revolution, to private charitable institutions, or to private enterprise. The task of the organisation of free, accessible, and skilled medical aid to the toiling population of town and country has been undertaken entirely by the central and local organs of the Soviet State. A People's Commissariat of Health, with the same powers as the other Government Commissariats, was established in June 1918. A health department was set up at each local Soviet. These bodies took charge of medical care, anti-epidemic measures, sanitary inspection of food, housing, and public utilities (waterworks, drainage, laundries, etc.); they are responsible for the protection of the health of the workers and peasants; provide for the health of children and adolescents, and protect maternity and infancy; control the health resorts; are in charge of pharmaceutical and medical supplies; provide for the sanitary education of the masses; train physicians, medical assistants, etc.

... This fact makes it possible to organise properly the medical service throughout the U.S.S.R., to distribute the medical personnel in such a way as to ensure the needs not only of the principal industrial regions, and of the collective and State farms in the heart of the country, but also of the most distant regions and districts. Every worker in the U.S.S.R. is thus able to benefit by the service of the medical and prophylactic institutions wherever he lives. The local health departments, as stated above, are departments of the Soviet of the province, town, or district. Their structure and functions correspond to those of the central Commissariat. Within their territory the local health departments have full control of all medical care of every group of the population. *Thus unity in the organisation of the health service is the first distinguishing feature of Soviet medicine.*

N. A. SEMASHKO: *Health Protection in the U.S.S.R.*

The planning of the health service is based on the following main principles. The health protection plan is co-ordinated with the general economic plan. With this object the health departments make a study of the economic situation of their region: the character of its industries, the most important factories and State collective farms. The plan must be calculated so as to provide the fullest service to the workers of these establishments in preference to the rest of the population.

The health departments also investigate the sanitary and hygienic conditions of the region: the general mortality rate and the mortality rate of infants under one year; the sickness rate, with particular reference to infectious diseases; the housing conditions and the condition of the public utilities (water supplies, drainage, bath-houses, laundries, etc.); the condition of communal feeding; the natural features of the region (i.e. swamps, condition of rivers, lakes, etc.).

N. A. SEMASHKO: *Health Protection in the U.S.S.R.*

. . . our country now has five times as many doctors as the Russian Empire had under the Tsar; and the 8 medical schools of Tsarist Russia have grown to 72 under the Soviets.

There are at present 214 medical research institutions in the Soviet Union. Chief among them is the All-Union Institute of Experimental Medicine, the uniting centre of medical thought, with a large number of branches and subsidiary organisations. Its laboratories have been the birthplace of many works of the greatest interest, which have attracted widespread attention in scientific circles both at home and abroad. These include the investigation of mitogenetic rays and of their rôle in cancer diagnosis, and the numerous works based on the theory of neurotropism, as well as certain extremely important researches in encephalitis.

N. N. BURDENKO: *In Defence of Civilization against Fascist Barbarism.*

The Soviet Red Cross Society, a voluntary organisation with a membership of over 20 millions, is playing an important part in the organisation of civil defence in the U.S.S.R. The society has 160,000 local branches in enterprises and institutions all over the country.

These branches carry out extensive work in organising the

health education of the population and training reserves for the army. Millions of Soviet citizens, with the assistance of Red Cross instructors, have gained first-aid badges inscribed "Ready for Health Defence." *Pravda*, 1941.

We all consider our children to be the most precious asset the country possesses, and whilst Soviet law recognises and enforces parental responsibility (that of the mother no less and no more than that of the father) both for the material and moral well-being of the child, our Government seeks to ensure for every Soviet child the best possible physical, intellectual, and moral care possible.

In 1940 over 1000 million roubles were spent on infant care, pioneer camps, children's sanatoria, and other children's institutions of a similar type.

The economic basis of the Soviet Union is, as is well known, a Socialist system of the national economy, in which private profit-making and the exploitation of man by man is excluded, and the training and education of our children is in conformity with this principle.

In crèche, school, and college our children and young people are trained to hate oppression or exploitation of one man by another or of one country by another. They are taught to love their own country, to be prepared to work, defend, and if necessary die for it, to be jealous of its honour but at the same time not to despise or hate other countries.

On the contrary, while our teachers and our leaders enjoin upon our young people the need to be loyal, devoted, brave Soviet citizens, they also stress the rights of all other countries to self-determination, to an equal place in the sun.

This we can do the more readily in our country since the U.S.S.R. is itself made up of a Union of many different national Republics and is inhabited by nearly 200 different nationalities, all of whom have equal economic, political, and cultural rights. The fraternity and amity existing between the peoples of the multi-national State of the U.S.S.R. act as a living example of the lesson of patriotic love for one's own country combined with an international fraternal regard for the rights of other countries which we endeavour to inculcate in our young people.

MADAME MAISKY, 1942.

The systematical growth of the national income of our country, and hence of the social wealth and the personal consumption of the working people, is due to the fact that new contingents of workers, collective farmers, and intellectuals are constantly being drawn into production, as well as to the increasing productivity of labour.

The size of the working class in the U.S.S.R. is growing from year to year. . . .

The rising standard of living of the people of the U.S.S.R. is attended by a rise in the level of culture. State appropriations for social and cultural services, which amounted to 35,200 million roubles in 1938, increased to 41,700 million roubles, or by 18·5 per cent. in 1940. The draft State budget for 1941 provides for an increase in expenditure on social and cultural services to 47,800 million roubles, 14·6 per cent. more than in the previous year.

N. Voznesensky: Report at the Eighteenth All-Union Conference of the C.P.S.U., 1941.

D. SCIENCE AND CULTURE

The U.S.S.R. is a country where scientists and creative thought are shown every respect. Our present-day culture has been produced by the collaboration of various peoples for many centuries. This respect for science in general is manifested particularly clearly in the Soviet Union. Proud though we are of our own writers, Tolstoy, Chekhov, and Dostoevsky; of scientists such as Pavlov and Mendeleyev, we admire to an equal degree the men of science and art of Great Britain, the U.S.A., France, Germany, Holland, Italy, and other countries. This proves that we have the same moral ideals and the same ideas about culture, ideals and ideas which are essential for the healthy growth of any country.

Professor Peter Kapitza: *In Defence of Civilization against Fascist Barbarism.*

In the first years of the existence of the Soviet Government, the Academy of Sciences consisted of one scientific institute and several museums and laboratories, while its staff was composed of 45 members of the Academy and 212 scientific workers. In 1941 we had under our auspices 76 large institutes with 118 members of the Academy, 182 corresponding members, and 4700 scientific and technical workers. We owe our successes to the constant solicitude of the Government and of Stalin personally for science and scientists, to the rapid development of the country's productive forces, and to the practical application of all scientific achievements.

    PROFESSOR VLADIMIR KOMAROV, on the Twenty-
    Fifth Anniversary of the Socialist Revolution.

There were great Russian men of science of international renown before the Revolution in 1917, but they were mostly isolated specialists working with little encouragement except from their colleagues at home and abroad. Under the Soviet Union there has been a wider and more rapid expansion of scientific education and more extensive applications of technical training to industrial, agricultural, and medical needs than any country has ever before experienced in a similar period of its history.

The few scientists who devoted their lives to the advancement of natural knowledge under the Tsarist State have become a great force of highly trained members working with deliberate plans to increase such knowledge in the service of science and the development of natural and national resources for the benefit of the community. In its system of State organisation of scientific research and the planning of discoveries of new facts and resources, the Union has departed from the monasterial tradition of scientific investigation and made the utilisation of science the purpose of activities in both the laboratory and the field.

The full story of achievements in this new Soviet world of science has not yet been told, but most British scientists know that within the past twenty years Russia has made advances far greater than ever before in her history. That is why the Union has been able to defy and repel the scientific forms of cultivated barbarity against which the United Nations are now fighting. Russia is undergoing martyrdom in defence of what are the fundamental rights of all peoples, and every human heart throbs to-day in sympathetic admiration of its strength and sacrifice.

    SIR RICHARD GREGORY, in *Labour Monthly*, 1942.

In the period between the first and second world wars a powerful chemical industry was built up in the Soviet Union on modern scientific and technical lines, such as Tsarist Russia did not possess. Soviet scientists have introduced a number of novel methods of production. Following the injunctions of the great scientists of our country, Lomonosov, Mendeleyev, Zinin, Butlerov, they have striven to combine theoretical research with the solution of practical problems, and have coped with this task by no means unsuccessfully.

A. N. FRUMKIN, Member of the Soviet
Academy of Science.

Our scientific work has always been closely related to the requirements of the people of our country, which coincide with the interests of all humanity. Our scientists have always put their work at the nation's disposal to make available its immense natural resources and to develop its national economy. The scientific development of this economy has permitted the creation in twenty years of a large-scale industry and a reorganised agriculture, which have increased the standard of living of all the peoples of the Soviet Union.

Our country grew in strength through the collaboration of all the nationalities inhabiting the Soviet Union. By the laws of our Constitution all nationalities have equal rights and are equally respected as members of our large Soviet family. Our scientists study the history of all the peoples of the Soviet Union, study their folklore and enrich Russian national culture. This work has fostered the unity of our people and their mutual respect for each other's culture.

Appeal of Soviet Scientists to the Scientists of
the World, October 12, 1941.

Science and culture are greatly valued in our country. The U.S.S.R. has built up a powerful industry. Agriculture has been highly mechanised and equipped with first-class machinery. Labour has become highly productive, and the soil bountiful in its yields. The country has been covered with an extensive network of educational establishments, research institutions, academies, institutes, and laboratories. . . .

The Soviet people and their scientists are filled with the common desire to defend the liberty and independence of their country.
> T. D. LYSENKO: *In Defence of Civilization against Fascist Barbarism.*

In common with the scientists of other countries, we Soviet scientists consider ourselves heirs and guardians of the cultural values created by mankind throughout history.

The cultural progress of the various peoples of the Soviet Union has always been our special concern. We restore their material and spiritual treasures and monuments. We join in honouring their best thinkers, poets, and scientists, and assist them in raising their cultural level, at the same time preserving and developing their own national characteristics.
> LINA STERN: *In Defence of Civilization against Fascist Barbarism.*

The latest figure of the total population of the Union is 193 millions. Among these millions of people we have something like 180 different languages, of which the more important number 70. I mean languages and not dialects.

Our newspapers are printed in 70 different languages, and so are our text-books for the schools. Our theatres give performances in 45 different languages. The Russians proper, numbering roughly 100 millions, or approximately a little more than half the total population, constitute the largest single nation in the Soviet Union.
> M. MAISKY, at the opening of the Russian Course for Teachers, 1942.

The Central Committee ascertains that, as a result of the successes of Socialist construction, literature and art have, in the past few years, exhibited a considerable growth, both in quality and quantity.

Some years ago, when literature was still under the strong influence of certain alien elements, which were particularly flourishing in the first years of New Economic Policy, and when the ranks of Proletarian literature were still comparatively feeble, the Party helped, by every means in its power, the creation of special Proletarian organisation in the spheres of literature and art, with a view to strengthening the position of Proletarian writers and art workers.

Now that the rank and file of Proletarian literature has had time to grow and establish itself, and that new writers and artists have come forward from factories, mills, and collective farms, the framework of the existing Proletarian literary-artistic organisations is becoming too confined and impedes the serious development of artistic creation. There is thus the danger that these organisations might be turned from a means of intensive mobilisation of Soviet writers and artists around the problems of Socialist construction into a means of cultivating hermetic groupings and of alienating considerable groups of writers and artists, sympathising with the aims of Socialist construction, from contemporary political problems.

Hence the necessity for a corresponding reconstruction of the literary-artistic organisations and for the extension of the basis of their work.

Therefore the Central Committee resolves:

(*a*) To liquidate the association of Proletarian writers.

(*b*) To unite all writers upholding the platform of the Soviet power and striving to participate in Socialist construction into a single Union of Soviet Writers with a Communist faction therein;

(*c*) To promote a similar change in the sphere of other forms of art;

(*d*) To entrust the Organising Bureau with the working out of practical measures for the application of this resolution.

> From a Resolution of the Central Committee of the
> All-Russian Communist Party, April 23, 1932.

Soviet literature has broken new ground. Conscious of its social task and its responsibility before life as a whole, it strives to integrate all the creative elements of the present and the past for the sake of a better future. And this brings us to that "Socialist realism" which was launched, in 1932, as the literary current of Soviet Russia.

What, then, is Socialist realism? Its elements can be found not only in the best Soviet novels since 1922, but also in Gorky, as well as in several intelligentsia authors, from Belinsky and

Herzen onwards. Gorky himself calls it Proletarian or Socialist humanism. The latter presupposes a Socialist society and that type of consciousness in which the individual and the community are no longer two hostile, but two complementary factors, helping each other's growth.

Our bourgeois realism is mainly one which criticises life. As long as it reflects our modern society in its process of disintegration, it is almost bound to be devoid of faith, of any perspective for the future. It is sceptical and pessimistic by its very nature. Losing the last traces of social consciousness, the modern individual, too, is liable to become a self-centred "decadent," either indifferent or even profoundly hostile to the community. He is critical of the present mainly in order to take revenge for his own frustrated will and for his inner devastation. Socialist realism, however, postulates not only an integrated society, but also a creative scope for the individual and collective will, stimulated by a new faith in man and life. It can be as minute in its description and relentless in its criticism as any bourgeois analysis, but the spirit is different. To quote Gorky, "we are interested in accurate description of reality in so far as this is necessary for a deeper and clearer understanding of all that we must abolish and that we must build up."

Socialist realism thus integrates literature and life. Its aim is not only to reflect life, but to shape it, to imbue it with significance, to direct the creative present towards a more creative future. Such art can be profoundly tragic at times, but it cannot be pessimistic.... One thing is certain: Soviet literature has bravely taken a new direction, and has come forward with new demands and values. The entire process is still one of fermentation. But when it has crystallised, the Russian novel may again play a leading part in world literature.

JANKO LAVRIN: *An Introduction to the Russian Novel.*

(1) Art by means of living images organises social experience not only in the sphere of knowledge, but also in that of feelings and aspiration. It is consequently one of the most powerful instruments for the organisation of collective forces and of class forces in a class society.

(2) A class art of its own is indispensable to the Proletariat for the organisation of its forces for social work, struggle, and con-

struction. Labour collectivism—such is the spirit of this art, which ought to reflect the world from the point of view of the labour collective—expresses the complex of its feeling and its militant and creative will.

(3) The treasures of ancient art must not be absorbed passively; otherwise they would educate the working class in the spirit of the ruling classes and in a spirit of acquiescence to a social order of their creation. The Proletariat must examine the treasures of ancient art in the light of its new critical doctrine, which reveals their secret collective foundations and their organisational significance. They will then prove a precious inheritance for the Proletariat and a weapon in its fight against that ancient world which created them, and an instrument for the building up of a new world. It is the task of Proletarian criticism to assure this artistic heritage.

(4) All organisations, all institutions, devoted to the development of the new art and the new criticism, ought to be formed upon a basis of comradely collaboration, which would directly educate its workers in the ways of social aspiration.

> The Resolution proposed by A. BOGDANOV at the First All-Russian Conference of Proletarian Cultural-Educational Organisations on September 20, 1918.

In front of the cathedral, facing the Red square, stands a bronze monument on an austere granite pedestal. Two powerful figures represent Kuzma Minin and Dmitry Pozharsky, heroes of the liberation war of 1613. The enemy was then enthroned in the very heart of the country, Moscow—and in the heart of Moscow, the Kremlin.

Minin of Nizhni Novgorod (now Gorky) raised national levies and invited Prince Pozharsky to be their leader. This people's army liberated the capital and the country. Since then the names of Minin and Pozharsky are inseparably linked in Russian history—two heroes, one representing the people, the other the army.

It was the unity of people and army that ensured victory over the powerful enemy of those days. That idea is expressed in the monument which the sculptor Matross created at the beginning of the nineteenth century, after the expulsion of Napoleon's army from Russia. Though it celebrates heroes of 1613, it reflects the spirit of the patriotic war of 1812, which ended in Russia's victory over the conqueror of Europe.

Minin stands with one hand outstretched imperiously, challengingly. The other hand rests on the hilt of a sword held by Pozharsky. The Prince, who has not recovered from wounds received in earlier wars, is seated, but his whole figure expresses his readiness to respond to the call of the national leader and to assume command of the liberating armies.

Matross, a master of the classical school, has given his heroes the dress and accoutrements of antique Russian warriors. But their faces are the faces of Russian peasants.

The spartan simplicity of the monument is peculiarly expressive against the background of St. Basil's traceries and coloured turrets. The Matross group expresses the stern imperative of civic duty, and St. Basil's the festive triumph of victory.

St. Basil's, the Matross monument, Lenin's tomb—in them are linked outstanding dates in Russian history. And all three testify to one thing: the inexhaustible latent energy of the Russian people, who at the darkest moments of their history acquire an inflexible staunchness and determination that ensures victory over the strongest enemy.

       PROFESSOR ARKIN, Member of the Soviet
       Academy of Architecture.

Shostakovich's Seventh Symphony was inspired by the war. The first three movements were written in September before the composer left besieged Leningrad, where he lives. He wrote the fourth movement in Kuibyshev.

The force which imbues the whole symphony is hatred for Fascism and faith in a new victorious world. Shostakovich's music has philosophical depth. The first movement (Sonata allegro) is dedicated to the common people "who forge our victories and our successes," as the composer himself puts it.

This movement, he says, is something in the nature of an antithesis to Richard Strauss's "Symphonica domestica." While the latter is a picture of the life of Vienna burghers, Shostakovich deals with a different sort of human material. He finds musical language which is simple and convincing enough to reach the people he is addressing.

Into the cloudless halcyon world of the first movement bursts the thunderbolt of war. The composer has carefully guarded his symphony from any pitfalls of naturalism, of musical photography. The sternness and relentlessness of the war sounds through his music.

In the scherzo (second movement) and adagio (third movement) the composer lapses into reminiscent pensive mood. It is a new Shostakovich we see here. In this music, perhaps autobiographical, he elevates human emotion to highly generalised levels. The music is original, but nevertheless clear and beautiful.

The symphony is long—52 minutes. We waited impatiently for the fourth movement, which we knew carried the promise of victory. When it came, it surpassed our expectations. The original organ-point is the foundation of the structure, a sort of magic portal leading to a new world, a wondrous, glorious, and at the same time stern world.   ALEXANDER OGOLOVETS.

Our intelligentsia has a part of exceptional importance to play in this historic work. Men of culture, men of science and technology, the old intelligentsia and the new, our students, and our skilled workers, whose ranks are being reinforced by youth, are all needed to enable the Soviet people to cope with the great new tasks, to accomplish the main economic task that now has to be performed, to successfully fulfil the Third Five-Year Plan. On their capacity to organise the labour of the workers and peasants, on their skill in applying their scientific knowledge to the utilisation of technology and to the attainment of the utmost increase in labour productivity, will depend the success of our work, the success of the competition with the other countries for economic primacy upon which the U.S.S.R. is now entering, and the success of the historic competition between Communism and Capitalism. Their creative efforts will be the more fertile and their achievements the more remarkable, the more consistently and deeply they delve into the essence of the fundamental modern science of society and the State—the essence of the great teachings of Marxism-Leninism, which is the basis for the growth and strength of Socialist construction in the U.S.S.R. We have already created so many of the requisites, so many potentialities for the further growth and full prosperity of our society, that the chief thing now is a conscious Communist attitude towards our work, and, especially, successful Bolshevik activity in the sphere of the ideological training of the swelling ranks of our Soviet intelligentsia.

The time has come when the work of education, the Communist education of the people, assumes prime importance. This estimate of the rôle of Communist education at the present juncture in no way detracts from the duty of which Comrade Stalin spoke, the duty of keeping our people in a state of mobilisation and readiness for any and every emergency. On the contrary, only that education may be called a Communist education which adds to our state of mobilisation and readiness, and enhances our capacity to engage in a supreme struggle, in new battles, for the victory of Communism.

> MOLOTOV: Report to the Eighteenth Congress
> of the Communist Party, 1939.

E. RELIGION

In the Soviet Union the Church is separated from the State. This means that the State grants no privileges to one or another religion, and does not undertake to maintain the Orthodox or Roman Catholic churches, mosques, synagogues, etc., at State expense. The citizens of one religion form a community which maintains its religious institutions at the expense of the congregation.

The U.S.S.R. grants the freedom of religious worship. This means that every Soviet citizen is free to worship according to his beliefs. This is a matter of conscience and world outlook of every citizen. Religion is a private affair of every Soviet citizen in which the State does not interfere and does not consider such interference necessary.

The Soviet Constitution grants every citizen not only the right to worship as he chooses, but also the right not to worship and to conduct anti-religious propaganda. The legislature of the Soviet Union does not consider it possible to compel citizens either to worship or not to worship at all. In its Constitution the U.S.S.R. proceeds from the following: Freedom of worship presupposes that no religion, Church, or religious community will be utilised for overthrowing the existing Government recognised in the country. The policy of the Soviet Union with regard to the religious question is concisely and clearly formulated in Article 124 of the Constitution of the U.S.S.R.

Official Statement by M. LOZOVSKY made in Moscow on October 4, 1941.

Religion in my country is not persecuted, and every citizen has the right to believe or not to believe, according to his or her own conscience.

Article 124 of the Stalin Constitution reads:

"In order to ensure to citizens freedom of conscience, the Church in the U.S.S.R. is separated from the State, and the school from the Church. Freedom of religious worship and freedom of anti-religious propaganda is recognised for all citizens."

This Article is quite clear, and it is by no means a dead letter. Indeed, in 1940, in the U.S.S.R. there were over 30,000 independent religious communities of every kind, over 8000 churches, and about 60,000 priests and ministers of religion. Believers practise their religions freely, they frequent services, they marry in church, christen their children, have religious funerals, celebrate religious festivals, and elect leaders of their congregations.

The Soviet Government did not, and does not, support any one religion in the U.S.S.R., but it puts at their disposal free of rent premises for religious observance, exempting all such premises from taxation. Soviet Courts of Law punish those who violate the rights of believers. Priests and ministers of religion enjoy equal rights to the Supreme Soviet and all other electoral institutions of the U.S.S.R. The Orthodox Church has the largest number of followers and is divided at the present time into two chief sections.: "The New Church" and "The Old Church," each of which has its own headquarters in Moscow. . . .

Side by side with assuring national and religious freedom, the Soviet Union also stands for the raising of the standard of life and education of the wide masses of the people. It stands for the progress of science and art, for assuring to all the right to work and the right to leisure.

The Soviet Union and Hitlerite Germany represent two entirely antagonistic worlds, and for this reason the Soviet people are fighting and will fight to the last drop of blood against the perfidious attack of German Fascism.

M. MAISKY, in a speech in London at the American
Chamber of Commerce, September 1941.

RELIGION IN THE SOVIET UNION:

There are 8338 churches, Catholic churches, synagogues, and mosques in the U.S.S.R. Without counting the Armenian-Gregorian Church and the preachers of different sects, there are 58,442 ministers of religious worship. In 1940 the number of religious communities registered, each having 20 or more members, was 30,000.

Believers freely practise their religious worship—baptize their children, marry, perform funeral ceremonies, celebrate religious festivals and fasts, attend church ceremonies, keep ikons in their homes, elect leaders of religious communities, and so on.

The Soviet Government provides buildings for religious purposes free of charge and exempt from taxes. The Soviet Government ensures that no one disturbs the rights of believers, offends their feelings or jeers at their belief. Soviet courts severely punish those who try in any way to infringe on the rights of believers.

The clergy in the U.S.S.R. enjoys rights with all other Soviet citizens. The most important right of citizens of the U.S.S.R.—to elect and be elected members of the supreme organs of the Soviet Government—is fully guaranteed to preachers, priests, mullahs, rabbis, etc.

Children of religious ministers work in the different spheres of the country's economic and social life equally with other citizens, as engineers, technicians, writers, artists, etc.

The Soviet Government has secured for each nationality the possibility to perform religious ceremonies in their mother tongue.

The Orthodox Church.—In the U.S.S.R. the Orthodox Church is represented by two movements—the Old Church and the New Church. The former is headed by Metropolitan Sergey, Acting Patriarch; the latter by the First Hierarch, Metropolitan Vitaliy. The Church Centres have their own buildings in Moscow, in which are housed their administrative offices.

The supreme authority of these Churches consists of 28 Metropolitans and Bishops, the principal ones being the Metropolitan of Leningrad, Alexei Simansky; the Metropolitan of Kiev, Nicolai Yarushevich, and others.

The Moscow Patriarchy (Old Church) extends its influence to some churches abroad, including the American Orthodox Churches. In the United States there is Benjamin Fedchenko, Exarch of the Moscow Patriarchy, who regularly reports to the Moscow religious Centre.

The Church Centres are supported by the voluntary contributions of their congregations and their own savings fund. According to the report of the Council of the Elokhovsky Cathedral in Moscow, where Metropolitan Sergey Stardorodsky holds his service, the savings of this Cathedral exceed a sum of one million roubles.

In the U.S.S.R. there are:

Churches	4,225
Monasteries	37
Priests	5,665
Deacons and Sacristans	3,100

In the total of acting churches there are in Yaroslavsky District, 346; Moscow District, 225; Ivanov District, 187.

Religious Sects.—There are numerous religious sects in the U.S.S.R., represented by different movements, the principal ones being: Evangelical, Old Church, and Adventist. All of these have their Centres in Moscow.

The All-Union Council of Evangelical Christians is headed by the Pastors Orlov, Andreyev, Urstein, and Karev. This sect comprises about 1000 societies and groups.

The All-Union Council of Adventists is headed by Pastor Gregoriev. The head of the Old Church is Archbishop Irinarkh Parfionov.

Moslem Church.—The Moslem Church in the U.S.S.R. is governed by its religious Centres in Ufa, headed by the Mufti Abdul Rahman Rassulayev. There are:

Mosques	1,312
Mullahs	8,052
Sheiks	282
Ishans	528
Murids	35,947

Catholic Church.—There are:

Churches	1,744
Priests	2,309

Armenian-Gregorian Church.—At the head of the Armenian-Gregorian Church is Archbishop Gevork Charekhchan, Assistant Catholicos. Working with him is a Council elected by the Armenian-Gregorian Church Congress. The last election took place in April 1941; Charekhchan, the Archbishop of the American Eparchies, Ovsipian (New York), and the Archbishop of Rumania, Zagrebian, and others were then elected to the Council.

All the foreign Eparchies of the Armenian-Gregorian Church (Rumanian, Bulgarian, Greek, French, Egyptian, Syrian, Iranian-India, American, and others) are subordinated to the Catholicos of Achmiadzinsk, who is the head of all the believing Armenians.

On the territory of the U.S.S.R. there are nine acting Armenian-Gregorian Churches.

Jewish Clerical Church.—There are:

Synagogues	1,011
Rabbis	2,559

In Moscow there are three synagogues, of which one is the Great Choral Synagogue, which has its own administration.

Up to 1941, religious books under 414 different titles were issued in the U.S.S.R. by the various religious bodies.

Soviet War News, 1941.

Chapter Six

SOVIET FOREIGN POLICY

To the question, what would be the attitude of the Proletarian Party in the event of its attaining to power through a revolution during the present war, the answer must be: We would propose peace to all belligerents on condition that all colonies and all oppressed, enslaved, and dependent nations received their freedom. Under their present Governments neither Germany nor England nor France would accept this condition. As a consequence of their refusal we would be forced to prepare and wage a revolutionary war. In other words—we would not only carry out with the most ruthless methods the least part of our programme (the demands put forward by Russian Social Democracy for the creation of a democratic Republic), but we would stir up all the peoples oppressed by Greater Russia as well as all colonies and dependencies in Asia, India, China, Persia, etc., and, above all, incite the Socialist proletariat of Europe, in spite of the Chauvinists among it, to rebellion against its Governments.
LENIN: Collected Works.

Capitalism has brought about such economic concentration that entire branches of industry are in the hands of syndicates, trusts, or corporations of millionaires; almost the entire globe has been parcelled out among the "giants of capital," either in the form of colonies or through the entangling of foreign countries by thousands of threads of financial exploitation . . . for the export of raw material, etc. Capitalism, formerly a liberator of nations, has now in its imperialist stage become the greatest oppressor of nations. Formerly progressive, it has become a reactionary force. It has developed the productive forces to such an extent that humanity must either pass over to Socialism, or for years, nay decades, witness armed conflicts of the "great" nations for an artificial maintenance of capitalism by means of colonies, monopolies, privileges, and all sorts of national oppression.   LENIN: *Socialism and War.*

The Government of the Soviet Union has never failed to avail itself of any opportunity arising in international politics for the furtherance of peace—and peace for all the peoples of the world as well as for its own country. All the diplomatic activities of the Soviet Union bear testimony to this aspiration for universal peace—never lost sight of in the darkest hour of defeat or the elation of victory. The Soviet Union holds the same language with regard to peace for all countries—for those that directly attacked it, for those that have entered into normal diplomatic relations with it, and for those who still refuse, despite its eleven years of existence and ever-increasing development, to "recognise" the Soviet State. . . .

Every year of the existence of the Soviet Republics has been marked by an unceasing and resolute struggle for peace, for the liberation of tortured humanity from the horrors of military catastrophes. In the whole eleven years' history of the Soviets no step has been taken that was not directed towards the effective realisation of peace. Despite the innumerable international obstacles put in the way of the Soviet Union by its imperialist foes and opponents, it has never lost an opportunity of demonstrating them, and never refused to take the initiative in advancing the affairs of peace.

HENRI BARBUSSE, in an Introduction to
The Soviet Union and Peace, 1929.

The Russian Government fully realises that with the present social-economic structure of the majority of countries, based upon the exploitation of man by man, and one nation by another, such measures as would completely remove the possibility of armed international conflicts are unthinkable. The attempts made and still being made by the Great Powers to regulate international relations, while removing some of the formerly existing injustices between nations, have created a set of new and still more crying injustices and new possible sources of war in the future. At the same time, the Russian Government is fully convinced that not only complete but even partial disarmament would greatly diminish the chances of armed conflicts, and would, moreover, give direct, tangible results in the form of the reducing of the burden of financial taxation. It is this aim which the proposals of the Russian Government are serving. These proposals are, in the opinion of the Russian Government, perfectly definite and practicable, and cannot be substituted by any talk of so-called "moral disarmament," of which so much is heard at international conferences when their participants want a high-flown excuse to abandon the effective realisation of the popular slogan of disarmament.

If the conference brings a resolution, based on the fundamental questions put forward by the Russian delegation, and really serving the affairs of peace, returning thousands of able workers to productive labour, lifting the burden of militarism from the peoples exhausted by years of war, it will have done work of vital significance not only for those countries which are directly represented here. It will be showing the way to those countries whose Governments are still grappling with post-war difficulties and have not yet understood that the first step to the issue out of these difficulties can only be made by lifting the yoke of militarism from the backs of the people. It will be laying the foundation for general disarmament—the aim which the Workers' and Peasants' Government has set itself in the interests of the toilers in its own country and those of the whole humanity.

M. LITVINOV, at First Sitting of Moscow Disarmament Conference, December 2, 1922.

... The attitude of the Soviet Government to the so-called League of Nations has frequently been expressed in the declarations of its responsible representatives. The Soviet Government's attitude to the so-called League of Nations remains unaltered. It regards it as a coalition of certain States, endeavouring to usurp the power over other States and masking their attempts on the rights and independence of other nations by a false appearance of groundless legality and in the form of mandates issued by the Council or . . . Assembly of the League of Nations, etc. The Soviet Government maintains its conviction that this pseudo-international body really serves as a mere mask to conceal from the broad masses the aggressive aims of the imperialist policy of certain Great Powers or their vassals. The Soviet Government finds confirmation for its convictions every time that a State assuming the leading rôle in the League of Nations makes a decision on international questions touching the interests of the Soviet Republic.

The Soviet Government cannot, however, sacrifice to such conceptions its constant aspirations to afford, by every means at its disposal, all possible assistance in the task of easing the burden of militarism lying upon all peoples, the task of preventing armed conflicts and the consolidation of general peace. Weak as are the hopes of the Soviet Government for the achievement of these aims in the present world situation, it would consider it out of the question to refrain from taking the least possible opportunity for doing somthing, however little, to assist the matter of the reduction of armaments. The Soviet Government, as the interpreter of the will of the toiling masses, has determined never to let slip a single opportunity for easing in any way the burden of armaments and world conflicts pressing upon the toiling masses the world over. . . .   From a Note sent by People's Commissariat for Foreign Affairs to General Secretary of League of Nations, March 15, 1923.

The Soviet State, of its very nature free from any imperialist designs and annexationist ambitions whatsoever, steadily pursues the policy of peace. It invited and still invites all its neighbours without exception, and not its neighbours only, in a spirit of real peaceableness, to conclude a pact of non-aggression. From the point of view of peace policy, the Soviet Union continues to insist on the necessity for full and general disarmament. If the capitalist countries consider the realisation of a plan for complete disarmament in one instalment or during the shortest possible term unacceptable, the Soviet delegation agrees to the gradual execution of such a plan, during a term to be established at the conference.
M. LITVINOV, from a Statement to Representatives of Soviet and Foreign Press, November 22, 1927.

The Soviet Government adheres to the opinion it has always held, that under the capitalist system no grounds exist for counting upon the removal of the causes which give rise to armed conflicts. Militarism and big navies are the essentially natural consequences of the capitalist system. By the very fact of their increase they intensify existing differences, giving a great impetus to all potential quarrels, and inevitably convert these into armed conflicts.

Despite the fact that the World War was called the "war to end war," the whole history of post-war international relations has been one of continuous, systematic increase of armed forces in the capitalist States and of a great increase in the general burden of militarism. So far none of the solemn promises of the League of Nations have been partially fulfilled, while in all its activities in this regard the League has systematically evaded setting the question in a practical light. . . .

In sending a delegation to the fourth session of the Preparatory Commission for the Disarmament Conference the Government has authorised it to present a scheme for general and complete disarmament. The Soviet delegation is authorised by its Government to propose the complete abolition of all land, marine, and air forces. The Soviet Government suggests the following measures for the realisation of this proposal:

(*a*) The dissolution of all land, sea, and air forces, and the non-admittance of their existence in any concealed form whatsoever.

(*b*) The destruction of all weapons, military supplies, means of chemical warfare, and all other forms of armament and means of destruction in the possession of troops or military or general stores.

(*c*) The scrapping of all warships and military air vessels.

(*d*) The discontinuance of the calling up of citizens for military training, either in armies or public bodies.

(*e*) Legislation for the abolition of military service either compulsory, voluntary, or recruited.

(*f*) Legislation prohibiting the calling up of trained reserves.

(*g*) The destruction of fortresses and naval and air bases.

(*h*) The scrapping of military plants, factories, and war industry plants in general industrial works.

(*i*) The discontinuance of assigning funds for military purposes both in State budgets and those of public bodies.

(*j*) The abolition of military, naval, and air Ministries, the dissolution of general staffs and all kinds of military administrations, departments, and institutions.

(k) Legislative prohibition of military propaganda, military training of the population, and military education both by State and public bodies.

(l) Legislative prohibition of the patenting of all kinds of armaments and means of destruction, with a view to the removal of the incentive to the invention of same.

(m) Legislation making the infringement of any of the above stipulations a grave crime against the State.

(n) The withdrawal of corresponding alteration of all legislative Acts, both of national and international scope, infringing the above stipulations.

>   Declaration by U.S.S.R. Delegation, pronounced by M. LITVINOV at Session of Preparatory Disarmament Commission on November 30, 1927.

What were their objections to our Programme? It was, you see, too simple. Yes, it is simple, requiring a similarly simple answer, and not permitting those lengthy arguments and discussions and those methods of delaying decisions to which the League of Nations is so accustomed; from this point of view the simplicity of our programme does indeed present, for some, a certain inconvenience.

Furthermore, it was stated that our programme is too good not to have been conceived by anyone else previously, and if our predecessors had not done so before, we had no business to do so now. We are also told that the Commission had already drafted a convention on which much labour had been expended, and it being impossible that this labour be wasted, it was therefore necessary to continue working on the old draft and not commence on a new one. The members of the Commission frankly admitted that the discussion on the project had led the Commission into a deep forest, with no path in sight, but they had comforted themselves by remembering that some wise philosopher had once said: "If you have lost yourselves in the woods, continue walking straight ahead, without turning either to the right or to the left, and you will eventually find yourself outside the forest." The Preparatory Commission, although it had lost its way, must

continue its dark path, paying no heed to any directions towards new and simple exits. . . .
>	From Report by M. LITVINOV to Fifteenth Congress of Russian Communist Party, on Work of Soviet Delegation at League of Nations Preparatory Disarmament Commission.

Much has already been said on the reasons why we do not participate in the League of Nations. I can point out some of these reasons.

The Soviet Union is not a member of the League of Nations and does not take part in it because, first of all, it does not want to take the responsibility for the imperialist policy of the League of Nations, for the "mandates" which are handed out by the League of Nations for the exploitation and oppression of colonial countries. The Soviet Union does not participate in the League of Nations because it is completely opposed to imperialism and to the oppression of colonial and subjugated countries.

The Soviet Union does not participate in the League of Nations because, secondly, it does not want to take responsibility for military preparations, for growing armaments, for new military alliances, etc., which are covered and sanctioned by the League of Nations and which cannot but lead to new imperialist wars. The Soviet Union does not participate in the League of Nations because it is utterly opposed to imperialist wars.

Finally, the Soviet Union does not participate in the League of Nations because it does not want to be a component part of that screen of imperialist machinations which the League of Nations represents and which are concealed by the honeyed phrases of its members. The League of Nations is a rendezvous for imperialist chiefs who do their business behind the scenes. What the League of Nations *says* officially is empty twaddle, intended to deceive the workers. But what the imperialist chiefs *do* unofficially behind the scenes is real imperialist business, which is pharisaically concealed by the eloquent orators of the League of Nations. What can there be surprising in the fact that the Soviet Union does not want to become a member and participant of this anti-peoples comedy?	STALIN: Speech, 1927.

Our policy is a policy of peace and of the development of

trading relations with all countries. . . . The result of this policy has been that we have actually succeeded in preserving peace, and that we have not let ourselves be involved in any military conflicts, despite a series of provocative acts and provocative raids which have been carried out by warmongers. It is our intention to continue this policy of peace with all our strength and with all the means in our power. We do not covet a hair's-breadth of foreign territory, but we are not prepared to surrender an inch of our own to anyone. STALIN, at the Sixteenth Congress of the
Communist Party, 1930.

DURANTY: Is your position in regard to the League of Nations always a negative one?

STALIN: No, not always, and not under all circumstances. You perhaps do not quite understand our view. Notwithstanding the withdrawal of Germany and Japan from the League of Nations—or perhaps just because of this—the League may become something of a brake to retard the outbreak of military actions or to hinder them.

If this is so, and the League could prove to be somewhat of an obstruction that could even to a certain extent hinder the business of war and help in any degree to further the cause of peace, then we are not against the League.

Yes, if historical events follow such a course, then it is not impossible that we should support the League of Nations in spite of its colossal defects.

STALIN, at an interview, December 1933.

We know the nature of capitalist States, the nature of imperialism, its foreign problems and functions; basically these problems and functions do not change. What changes is the tactics pursued for solving these problems and their application to the historically changing circumstances. It is these changing tactics which it is the custom to call diplomacy. The fundamental feature of a capitalist and particularly of an imperialist State is that it places before itself foreign objectives the realisation of which it cannot conceive without the application of force, without war. If an additional proof of this were required, it is certainly furnished by the reply given in Geneva to our proposal for complete disarmament, for the complete annihilation of the means of warfare. We were informed that there could be no question about renouncing war, that one may temporarily speak about peace, but that one must always prepare for war. We were given this answer both before and after the general signature of the Kellogg-Briand Pact, which would seem to have renounced war as a method for the solution of international disputes.

But *not all* capitalist States, at any or every time or always, desire war to the same extent. Any, even the most imperialist, State, at any given time, may become strongly pacifist. This happens when it has either suffered a defeat in war, and therefore requires a certain interval before it can be ready for a new war, or when it has as antagonist a far more powerful State or group of States and the general political situation is unfavourable; or it may happen when a country has become over-satiated with victories and conquests and requires a certain period of time for the assimilation of these conquests. There are also other factors which may predispose countries against war. For instance, internal disturbances, economic weakness, etc.

> M. LITVINOV, the Soviet Foreign Minister, at the Session of the Central Executive of the U.S.S.R., December 1933.

It would, however, be an altogether erroneous deduction from what I have said to conclude that all the capitalist States are now aiming at war and are directly preparing for it. That is far from true. Side by side with the very few countries which have either already replaced diplomacy by military operation or, not being yet ready for it, are preparing to do so in the near future, there are countries which have no such immediate aims. They have their own antagonisms with other countries which they do not imagine can be solved other than by war, but these antagonisms have not yet become so acute as to make war an actual present possibility.

Considering, however, that war is inevitable, and on the other hand not being any too interested in the preservation of general peace, they do not wish to bind themselves, and therefore avoid assuming obligations which in their view would quite unnecessarily consolidate peace, such as Pacts of Non-Aggression, of the Definition of an Aggressor, etc. Possibly they might even not be averse to a small fight between other States in which they themselves would not be involved, and from which they might obtain some advantage, particularly if the U.S.S.R. suffered thereby.

Finally, there are also such bourgeois States, and a fair number of them indeed, who are at the present moment interested in the maintenance of peace and are prepared to direct their policy to the defence of such peace. I am not entering into any estimation of the motives of this policy. I merely affirm the fact which is of great value to us. I have, of course, dealt only with the fundamental groups of countries, the conflicts between whom now occupy the international arena. It is easy to follow this struggle in all international events, at all congresses, conferences, and international organisations. In the League of Nations this struggle is shown up particularly clearly.

One may, however, concede that the tendencies which are interested in the preservation of peace would seem to be gaining the upper hand in the League of Nations, and probably this is the explanation of the deep changes noticeable in the composition of the League.   M. LITVINOV, December 1933.

President Roosevelt once told me that it had been reckoned that 92 per cent. of humanity desire peace, and only 8 per cent. desire to violate it.

This 8 per cent. was intended to represent the entire population of those countries who were placed in the belligerent category. I consider that it would be unfair to ascribe to any population, or even the bulk of it, the criminal intention of violating peace, so that the actual percentage is even less than the above.

This fact in itself gives rise to the task of uniting this vast mass of people for the purpose of preventing the puny minority from hindering their peaceful aspirations.
      M. LITVINOV: Speech, 1933.

That the danger of new wars has become particularly imminent this year is clear, if only from the following fact. This year Germany and Japan have announced their decision to withdraw from the League of Nations. Germany has done this evidently in order to untie her hands for rearming, considering her participation in the League of Nations as a hindrance thereto. On the other hand, Japan announced her exit from the League of Nations in connection with her desire to have a completely free hand for her intervention in China. It has thus happened that even the League of Nations has, to a certain extent, stood in the way of the "liberty" of the interventionists. In connection with all this it must be recognised that the League of Nations has exerted a certain restraining influence upon those forces which are preparing for war. However different may be the reasons which have led to their withdrawal from the League of Nations, one cannot but bear in mind that these acts are certainly not helping the consolidation of general peace, but, on the contrary, they have assisted the more aggressive reactionary forces.

So much the more decisively and consistently shall we defend the progress towards peace and expose all and every attempt to accelerate the outbreak of new imperialist wars and new attacks on the U.S.S.R., utilising for this purpose every possibility of the given moment. In connection with this, our first duty is to keep the labouring masses informed as to the real position of the U.S.S.R. in the present capitalist surroundings, so that the wide masses of the workers and peasants should comprehend the fundamental factors menacing peace and should at the same time understand those factors which strengthen our peace position and universal peace.   M. MOLOTOV, December 1933.

Our foreign policy is clear. It is a policy of preserving peace and strengthening commercial relations with all countries. The U.S.S.R. does not think of threatening anybody—let alone of attacking anybody. We stand for peace and champion the cause of peace. But we are not afraid of threats and are prepared to answer blow for blow against the instigators of war. Those who want peace and are striving for business intercourse with us will always receive our support. And those who try to attack our country—will receive a stunning rebuff to teach them not to poke their pig's snout into our Soviet garden again.

STALIN, at the Seventeenth Congress of the
Communist Party, 1934.

An army created by the people and owing its origin to the difficult years of the civil war, an army enjoying the confidence of the people, an army knowing what it is fighting for and against whom it must fight, cannot be beaten. Our hard-working people can look to the future without fear—its defence is excellent—not only because it has good bayonets, but first and foremost because it is armed with the truth, which is invincible. . . .

The Soviet people, peacefully building up its own life, must be prepared for the onset of the enemy, a powerful and cunning enemy. It is stupid and even criminal to underestimate the strength of the enemy. We all know perfectly well how strong his industrial technique is, and in particular his war machine, which sooner or later will be directed against us. . . . We must be prepared for the fact that it will be no easy matter to conquer the enemy. Obsessed with the fear of death, he will fight to desperation for the remnants of his shattered existence. . . .

Is the Soviet Union strong enough to withstand the onset of this powerful and vile foe? Yes. The basis of this conviction was first and foremost the unconquerable love of freedom of the Soviet people, its solidarity, its heroism, and its readiness to fight to the last drop of its blood for its homeland. Great is the strength of the Russian people! For centuries they beat it on the face, trampled its face with their feet, beat it with whips, set it to die in prisons, in Siberian exile, shot it by the thousand against the wall—all this it bore, all this it endured patiently and rose again to its feet, and now the Russian people governs itself, working unceasingly, courageously. . . .

>> GORKY, at the First All-Union Conference of Soviet Writers, 1934.

There is not a single country, not even the smallest State bordering on the frontiers of the U.S.S.R., which has any grounds for uneasiness with regard to the Soviet Union, and this is more than can be said of certain other large States. The prestige and might of the Workers' and Peasants' State in international relations now serve only one cause—the cause of general peace. The Soviet Union has become the spokesman of the vital interests of the toilers of all countries in the sphere of international relations. Whatever our class enemies may say, the political significance of the dictatorship of the proletariat in the U.S.S.R. under present conditions, when the danger of war is becoming more and more real, is that nowhere in the world can there be found a more reliable stronghold of peace than our Workers' and Peasants' Government.

M. MOLOTOV, at the Seventh Congress of Soviets, 1935.

You remember how the first World War arose. It arose out of a desire to redivide the world. To-day we have the same background. There are capitalist States which consider that they were cheated in the previous redistribution of spheres of influence, territories, sources of raw material, markets, etc., and which want another redivision that would be in their favour. Capitalism in its imperialist phase is a system which considers war to be a legitimate instrument for settling international disputes, a legal method in fact, if not in law. . . .

If you imagine that Soviet people are themselves desirous, and, what is more, by force, of changing the aspect of surrounding States, you are seriously mistaken. Soviet people are, of course, desirous that the aspect of the surrounding States should change, but that is the affair of the surrounding States themselves. . . .

STALIN, in an interview with Roy Howard, 1936.

The Soviet Union was and is guided in its foreign policy by the principle of self-determination of nations. . . . Accordingly the Soviet Union defends the right of every nation to the independence and territorial integrity of its country, and its right to establish such a social order and to choose such a form of Government as it deems opportune and necessary for the better promotion of its economic and cultural prosperity.

The Soviet Union has untiringly and resolutely advocated, and advocates to-day, the necessity of collective action against aggressors, as one of the most effective means of bringing about the triumph of those principles and advancing the peace and security of nations.

It has been, and still is, building its foreign policy upon the desire to maintain peaceful and neighbourly relations with all countries which respect the integrity and inviolability of its borders. The Soviet Union was, and is, willing to render all possible assistance to peoples becoming victims of aggression and fighting for the independence of their native land.

The Soviet Government proclaims its agreement with the fundamental principles of the declaration of Mr. Roosevelt, President of the United States, and of Mr. Churchill, Prime Minister of Great Britain. . . . Considering that the practical application of these principles will necessarily adapt itself to the circumstances, needs, and historic peculiarities of particular countries, the Soviet Government can state that a consistent application of these principles will secure the most energetic support on the part of the Government and peoples of the Soviet Union.

M. MAISKY, at the Inter-Allied Conference, September 1941.

We stand for peace and the strengthening of business relations with all countries. That is our position; and we shall adhere to this position as long as these countries maintain like relations with the Soviet Union, and as long as they make no attempt to trespass on the interests of our country.

We stand for peaceful, close, and friendly relations with all the neighbouring countries which have common frontiers with the U.S.S.R. That is our position; and we shall adhere to this position as long as these countries maintain like relations with the Soviet Union, and as long as they make no attempt to trespass, directly or indirectly, on the integrity and inviolability of the frontiers of the Soviet State.

We stand for the support of nations which are the victims of aggression and are fighting for the independence of their country.

We are not afraid of the threats of aggressors, and are ready to deal a double blow for every blow delivered by instigators of war who attempt to violate the Soviet borders.

Such is the foreign policy of the Soviet Union.

STALIN, at the Eighteenth Congress of the Communist Party, 1939.

The tasks of the Party in the sphere of foreign policy are:
(1) To continue the policy of peace and of strengthening business relations with all countries.
(2) To be cautious and not allow our country to be drawn into conflicts by warmongers who are accustomed to have others pull the chestnuts out of the fire for them.

(3) To strengthen the might of our Red Army and Red Navy to the utmost.

(4) To strengthen the international bonds of friendship with the working people of all countries who are interested in peace and friendship among nations.

Stalin, at the Eighteenth Congress of the Communist Party, 1939.

For many years the Soviet Government called untiringly for collective security, which means united efforts, at the same time preparing the material basis for its own efforts. But, in spite of its sincere attempts, it became finally convinced there was an absence in other Governments of any real desire for the organisation of a common, active front against Hitlerism on the basis of equal rights and common effort and sacrifice.

Litvinov, at the Annual Meeting of the American Academy of Political and Social Science, April 1942.

Chapter Seven

THE TESTAMENT OF FAITH IN SOVIET RUSSIA

RUSSIA, the mother of a new humanity.
JOHN S. HOYLAND.

The Revolution has raised up a new man: the citizen of the Republic of Labour.   HENRI BARBUSSE.

The U.S.S.R. is the only real Socialist experiment that has ever been made, and it affords a real concrete proof that Socialism is feasible in this world. The results of Socialism are there; you have only to look at them. That is the country in which, by the hands of two super-men, have been united ''the practical genius of the American and the enthusiasm of the Revolutionary,'' the country of intelligence and of duty—with its yearning for truth, its enthusiasm and its youth. It stands out from the map of the world, not only because it is new, but because it is clean.
HENRI BARBUSSE.

Russia's civilisation has not yet burst forth into blossom: it still belongs to the future. . . . Not yet has the soul of the Russian people been able to cast off the yoke of Western Europe and to achieve its free development; not yet has it found a way to express *its own* truth. But its time will come.

When we read the literature of Russia, and perhaps even more when we listen to the national music of the Russian people, its strange charm, vibrant with the suppressed glow of passion, makes us conscious of the mighty, stirring echoes of melancholy from the limitless steppes, from the unknown depths of an alien existence; we seem to hear a soul still in bondage utter its eternal yearnings for liberty, and deep down in that soul we recognise a world still unborn.

One cannot be brought into close association with this great people, in prosperity or adversity, without feeling an affection for it and acquiring faith in its possibilities.

One must needs admire its stoical fortitude and boundless resignation, which may prove a weakness in time of development but which is its great strength in the day of misfortune. Even against our will we are attracted by the high-strung emotionalism of its character, which may easily lead to excesses, but nevertheless bestows that remarkable gift of devotion and unhesitating readiness for sacrifice even unto death on behalf of its ideals or ideas, which we meet with again and again. . . .

It appears probable to me that not only will Russia some day, and at a date not far distant, save Europe in all things material, but that the sorely needed spiritual renewal will also come from there.
FRIDTJOF NANSEN, 1923.

In Russia I see a nation which at the cost of unspeakable suffering is endeavouring to bring into life a new order. This new order is all smeared with blood like a human child just drawn from its mother's womb. In spite of the horror, in spite of the terrible mistakes and the crimes, I go up to the new-born and take it in my hands; it is hope, the pitiful hope of the future of mankind.
ROMAIN ROLLAND, in a letter to Balmont, 1923.

Russia's cause is true democracy's cause, always and everywhere, for Russia has done more already for the common man than any country recorded in history.
THEODORE DREISER: *In Defence of Civilization against Fascist Barbarism.*

The fundamental principles of the New Order in Russia—justice and an equal chance for the average man, childhood first, the elimination of private selfishness and greed, co-operative activity for the sake of the community—are profoundly and radically Christian. . . .

Soviet Russia demonstrates also the possibility of building up, especially amongst the young people, a new code of morality, which stigmatises the making of private profit out of one's neighbours as odious, and even repudiates any tendency to take advantage of chance opportunity for personal advantage in which one's fellows cannot share. Side by side with this disinterestedness there may go a positive community sense, which makes it the natural thing that every young person should spend his or her leisure in working at jobs—often involving arduous physical labour—which are of service to the community. These jobs may vary widely, from teaching illiterate peasants to unloading goods-trains or gathering rabbit-food; but a spirit may be bred, in the right social and educational environment, under the influence of which the young people shall find a genuinely creative joy in thus helping forward the new social order, in a gay and jolly fellowship, and without regard to personal advantage. JOHN S. HOYLAND: *The New Russia*.

I am happy that I have been able to come to the U.S.S.R., to the promised land of the whole of mankind. For the first time for many years the state of my health has made it possible for me to undertake such a long journey. I am glad to be able to be inspired by your energy, to see your life, full of tireless activity, to make common cause with it. If I were young I would travel through and see the most distant corners of the U.S.S.R. First and foremost the new young republics: Tatary, Kazakhstan, Daghestan, Uzbekistan, and Tadjikstan—young countries where most deeply of all is there to be felt the blossoming of vital forces, in so far as they are inhabited by peoples that were oppressed and backward under Tsarism.

My comrades! In leaving Soviet soil I have one feeling: your soil is not foreign, it is my soil as well. I have met here much love, and I respond to you with the same feeling. There is not a single success, not a single victory of the great Socialist construction that you have achieved in which I have not participated with all my thoughts. I am confident that the future is yours. It belongs to us, my friends.

ROMAIN ROLLAND, on his journey to the U.S.S.R., in an interview with Representatives of Soviet Press in 1935.

We also, your French brothers, had at one time, like you, to conduct a furious struggle against a world of enemies, both at home and abroad; and despite the heroism of our great forefathers of the Convent, our revolution, betrayed, mortally wounded, was forced to stop half-way, decapitated of its Robespierre. You, Soviet comrades, have raised the torch which fell from our hands, and in the hands of your great Lenin the torch of liberty, which he lit again, now shines over the whole world.

The unfinished work of the Convent now continues, and the new world of which we dreamed is being built by you.

. . . . .

At the International Exhibition, high over the banks of the Seine, two young Soviet giants, "the collective farm woman and the worker," hold the sickle and hammer in indomitable transport before the Hitler eagle. And we hear the heroic hymn burst forth from their breasts which, like a new "Marseillaise," calls the people to freedom and unity and leads them to victory.

ROMAIN ROLLAND: A Message to the Union of
Soviet Socialist Republics.

In Russia at last! Whichever way I look, I am filled with wonder. It is unlike any other country. It is radically different. From top to bottom they are rousing the whole community up without distinction.

Throughout the ages, civilised communities have contained groups of nameless people. They are the majority—the beasts of burden, who have no time to become men. They grow up on the leavings of society's wealth, with the least food, least clothes, and least education, and they serve the rest. They toil most, but theirs is the largest measure of indignity. They are starved and are humiliated by their superiors at the least excuse. They are deprived of everything that makes life worth living. They are like a lamp-stand bearing the lamp of civilisation on their heads: people above receive light while they are smeared with the trickling oil.

I had often thought about them, but came to the conclusion that they were beyond the reach of help. If there were no lower classes, how could there be any upper classes? It is a necessary division, for if there is nobody above, it is impossible to see anything beyond one's immediate ken; mere animal existence can never be man's destiny. His civilisation consists in going beyond the limits of bare subsistence. Its most cherished fruits have flourished on the field of leisure. There is need to preserve a corner for leisure in human civilisation. So I used to think that the utmost should be done to improve the education, health, and comforts of those who are compelled to labour at the bottom of society, not merely by circumstances, but by reason of their body and mind.

But the trouble is that nothing permanent can be built up on charity: to try to do good from without is vitiated at every step. Only from equals can one expect real help. I have not been able to think it all out satisfactorily, but to assume that progress can be maintained only by keeping down the bulk of humanity and denying them their human rights is a reproach to the mind. . . .

Man cannot do good to those whom he does not respect. No sooner is one's self-interest at stake than a clash arises. A radical solution of this problem is being sought in Russia. It is too soon for a final judgment of this attempt, but for the present whatever catches my eye strikes me with amazement. The royal road to the solution of all our problems is education. The bulk of human society has so far been deprived of full opportunities for education: in India well-nigh completely so. It is astonishing to watch the extraordinary vigour with which education spreads throughout Russian society. The measure of education is not merely the number involved, but its thoroughness: its intensity. What abundant preparation, what tremendous effort, so that no one should remain helpless or idle! Not in European Russia alone, but also among the semi-civilised races of Central Asia, they have opened the flood-gates of education. There is no limit to the effort made to bring the latest fruits of science to them. The theatres here are crowded to overflowing, but those who come to them are peasants and workers. Nowhere are they humiliated. In the few institutions I have visited so far, I have seen the awakening of their spirit and the joy of self-respect.

> RABINDRANATH TAGORE: *Letters from Russia*
> (trans. by Dr. S. Sinha).

In stepping on the soil of Russia, the first thing that caught my eye was that in education, at any rate, the peasant and working classes have made such enormous progress in these few years that nothing comparable has happened even to our highest classes in the course of the last hundred and fifty years. And yet eight years ago they were as helpless, hungry, oppressed, and illiterate as our Indian masses: indeed, in certain respects their misery was even greater, not less, than ours. The vain picture of national education, our heart's desire, which I dared not draw even on the canvas of mirage, is here a reality stretched from horizon to horizon.

Again and again I have asked myself: How has such a great miracle been possible? The answer that I have received in my mind is that here there is no barrier of greed. To think that by education everybody will become adequately competent seems so natural. The people here are not at all afraid of giving complete education even to Turkomans of distant Asia; on the contrary, they are dreadfully earnest about it. They have not relapsed into indifference after pointing out in their report that the root cause of all the misery of the people of Turkoman Republic lies in their traditional ignorance.

RABINDRANATH TAGORE: *Letters from Russia*
(trans. by Dr. S. Sinha).

I have been privileged to witness the unstinted energy with which Russia is trying to fight disease and illiteracy. Her industry and application has helped Russia in steadily liquidating poverty and ignorance and abject humiliation from the face of a vast continent. Her people have not observed distinction between one sect and another, one race and another. They have spread far and wide the influence of that human relationship which is above and beyond everything petty and selfish. Their astonishingly quick progress has made me happy and jealous at the same time. . . . While in Moscow I particularly liked one characteristic of Soviet administration, and that was the pleasing fact that there was here no conflict of interest between the different races and religions; a truly civilised administration impartially served their common interests.

RABINDRANATH TAGORE, on his eightieth birthday (1941).

The Bolshevik experiment has, in the course of the past decade, demonstrated beyond all denial that neither the incentive of profit-making nor the existence of a capitalist class as the leaders and directors of industry is indispensable to wealth production on a colossal scale, or to its continuous increase.

... Assuming that the increase in wealth production and in population continue at their present compound rates, it seems likely that, in the course of two or three decades, the U.S.S.R. will have become the wealthiest country in the world, and at the same time the community enjoying the greatest aggregate of individual freedoms.

... It is these outstanding features of the emergent morality of Soviet Communism that seem to us to mark it off from that of all other civilisations. In particular, it is just these features that enable Communist morality to embrace more than the exaction of the performance of duty. Within its sphere is also the positive provision not only of universal opportunity for the enjoyment of life, but also of equal provision of leisure for individual disposal. It is an essential part of the Good Life in the U.S.S.R. that every person should actually have the opportunity of working at the job that he finds within his capacity and chooses as that which he likes best. Labour, the Bolsheviks declare, is to cease to be merely continuous drudgery of an inferior class or race, and is to be made a matter of honour and a joy for every member of the community.

SIDNEY and BEATRICE WEBB: *Soviet Communism, a New Civilisation.*

We are still sometimes told that under Socialism the State must be the only employer! As a matter of fact, more than one-half of the adult inhabitants of the Soviet Union find themselves outside the ranks of public employees, even in the widest sense of that term. They are not in receipt of wage or salary at all, but work on their own account as handi-craftsmen, fishermen or agriculturists, calling no man master, but producing either each for himself and family, or jointly as partners in co-operative production societies (artels or kolkhozi); after payment of the Government dues, selling their own products freely to consumers at the best price they can get....

... In 1917 no economist in the Western world imagined that the elimination of competitive profit-making could possibly result in greater initiative and inventiveness in all fields: increased investment and rationalisation by the captains of industry, when these were merely employed at salaries; augmented zeal and diligence among the rank and file of manual workers, when the trade unions arranged the wage rates; and positively a larger dividend per head among a larger number of workers by hand and by brain than had ever previously been distributed throughout this one-sixth of the surface of the globe. In 1937, twenty years later, this is what the economists who deign to look at the U.S.S.R. are now enforcedly recognising.

And the progress in material production has been, during the past decade, at least equalled by the advance in the physical health and cultural development of the people, whose numbers have gone on increasing each year—in spite of the so-called famines of which we still hear from enemies of the régime—by about as many as the whole of the rest of Europe put together. The crude death-rate has been reduced below two-thirds of what it was under the Tsar, whilst the infantile mortality has been halved.

. . . And, most important and most significant of all, there has been, since 1930, no involuntary mass unemployment among able-bodied men and women in the whole length and breadth of this immense country. Nor is such unemployment expected to recur. . . .

. . . One of these well-marked features in the Soviet pattern of social organisation is the constant insistence, throughout all collective activities and every branch of social life, on the widest possible participation. Not only is the political electorate the widest in the world, but it is now being cleared of all remaining exclusions and inequalities. In the trade union and co-operative organisations, with their tens of millions of members, the meetings are not only more numerous and frequent than in other countries, but also they are habitually attended by a majority of the membership and by women equally with men. The daily administration of the public services, in populous cities as in rural villages, is largely undertaken, not by the salaried officials, not even mainly by the elected councillors themselves, but, without remuneration, to a considerable extent by private citizens, as part of their voluntary social service. Fifty thousand men and women are reported to be habitually thus engaged in the city of Moscow. . . .

. . . More important, however, than this or that definition of democracy is the question of personal freedom. Leaving aside any quibbling about terms or their verbal definitions, the substantial issue is whether the indication, for the future of the Soviet Union, is towards greater or lesser freedom for its individual citizens than at present exists. . . .

It may fairly be said that there is much reason for expecting that the Soviet Union will, in another decade or so, be able to demonstrate beyond cavil its actual superiority, in a greater aggregate per head of individual freedoms, over any highly evolved large State, organised on the basis of capitalism and the direction of wealth production by competitive profit-making, with all the economic insecurity, and all the inequality of wealth and social conditions involved. . . .

. . . When nearly all the world seems staggering towards social and economic catastrophe, the pattern of the U.S.S.R. stands out as supremely that of a Land of Hope.

>   SIDNEY and BEATRICE WEBB: From an Article written for the Twentieth Anniversary of the October Revolution.

It may be the fate of Russia not only to prove to the world that Socialism can be made to work, but actually to save political freedom for mankind as well. To put it bluntly, the democracies who, irrespective of economic theory, still value political freedom will henceforth feel much more disposed to co-operate with Russia as a valuable aid in stemming the flood of militarist and nationalist dictatorship which threatens to spread over the world.

With the aid of Russia the fight for democracy can be won; without it, that fight may well go to the military autocracies based upon violence, racial discrimination, the suppression of all freedom of speech and thought.

>   NORMAN ANGELL, 1936.

No intelligent Socialist can deny that the Revolution represents one of the supremely beneficent epochs of history.

It has awakened a whole people from its slumber. In education, in public health, in economic construction, in the degree to which *it has ended the exploitation of man by man, in its reclamation of* wealth from the few for the masses, in its opening-up of the potentialities of production for the many, revolution has made possible in Russia a new epoch in the history of the world. ...

There is in the new Russia for the masses what there was never for them in the old: the right to hope. That is what gives the Soviet Union to-day a significance for the working class which it is fundamental to recognise.

Compared with the Tsarist regime, there has been in every aspect of life immeasurable improvement. ...

But where the old Russia faced its future with dread, the new faces its future with confidence. Where life for the peasant and the industrial worker in the old Russia was, as Hobbes put it, "nasty, brutish, and short," life for them in the new offers the right to a sense of mastery over their lives. ...

The career is open to the talented.

New and immense reserves of talent and energy have been revealed which, in the old Russia, it was dangerous even to explore. As new wealth is discovered it does not go to the few; it is garnered to the service of the many.

Compare the status of women in the old Russia with that of the new.

Measure the significance of children in the epoch of the Tsars with that in the epoch which Lenin founded.

Set the Red Army alongside the army of the Tsars. ...

Like the Renaissance, like the French Revolution, amid all its blood and tears, the Russian Revolution marks an immense stage in the liberation of mankind. ...

Its purposes and its achievements entitle us to hope for the future. HAROLD LASKI: From the Article in the *Daily Herald* of March 12, 1937.

I have followed the affairs of the U.S.S.R. during the past twenty years with most careful attention. I do not believe that ever before in the history of mankind have the masses of the people made such great progress, culturally, politically, and economically.

UPTON SINCLAIR, 1937.

In *Mammon Art*—an Essay in Economic Interpretation—speaking about "Art and the Future," I greeted the "great new force shaping itself in our world, preparing for the making of the future." I meant the U.S.S.R., and asked: "Shall men not thrill to this vision, and rouse others to make it real? Here lies your task, young comrade; here is your future—and not the timid service of convention, the million-times-over repetition of ancient lies, the endless copying of copies of folly and cruelty and greed. The artists of our time are like men hypnotised, repeating over and over a dreary formula of futility. And I say: Break this evil spell, young comrade; go out and meet the new dawning life, take your part in the battle, and put it into new art; do this service for a new public, which you yourselves will make. That is the last word I have to say: that your creative gift shall not be content to make art works, but shall at the same time make a world; shall make new souls, moved by a new ideal of fellowship, a new impulse of love, and faith, and not merely hope, but determination."

And now, in greeting my Soviet fellow-writers, whose country is one of the decisive bastions of civilisation, I am glad to stress, again and again, that U.S.S.R. shows tremendous forces not only in the political, economic, and military fields, but also in all its intellectual and artistic manifestations. That is why Soviet Russia is locked up in the hearts of the masses. That is why U.S.S.R. will triumph once more.

UPTON SINCLAIR: *A Message to Soviet writers, 1942.*

A peaceful solution of racial conflicts demands equal opportunities for all races in all occupations and professions and equal rights in the exercise of citizenship. It cannot be attained without vastly increased facilities for the backward races in education, in capital equipment, and in the development of resources in their interest. Racial relations to-day present more dangerous features in the field of interhuman relations than any other point of conflict. Nowhere are mob passions, prejudices, and fears so easy to evoke and so difficult to check. If they are to be prevented from crystallising into custom, and sometimes even into law, there must be a conscious and persistent effort by all religious and rational forces which subscribe to the idea of equality of men and of races. Unless decisive changes are made in the attitudes and practices of dominant toward backward races—and such changes are not now in prospect outside of the Soviet Union—wars and revolts must inevitably result.

HANS KOHN: *Encyclopaedia of Social Sciences.*

I did not become a Marxist because I was convinced by abstract arguments for Marxism; I did so because I found not merely that the Marxist theory worked, but that I had to adopt it if I wanted to get practical results.

Marxism helps me in my scientific work. For example, I am investigating the genetical structure of human and animal populations. Until I became a Marxist I could not design my experiments properly. I did not see that what I had described as equilibrium was really in many cases a struggle which was transforming the species.

J. B. S. HALDANE, in *The Daily Worker*.

At the present time, the struggle between two systems—capitalist and socialist worlds—has become extremely acute. The economics of the Soviet Union have finally become consolidated on Socialist principles. The First Five-Year Plan of the Soviet Union was fulfilled in four years. The Soviet Union has long ago liquidated unemployment and has raised the cultural life and living conditions of the mass of working people to a high level. . . . It is clear that such widely developed democracy has never existed before under any form of government in the history of mankind. Based upon this system and in contact with the broad masses, the Soviets are becoming organs which develop in the widest degree the creative ability of the masses, organs capable of mobilising the masses. No Government in history, except in the U.S.S.R., has ever been able to achieve this.

MAO TSE-DUN, at the Congress of the Chinese Soviets.

I had long been drawn to Socialism and Communism, and Russia had appealed to me. Much in Soviet Russia I dislike—the ruthless suppression of all contrary opinion, the wholesale regimentation, the unnecessary violence (as I thought) in carrying out various policies. But there was no lack of violence and suppression in the capitalist world, and I realised more and more how the very basis and foundation of our acquisitive society and property was violence. Without violence it could not continue for many days. A measure of political liberty meant little indeed when the fear of starvation was always compelling the vast majority of people everywhere to submit to the will of the few, to the greater glory and advantage of the latter.

Violence was common in both places, but the violence of the capitalist order seemed inherent in it; whilst the violence of Russia, bad though it was, aimed at a new order based on peace and co-operation and real freedom for the masses. With all her blunders, Soviet Russia had triumphed over enormous difficulties and taken great strides towards this new order.

JAHWARLAL NEHRU: Autobiography.

Socialist realism or revolutionary romanticism are two names for one and the same thing. To render such a synthesis possible required the downfall of capital and the victory of Socialist economy.

The proletariat, which is in power, has nothing to hide. It is rich in the whole of human truth. It has no need of lies, it can look truth, reality straight in the face.

For among its activities there is not the robbery of the working class, the discovery of which is so unpleasant for the robber.

In the land of the victorious proletariat, culture is not a light shining down from above; it is not the creation of a handful of people; there it is engendered by all, there it grows out of the earth, there it washes and transforms everything, even the everyday manifestations of labour and everyday life. For in that land there is already to-day what we shall have to-morrow. There, in the U.S.S.R., miracles are being performed not on church pictures, but are being created in actual life by living working people.

I demand a return to reality in the name of the reality which is ruling to-day on one-sixth part of the earth, in the name of him who was the first to foresee this reality and who in the spring of 1845 wrote in Brussels:

"Philosophers have merely *explained* the world in different ways, but the thing is to *change* it."

LOUIS ARAGON, at the Congress in Defence of Culture, 1935.

All the bright manifestations of Soviet life: the building of the Moscow–Volga Canal, the building of Polar stations, and the two big flights from Moscow through the North Pole to the United States of America, performed by the hero pilots Chkalov, Baidukov and Belyakov, Gromov, Yumashow and Danilin,—all these show what a tremendous degree of perfection can be achieved by a country possessed of a political organisation created by such leaders as Lenin and Stalin. Thanks to them, the citizens of the Land of the Soviets are inspired with the desire to outdo even themselves in the interests of the common weal. Your country is free of dirty, imperialist aims.

JOSE ROYO I GOMEZ: A Message to the Communist Party, 1937.

I think that to-day all men of good faith who have sufficient information about the Soviet Union must agree that it is in the U.S.S.R. that the social régime is being built which will assure to man a life more worthy, more human, more just; a life that will no longer permit the exploitation of man by man. The abolition of this exploitation denotes so much human progress that it seems to me impossible not to subscribe fully to it, if one is not lacking entirely in all dignity, all sense of justice.

All we know, all we have seen of the Soviet achievements are a certain guarantee that the end which the builders of Socialist society are pursuing will be achieved. In all spheres there is not only the guarantee of future victories, but much more: there are the achievements which not infrequently supersede the latest achievements of more advanced countries.

. . . . . .

I consider it essential to mention here how much the policy of the U.S.S.R. seems to me to be one of the principal guarantees of peace. If there is one country in the world that does not want war, it is, indeed, the U.S.S.R. What particularly strikes the foreigner in the U.S.S.R., the foreigner who speaks the language and wants to make a close study of all he sees, is the tremendous yearning for knowledge, education, which is characteristic of all the Soviet people, so different among themselves, for whom Stalin has created the new Constitution of the U.S.S.R. Everywhere, beginning with the children right up to the aged, the thirst for culture is astonishing, and the means are given to all to quench this thirst or to perfect themselves in any direction.

A country that makes such an effort for culture in general is a country in which one must believe and on which one must lay one's hopes, because everything is done there by everybody for the well-being of all.

FRANS MASEREEL: A Message to the Communist Party, 1937.

Power is concentrated in the hands of a body of men and women wholly consecrated to the service of the community, precluded from using the power to obtain money for themselves, trained from youth up to regard the interests of the future as superior to those of the present, pledged to go anywhere and to do anything for the sake of the new world which they are building. They remind one of Plato's Guardians in the *Republic*. They know whither they are going: and are confident that they can lead mankind out of the morass of self-frustration in which we wallow. They discipline themselves most strictly, and live strenuous puritanical lives. They sacrifice their own comfort and well-being ruthlessly, as in the matter of giving the best food to the children, and in that of the feeding of hand-workers on a scale far beyond that employed for brain-workers. Throughout Russia the Party membership forms the steel-framework of the Bolshevik system.
JOHN S. HOYLAND: *The New Russia*.

All our lives we have suffered much at the hands of the State that has been against us, against our conscience, against the rational idea of justice, and humanism.

And then a State arises which has as its aim that of which we have always dreamed, namely, to convert people into rational beings who work communally for the sake of the happiness of each, and who strive to make each more elevated and better, in a society which is constantly being perfected. The consciousness that such a state exists makes one happy. Many who live on the earth are saved from despair by the hope that their own country will one day follow this example.

The existence of the Soviet Union and its example save people the thought of the need to turn their backs on living realities. We are not living in a world of fantasy, our duty is to watch living realities and the facts of human life.

A few days ago I saw on the first page of a magazine in which a novel of mine is being printed, the speech of the leader of the Soviet Union about the new Constitution of that country. I admit that perfect democracy and realistic humanism cannot be accomplished in such a short space of time. Whole generations of Soviet people must pass through the school of democracy and humanism before they can answer all the demands of the new Constitution. But the hope that it will, in spite of all, be possible is extremely heartening when you read the words of Stalin; so full of confidence, kindness, and clarity of mind they are. For me it was a surprise that the head of such a gigantic State could combine all these qualities with tremendous energy. Nor had I ever come across the works of the head of a State on the first pages of a literary magazine; never before did I think that he could have the right to it by virtue of the talented form and effectiveness of his works. This undoubtedly is something new. Besides the material satisfaction, which, of course, is of great importance, the people also feel a moral and spiritual satisfaction. To feel that you are growing, to be pleased with yourself, to give all your leisure to science, to find in the theatre a reflection of the life that surrounds you, and that does not deprive one of courage but strengthens his spirit, all these as well are great factors. What profound satisfaction a writer must feel who takes part in such experiences!

Collaboration between the intelligentsia and proletariat is the only rational way out, because the proletariat will remain henceforth as well the bearer of culture and the class which creates the State. And we in the West are already setting about this collaboration. The type of intellectual who is afraid of proletarianisation is fading into the past. We must see to it that the proletariat becomes intellectual. Incidentally, if non-committal emotional sympathy for the Soviet Union is simply a pleasant feeling, the rational confidence that in the history of mankind henceforth and evermore there is only one road to progress is still more important.

HEINRICH MANN: A Message to the Communist Party, 1937.

The Soviet Union is uninterruptedly pursuing its line of defending peace. The Soviet Union came to support the League of Nations at a time when other Powers had already begun their hostile actions against it. A series of obstacles has been systematically put forward against the Soviet criterion of indivisible peace down to this very day. This principle is constantly being attacked. The principle of collective security is being countered by one-sided acts having no force at all. Concessions are being made to the instigators of war. In face of the invasion of Spain, there is being applied the principle of so-called "Non-intervention," which bears in it the embryo of a future European war. In Europe the right of peoples to free self-government and to determine their own fate according to their own wishes is absent. Under the sign of Fascism, which in itself is the negation of human dignity and civilisation, the rough mask of voracious imperialism, fraught with racial and other prejudices—the totalitarian States are waging a war of intervention on the territory of other European States and their colonies. For Fascism no value at all attaches either to the independence of other nations or to the age-old dignity of countries marked by a fruitful and civilising mission that has been extended over many years.

The Soviet Union has demonstrated to Europe its rôle as a civilised people, which is the disinterested friend of peace and maintains respect for other peoples.

JUAN NEGRIN: A Message to the
Communist Party, 1937.

We are accused that Communism destroys civilisation. It is a well-known fact that present-day civilisation is indeed greatly menaced. However, the menace comes not from the direction of the Soviet Union or Communism, but from the direction of the new war prepared by the imperialists. Moreover, culture and science are being made every use of in order to prepare the most destructive means for destroying in the shortest space of time all cultural and economic centres, all big towns, which cannot be restored again.

The Soviet Union and the Communist movement alone stand out against this catastrophe, which menaces the whole of modern civilisation. It is enough to glance at the events of the last decade to understand what a tremendous factor is the U.S.S.R. in the struggle against the outbreak of a new world war. Were there no Soviet Union, war would have broken out long ago.

The Soviet Union is now the only country in the world

where the cultural level of the masses is continually growing, and where science and art are surrounded by care, honour, and attention.

From the Last Speech of MATIAS RAKOSHI,
at the Trial in Budapest on July 1, 1935.

The concise planning of economy, the planning of the whole of the life of the State, reconciles the individual personality to the shortcomings in living conditions, if they are noticed at all; for the undoubted difference beteen the past and the present forces one to forget these privations. Anybody who has eyes to see, who has ears to distinguish the sincere notes of human speech from the insincere, feels at every step that when people tell you of their happy lives these are no empty phrases. And they know that their well-being is not the consequence of a passing favourable situation, but the result of rational planning.

. . . . . .

The knowledge that the State does not deprive the majority, in the interests of the minority, of the use of the good things of life, that it really helps everybody in all kinds of ways, this knowledge, confirmed by the experience of twenty years, has become part of the flesh and blood of the whole population and has created a confidence in the leadership such as has never been observed in any other place.

. . . . . .

The majority of letters which young people address to me outside the Soviet Union are S O S appeals. Large numbers of young people in the West do not know how to fill up their lives, either outwardly or inwardly; not only have they no chance of obtaining the work they would like to have: they have no chance in general of getting work. They do not know what to do, they see no sense in their own lives, all roads to them seem aimless. What a joy, after these impressions, to meet young people who have had an opportunity of gleaning the first-fruits of Soviet education, to meet young intellectuals of peasant and working-class origin. How firmly, with what confidence and calm they march through life, feeling themselves an organic link in one intelligent whole. The future lies before them like a road traversing a beautiful landscape. Whether speaking at meetings or talking to one *vis-à-vis*, the naïve ardour with which they tell of their happy lives is artless: their lips do indeed give expression to that which fills their hearts.

The air in the West is bad, oppressive. There is no longer clarity and resolution in Western civilisation now. People hesitate to defend themselves against the offensive of barbarism, either by fists or strong words, they do it unwillingly, with indefinite gestures; the utterances of responsible persons against Fascism are sugared, are drowned in reservations. Who is not revolted by the indifference and hypocrisy with which these responsible persons have reacted to the aggression of the Fascists against the Spanish Republic? One draws a sigh of relief when one leaves behind this depressing atmosphere of falsified democracy and hypocritical humanitarianism, and arrives in the severe atmosphere of the Soviet Union.

FEUCHTWANGER: Moscow, 1937.

Soviet patriotism is not expressed in florid talk or histrionic gestures. It is a sober, matter-of-fact patriotism, a patriotism of everyday life. It manifests itself as a natural sentiment, in the acceptance of discipline and the self-sacrificing discharge of civic duty. This patriotism springs from a consciousness that all citizens are equal, from a social system in which all have equal rights, equal duties and equal responsibilities. . . .

People abroad who were unable to appreciate the significance of the Russian Revolution and its historical perspectives were amazed when, through the smoke of war, they discerned its true nature. The great Russian Revolution has endowed the Soviet citizen with faith in himself and inculcated in him a sense of responsibility. It has rid the Russian of all that used to hamper his cultural development and stifle his striving for a better life. Soviet patriotism is a patriotism purged of all earlier impurities, since the full utilisation of productive forces purges a people of all imperialist aspirations.

The Russian Revolution is a true heir of the humanism engendered by the French Revolution, which later led the cultural progress of Germany, and which expedited the national regeneration of the central European nations. It was our century, of course, that provided the conditions for the realisation of the humanist ideal, which was only possible in a classless society.

This ideal could have been carried into real life only on the crest of a popular wave. It embodied the moral aspirations of all eras and races. It was a people's, and at the same time an international ideal.

It is only natural that in the Soviet Union there should be a high appreciation of everything fine in Russian history and folklore, that there should be a veneration for great men in the fields of science and culture and for the people's great military leaders; that historic figures like Peter I, who admitted the influence of Western civilisation into Russia, should be revered.

The trends which led finally to the Russian Revolution were already in existence at the beginning of the nineteenth century. These were romantic trends, it is true, but they strove to check reaction. One of these trends was represented by the Decembrists, who were recruited from the most cultivated section of Russian society. In the shade of the gallows, where the Decembrists met their end, arose a new generation of patriots, writers, and poets who were opposed to the existing régime. First among them were Pushkin and Lermontov. Never has the memory of these great poets been so alive in the Soviet Union as it is to-day.

ZDENEK FIRLINGER, Czechoslovakian Ambassador in the U.S.S.R., in *Soviet War News*, 1942.

There is no Russian Enigma : it is the country whose policy, given a genuine desire for understanding, it is easy to comprehend. The Soviet Union is a Socialist country developing a Socialist society, aware that hostile peoples are planning to attack it. There is no secret hidden motives behind the action of the leaders. Their motives are to save the Socialism which their people have created at a cost of so much effort, and steadfastly to increase the well-being of the country. Their profession of solidarity with the workers of the world is genuine, as is their love of the common people, particularly Stalin's love for the people. Those who have seen him among the people, those who have listened to the people—to a peasant, a railwayman, a factory worker, a young Jewish lawyer, or a woman doctor—and felt their love for Stalin, will find this easy to believe. It is this passionate desire for the happiness of the common people, found not only in Stalin but in all the leaders, which actuates Soviet policy. Editor, *The Anglo-Soviet Journal*, 1941.

As President of the Anglo-Soviet Public Relations Association, I wish to join heartily in your celebration of the twenty-fifth anniversary of the foundation of the U.S.S.R. Few of us foresaw how magnificently the young and vulnerable Republic would withstand the shock of the present Nazi attack upon its very existence. Its intrepid courage and its loyalty to the Fatherland and to the social ideal of the people surely must lead every thinking nation to exclaim: "Oh! be my friend and teach me to be thine."
> LORD HORDER: A Message (in *Labour Monthly*)
> on the Twenty-Fifth Anniversary of the Union
> of Soviet Socialist Republics.

British people are conscious after all the years of deception that the U.S.S.R. has made an outstanding contribution to humanity. It is obvious that the immediate phase of this contribution is the amazing resistance offered by the Red Forces, but perhaps there is an even greater part which the Soviet Republics are playing.

The "Russian Glory" is not only the quality of the fighting by the Red Army, but the astonishing unity of the whole Russian people. They are inspired by an ideal or national purpose which has bound them into one people. They have shown the world that when a nation is inspired by a Purpose its achievements are almost unlimited.

We hope that the example of a Purpose may be an inspiration to the British people to find a Purpose which shall bind them into one united nation both now and after the war. Only by such unity and moral zeal can the peace both for ourselves and the whole world truly be won.
> Dr. ALECK BOURNE: A Message (in *Labour Monthly*)
> on the Twenty-Fifth Anniversary of the Union
> of Soviet Socialist Republics.

In the U.S.S.R. there is no place for racial prejudice. The numerous peoples of the Soviet Union have preserved their own languages and traditions. Man is valued for his abilities. All peoples are citizens. Women have the same rights as men. The right of education is given to all.

In the course of the years the Soviet Union became a powerful industrial State and the most important agricultural country in the world. At the same time it created a powerful army and a strong fleet prepared for the growing danger of attack.

The Russians are numerous and strong. They are young. One hundred and ten million of the population are not more than thirty years old. They know only the new Russia. They are ready to fight and suffer for the new Russia as Russians and Socialists. They are doing so.

Some say that this has been accomplished by the Socialist State. Others say that it is the result of the age-old Russian tradition. The more clear-sighted know that it is the result of both. From a Memorandum by The United States Government Bureau of Facts and Figures, 1942.

Comrades, the Soviet Union was never more threatened than to-day by decadent imperialism. But at the same time we see the Communist proletarians, the Socialists, and many of those who are still attached to the forms of bourgeois democracy, the best intellectuals, the best artists, the greatest scientists in the world, are turning from imperialism and are being drawn towards the fatherland of Socialism.

All those who think realise that an eclipse of the Soviet Union would mean darkness over the whole world; they all realise that the World Soviet Union is the only way out for human civilisation. And that is why the toilers throughout the world will rise in revolt against all attempts at anti-Soviet aggression. Since the October Revolution they have repeatedly and concretely manifested their resolution not to let the U.S.S.R. be touched. But in the stage of decisive social struggles that we now have reached, everyone understands that he must give himself without reservation to the defence of the Soviet Union, must identify it with his own defence. MARCEL CACHIN, at Seventh World Congress Communist International.

We Russians love our country profoundly and ardently. We

love its nature, mighty and varied, from the far northern inland polar ice to the hot south at the feet of the dazzling snows of Caucasia.

We love its history, the beginnings of which are lost in the mists of Scythian legend. We recall the days of Kiev's brilliance. We are proud of the stern glory of those days when our country, locked in a desperate struggle with the mightiest of enemies who devastated half Europe, warded off the blow he aimed, through us, at all the freedom in the world. Our shrine, our heart, Moscow, was in flames. Vast hordes of arrogant enemies trampled our countryside, yet our people never wavered, and finally our two peoples defeated the conqueror of all Europe.

We are proud of the treasures of our art; our *Saga of Igor* is more powerful and humane than the *Niebelungslied* or the *Song of Roland*: ancient temples weird and beautiful like fairy-tales of the hoary past: our poets and novelists who came late in time, but in one century managed to contribute so many treasures to the world's storehouse.

We have had generals comparable to Hannibal (I refer to Souvorov) and creative rulers like Peter the Great beyond parallel.

Finally, we have given mankind men whose incomparable significance will be appreciated fully only in the future: him whom you, Mr. Wells, once described as "the dreamer in the Kremlin," and Stalin his friend, associate, and successor—we have given the world Lenin and Stalin.

COMMANDER LEV USPENSKY, to H. G. Wells, 1942.

Chapter Eight

THE RUSSO-GERMAN WAR (1941)

IF we talk about new soil and territory in Europe to-day, we can think primarily only of Russia and its vassal border States.
        ADOLF HITLER: *Mein Kampf.*

I remember Maxim Gorky, kind, yet stern and steeled in battle. One day, some four months before his death, Gorky was sitting with eyes half-closed listening to the radio reports about the Italian invasion of Ethiopia. With every word his face grew more overcast; his brows were knit, and he kept stroking his rough moustache. Finally he got up, switched off the radio, and said in his soft voice, as though speaking to himself:

"When will those cut-throats be stopped? How much longer will they roam around footloose?"
      S. MARSHAK: *In Defence of Civilization*
          against Fascist Barbarism.

The theory and practice of Fascism is that of adventurers. . . . Fascism advanced the theory of the right of the German race to dominate over all races. This theory of the right of the white races to domination over the whole world makes distinctions, and regards not only all coloured races but also the white European neighbours of the race in question as barbarians who must submit to enslavement or annihilation. . . . To-day they [the Nazis] preach, and are already putting into vile practice, anti-semitism; to-morrow they will return to the doctrine of anti-slavism, well mindful of the shameful opinions of the Slavs they earlier expressed . . . and completely forgetful how many talented people the Poles, Pomeranians, and Czechs have given to German culture. They are creating a cult of enmity and war of the German race against the Romance race just as they are doing also against the Anglo-Saxon.

The racial theory serves as organising ideational force for

Fascism, a theory which holds up the German race as the only force capable of effecting the continued development of culture, a pure-blooded racial culture based, as is well known, on merciless and ever more cynical exploitation of the great mass of the people of the world by a numerically insignificant minority. This numerically insignificant minority is insignificant if only judged by the intellectual powers it displays in the task of thinking out methods for exploiting people. They [the Nazis] equip striplings and young men not only with revolvers but also with a battery of outworn ideas of nationalism and race-doctrine, nourishing in the youth of the nation a kind of cynicism with regard to social life and a sadistic lust for murder and destruction.

GORKY: *On Fascism.*

Citizens of the Soviet Union! The Soviet Government and its head, Comrade Stalin, have authorised me to make the following statement:

To-day, at 4 o'clock a.m., without any claims having been presented to the Soviet Union, without a declaration of war, German troops attacked our country, attacked our borders at many points, and bombed from their airplanes our cities— Zhitomir, Kiev, Sebastopol, Kaunas, and some others, killing and wounding over 200 persons. There were also enemy air raids and artillery shelling from Rumanian and Finnish territory. This unheard-of attack upon our country is perfidy unparalleled in the history of civilised nations.

The attack on our country was perpetrated despite the fact that a Treaty of Non-Aggression had been signed between the U.S.S.R. and Germany, and that the Soviet Government most faithfully abided by all the provisions of this Treaty. The attack upon our country was perpetrated despite the fact that during the entire period of the operation of this Treaty the German Government could not find grounds for a single complaint against the U.S.S.R. as regards observance of the Treaty. The entire responsibility for this predatory attack upon the Soviet Union falls fully and completely upon the German Fascist rulers.

At 5.30 a.m., that is after the attack had already been perpetrated, Schulenburg, German Ambassador in Moscow, on behalf of his Government, made a statement to me as People's Commissar for Foreign Affairs to the effect that the German Government had decided to launch war against the U.S.S.R. in connection with the concentration of Red Army units near the Eastern German frontier. In reply to this, I stated on behalf of the Soviet Government that until the very last moment the German Government had not presented any claims to the Soviet Government, that Germany attacked the U.S.S.R. despite the peaceable position of the Soviet Union, and that for this reason Fascist Germany is the aggressor.

Address by M. MOLOTOV, June 22, 1941.

By virtue of this war which has been forced upon us, our country has come to death-grips with its most malicious and most perfidious enemy—German Fascism. Our troops are fighting heroically against an enemy armed to the teeth with tanks and aircraft.

Overcoming innumerable difficulties, the Red Army and Red Navy are self-sacrificingly disputing every inch of Soviet soil. The main forces of the Red Army are coming into action armed with thousands of tanks and airplanes. Men of the Red Army are displaying unexampled valour. Our resistance to the enemy is growing in strength and power. Side by side with the Red Army, the entire Soviet people are rising in defence of our native land.

What is required to put an end to the danger hovering over our country, and what measures must be taken to smash the enemy? Above all it is essential that our people, Soviet people, should understand the full immensity of the danger that threatens our country, and abandon all complacency, all heedlessness, all those moods of peaceful constructive work which were so natural before the war, but which are fatal to-day when war has fundamentally changed everything.

The enemy is cruel and implacable. He is out to seize our lands watered with our sweat, to seize our grain and oil secured by our labour. He is out to restore the rule of landlords, to restore Tsarism, to destroy national culture and the national State existence of Russians, Ukrainians, Byelo-Russians, Lithuanians, Letts, Estonians, Uzbeks, Tartars, Moldavians, Georgians, Armenians, Azerbaijanians and the other free peoples of the Soviet Union, to Germanise them, to convert them into the slaves of German princes and barons.

Thus the issue is one of life or death for the Soviet State, for the peoples of the U.S.S.R.; the issue is whether the peoples of the Soviet Union shall remain free or fall into slavery.

. . . . .

The aim of this national war in defence of our country against the Fascist oppressors is not only the elimination of the danger hanging over our country, but also to aid all European peoples groaning under the yoke of German Fascism.

In this war of liberation we shall not be alone. In this great war we shall have loyal allies in the peoples of Europe and America, including the German people enslaved by the Hitlerite despots. Our war for the freedom of our country will merge with the struggle of the peoples of Europe and America for their independence, for democratic liberties. It will be a united front of peoples standing for freedom against enslavement and threats of enslavement by Hitler's Fascist armies.

STALIN, July 1941.

Hitlerite Germany's treacherous attack on the peaceful Soviet Union in face of the Non-Aggression Pact between the two countries, confirmed by Hitler's "own" repeated solemn declarations, has furnished the world with fresh and striking evidence that no country, whatever its policy, can feel secure so long as Nazism and Hitlerism exist. No agreements or treaties, no undertaking signed by Hitler and his henchmen, no promises or assurances on their part, no declarations of neutrality, no relations with them whatsoever can provide a guarantee against a sudden unprovoked attack.

In his diabolical plans for attacking other countries in order to fulfil his dream of world domination, Hitler has always been ruled by the principle "divide and attack!" He uses the most insidious means to prevent his intended victims from organising common resistance, taking special pains to avoid war on two fronts against the most powerful European States. His strategy is to mark down his victims and strike at them one by one, in the order prompted by circumstances.

He intended first to deal with the Western States so as to be free afterwards to fall upon the Soviet Union. This did not quite come off. There was a hitch somewhere. Hitler has not the training for a Channel swimmer yet. And so another plan matured in his brain. Believing that he had secured himself a *de facto* truce in the West, he decided to have a "blitzkrieg," lightning war, in the East in order immediately afterwards to fall with added strength upon Great Britain and finish her off.

He hoped at the same time to prevent simultaneous action against himself in the West and East by driving between them an "ideological" wedge. But it is already clear that this time Hitler was out in his reckonings both as to the lightning quality of his blow in the East and as to the miraculous power of his "ideological" propaganda.

Mr. Churchill, Prime Minister of Great Britain, with that statesmanlike acumen which is characteristic of him, immediately informed the world that he was not taken in by Hitler's wiles, declaring that victory over the Soviet Union by Hitler would be fraught with innumerable disasters and catastrophes for the British Empire. We no less recognise the menace which Hitler's victory in the West would constitute for us.

M. LITVINOV, July 1941.

My people are building no half-way house. We fight to the end until Hitlerite Germany is utterly and completely crushed. The best token of our determination is the destruction of the great Dnieper Dam.

The hearts of millions must have contracted at the news of the blowing up of the dam, but no one flinched. The sacrifice was made without any hesitation. My people knew the struggle would be hard, difficult, and long, but they had not the slightest doubt of the final issue.

But what of the price? The Soviet people have already sustained many losses and sacrifices in men, material, and territory, with the possibility of future losses and sacrifices, but every one of them knows, and every one here knows, that the closest possible military, economic, and political co-operation between the peoples of Great Britain and the Soviet Union is the way to reduce those sacrifices to as low a level as possible. The closer it is, the sooner will victory come with a just and stable peace.

M. MAISKY, August 1941.

Lenin distinguished two types of wars—predatory, i.e. unjust wars, and wars of liberation, i.e. just wars.

The Germans are carrying on now a predatory, an unjust war, aiming at the seizure of foreign territory and the subjugation of foreign peoples. That is why all honest people must rise against the German invaders as their enemies.

In contradistinction to Hitlerite Germany, the Soviet Union and its Allies are carrying on a war of liberation, a just war, aiming at the liberation of the enslaved peoples of Europe and the U.S.S.R. from Hitler's tyranny. That is why all honest people must support the armies of the U.S.S.R., Great Britain, and the other Allies, as armies of liberation.

We have not, and we cannot have, such war aims as the seizure of foreign territory, the subjugation of foreign peoples, whether it concerns the peoples and territories of Europe or the peoples and territories of Asia, including Iran. Our first aim consists in liberating our territories and our peoples from the German Fascist yoke.

We have not, and cannot have, such war aims as the forcing of our will and our régime on the Slavonic or any other enslaved European peoples who are expecting our assistance. Our aim consists in helping these peoples in their struggle for liberation against Hitlerite tyranny, and later permitting them freely to settle their own destiny in their own land. No interference in the internal affairs of other people! But in order to achieve these aims we must first crush the military might of the German aggressors. We must destroy all the German invaders to the very last one; all those who have penetrated into our country in order to subjugate it.

  STALIN, to the Moscow Soviet on the occasion of the Twenty-Fourth Anniversary of the Revolution, November 6, 1941.

Remember the year 1918 when we celebrated the first anniversary of the October Revolution. At that time three-quarters of our country was in the hands of the foreign interventionists. We had temporarily lost the Ukraine, Caucasus, Central Asia, the Urals, Siberia, and the Far East. We had no Allies, we had no Red Army—we had only just begun to create it. We experienced a shortage of bread, a shortage of arms, a shortage of clothing. At that time fourteen States were pressing against our country.

But we were not despondent, we did not become disheartened. In the midst of the conflagration of war we organised the Red Army and converted our country into a military camp. The spirit of the great Lenin inspired us at that time for the war against the interventionists.

And what happened? We defeated the interventionists, recovered all the lost territories and achieved victory.

Now our country is in a far better position than twenty-three years ago. Now our country is many times richer as regards industry, raw materials, and food than twenty-three years ago. Now we have allies, who jointly form a united front against the German invaders. Now we enjoy the sympathy and support of all the peoples of Europe who have fallen under the yoke of Fascist tyranny. Now we have a splendid Army and splendid Navy defending with their lives the freedom and independence of our country. We experience no serious shortage of either food, arms, or clothing.

Our whole country, all the peoples of our country, are backing our Army and Navy, helping them to smash the robber hordes of German Fascism. Our reserves of man-power are inexhaustible. The spirit of the great Lenin and his victorious banner inspire us now for patriotic war just as twenty-three years ago.

STALIN, November 1941.

During decades of stubborn and intense battles the peoples of our country won their fatherland for the construction of a new society.

Because the old world refused to make way for it, this new society came into being in blood and suffering. Those who for centuries had stunted the development and growth of the people, who were responsible for incalculable suffering and torture, would not surrender power to the people. They wanted to restore their domination and privileges by blood, fire, and sword.

The great ideal of the defence of the fatherland which has always animated our people, particularly in the days of our country's hardest trials, has been reborn. It has found new expression and new content.

"The Russia which was set free, for which we have suffered

for two years during our revolution—this Russia we shall defend to the last drop of our blood," said Lenin at the first All-Russian Conference of Cossack toilers on March 1, 1920, when the war against the White Guard interventionists was not yet finished.

The Soviet fighters knew that they were defending their native land—their soil, which had been amply drenched in blood, tears, and sweat; on which their forefathers toiled and on which their children lived and would live a happier and more joyous life. They fought for the right to make this new happy life.

Lenin and Stalin created the Red Army and educated it politically. The Bolsheviks transformed the country into a united military camp, supplying the front with arms, military equipment, uniforms, provisions, and reserves.

After the victory of the Red Army in the Civil War of 1918-1920, the Soviet State devoted its strength to peace-time construction. But it never forgot that the enemies of the Soviet Union were preparing to interrupt this respite.

Lenin warned: "Having taken up our peace-time construction, we shall exert every effort to carry it on without interruption. But at the same time, comrades, be on the alert, take care of the defence of our country and of our Red Army, like the apple of your eye."

Led by Stalin, the Soviet people during all these years have devoted tremendous attention to the Red Army and the Red Fleet, to their organisation and armament, to the training of their commanding staff and to their political enlightenment, military fitness, discipline, and endurance in battle.

To-day we are again fighting for our land. Some day a new epic will be written of our mass heroism and the exploits of individual men. . . .

But not only soldiers are heroes. Ordinary workers and famous engineers who have devoted all their knowledge and inventive ability to the production of new types of arms; men who produce aeroplanes, air armaments, engines, tanks, machine-guns, guns,—all these defend their fatherland.

Pravda, quoted in *Soviet War News*, 1942.

Comrades, Red Army and Red Navy men, commanders and political workers, men and women guerrillas!

The peoples of our country meet the twenty-fourth anniversary of the Red Army in the stern days of the patriotic war against Fascist Germany which has basely and insolently encroached upon the life and freedom of our motherland. Along a tremendous front, from the Arctic Ocean to the Black Sea, men of the Red Army and Red Navy wage fierce battles in order to oust the German Fascist invaders from our country and safeguard the honour and independence of our motherland.

This is not the first time that the Red Army has had to defend our native land from attack by enemies. The Red Army was created twenty-four years ago to fight the troops of the foreign interventionist invaders who strove to dismember our country and destroy her independence. Young detachments of the Red Army, which were taking part in war for the first time, inflicted utter defeat on the German invaders at Pskov and Narva on February 23, 1918.

For this very reason February 23, 1918, was proclaimed the day of the birth of the Red Army. Since then the Red Army has been growing and gaining strength in the struggle against the foreign interventionists and invaders. It safeguarded our native land in battle with the German invaders in 1918 and ousted them from the Ukraine and Byelo-Russia. It safeguarded our native land in battles with foreign troops of the Entente in 1919-1921 and ousted them from our country.

The defeat of the foreign interventionist invaders in time of civil war secured for the peoples of the Soviet Union lasting peace and the possibility of peaceful constructive work. During those two decades of peaceful constructive work, Socialist industry and collective agriculture grew up in our country; science and culture flourished; the friendship of the peoples of our country grew strong.   STALIN: Order of the Day, February 23, 1942.

In reply to your call, the movement of innovators in science and production will grow enormously and the creation of new and more perfect technical equipment and destructive arms for the Red Army and Navy will be furthered. Soviet science will solve the complex scientific and technical problems involved in extending production and exploiting the natural resources of the Urals, Siberia, Kazakhstan, and Central Asia. . . . It will help in the rapid restoration of the western and southern districts which are being liberated by the Red Army. It will evolve new curative methods for military use. . . .

The Academy of Sciences gives you its solemn promise to raise against the enemy the boundless powers of modern progressive science which keeps advancing, knowing no limits and transcending all boundaries.

From a Message of Greeting addressed to
Stalin by the Soviet Scientists, 1942.

For scores of years I, an old Russian scientist, have been in close contact with youth, teaching it precise and rigid laws of science, opening to it nature's secrets. To-day I address not only my students, but the citizens of my country. I want the whole of the Soviet nation to hear the wrathful words of a Russian scientist.

Human monsters and degenerates are stretching their talons to Leningrad. They want to transform our beautiful city into the same desolate waste into which they have turned Prague, Warsaw, Belgrade, Vienna, and Amsterdam.

I am an old engineer and accustomed to think that there is nothing stronger than steel. Now I see I am mistaken, for there is something stronger even than steel itself, and that is the will of the Soviet people. Now that the huge battlefront stretches across our country, when Leningrad has become a battlefield, I see that there is no limit to the courage of Soviet men and women.

PROFESSOR ALEXANDER BAIKOV, in *Soviet War News*, 1942.

To-day the hearts and minds of all Russians are imbued with one thought, one fervent desire: to devote every energy to the fight, to strain every nerve for victory over the enemy of freedom, culture, and democratic civilisation.

The whole of Soviet Russia, from the Pacific Ocean to the battlefields where our armies oppose the universal foe, has rallied in energetic and unanimous action, in unconquerable hatred for the bearers of slavery and death. ALEXEY TOLSTOY.

History has known many just and noble wars for freedom and independence. Not a few of them belong to the history of Russia. When our people were overthrowing the Tartar yoke their leader, Dmitri Donskoy, said: "I know that I came not to stand guard on the River Don, but to free the Russian land from captivity, or to give my life for all of you. It is better to die honestly than to live in disgrace."

Two centuries later he was echoed by Kuzma Minin, the Moscow citizen who organised the capital's defence against the invaders: "Better death than a foreign yoke!"

During the war of 1812 Mikhail Kutuzov, commander-in-chief of the Russian forces against Napoleon, said: "The Russians would not wish to taste the sweetness of peace before they had exterminated the treacherous foe who defiled the land of our forefathers by his attack."

Never has a people anywhere so loved their native land as in our time and in our country, where the whole wealth, all the fruits of labour, all the treasures of national genius belong to the people themselves.

We defend our State and the life and dignity of every citizen whoever he may be. We are humanists. We treasure the wealth of our native land, but we treasure our fellow human beings a thousand times more.

PROFESSOR KOMAROV, *in Soviet War News*, 1942.

There is no citizen of our country who remains aloof from the struggle. The self-denial of the workers, the industry of the collective farmers and the spirit of research which inspires our scientists, the boldness of our designers, the lyricism of our poets, the creative imagination of our composers—everything must be wholly devoted to the sacred goal for which we live and breathe: victory.

The upsurge of patriotic feeling which has seized the people of the Soviet Union, who are defending their free life, has provided splendid soil for the growth of new artistic achievements during the war.

Our theatres are working intensively, staging new plays, creating new characters, and arousing heroic sentiments among the people. In addition to producing new works, they are devoting much attention to the great world classics of the past.

Our orchestras are holding their usual concert season with enormous success. Exacting audiences keenly follow their performances. This fact, of such good omen for us, is one of terrible import for Hitler.

Art, which in any other country would recede into the background at such a time, which would take shelter in the "tranquillity of the rear," in our country has become a weapon striking against the enemy. From the inspired sounds of symphonies and songs, marches and oratorios the Soviet people draw resolution for their struggle.
> DMITRI SHOSTAKOVICH, in *Soviet War News*, 1942.

The "mystery of Russian resistance" is simple. Our people know what the Germans bring them. Never has there been a war so clear in purpose and so just. Why have even the Russian émigrés, sworn enemies of the Soviet Government, refused to take part in the German "crusade"?

Why do Russian priests pray for the victory of the Red Army? There is food for thought. Our people understand that the existence of Russia is at stake, and they defend that which at all times men and peoples have defended—their country.

In times of peace there are hundreds of issues before men and nations. There are wars which can be settled in various ways—by compromise, by an adjustment of frontiers, by a financial agreement. But in this war, imposed on our people, we have no choice. We must win or die. The "war aims" which we pursue are very simple—to defend our land and our independence.
> ILYA EHRENBURG, in *Soviet War News*, 1942.

Under the slogan, "Every city a bastion, every house a fortress," the entire adult male population is being trained to wield arms, to use machine-guns, build barricades, throw hand-grenades, fight fires and poison gas. There is no relenting in the grim determination to fight the most critical battle in Russian history "to the last man," in the words of the defenders of Leningrad.
> HENRY SHAPIRO, the Representative of the Mutual Broadcasting Company, from Moscow Radio, on September 21, 1941.

During the years of the Civil War [when the young Soviet Government was consolidating its power against the White Guards], Soviet women worked in first-aid detachments, guarded factories, fought in the firing-line, joined guerrilla detachments and derailed enemy trains.

To-day they are again in the vanguard as active helpers of their husbands, sons, and brothers, in the war for the defence of the motherland.

> KLAVDIA NIKOLEYEVA, a leading Woman Trade Unionist and Secretary of the Soviet Central Council of Trade Unions, 1941.

O son of mine, forgive these tears,
The tears that from my heart are wrung!
E'en birch-trees for their reft boughs weep,
The wild beasts for their young.

And, dearest, how should I not weep?
Nor dolorous grief o'er me prevail?
Where strength and calm endurance draw
To choke . . . a mother's wail?

In offering to our native land
We needs must of our own will part
With what is lovelier than life,
E'en though it break our heart.

And so I freely offer thee
To deadly battle with the foe.
Though dearer to me than my life. . . .
Farewell! God with thee! Go![1]

GRINEVSKAYA.

Trade unions must first of all strive to achieve the fulfilment of industrial tasks, and above all to popularise widely the most advanced technique so as to bring it within the knowledge of the broadest sections of the people.

They must give every possible support and assistance to workers who put forward inventions or proposals for rationalisation, and to all those who strive to raise the productivity of labour and the quality and economy of production.

[1] Written during the last war (1914-1918).

They must give assistance to the managers of factories and undertakings in their work of reorganising industry on a war footing. Work must be considered from the point of view of fulfilling the requirements of the front. The mastery of new production methods; the rapid change-over of equipment to war needs; active assistance to the factory management based on the experience and knowledge of the lower technical and management personnel,—these are the tasks demanding the immediate attention of trade unions.

New recruits are replacing the men who have left factories for the front. Women are mastering industrial work to replace their husbands and brothers. But these recruits still lack industrial experience. They must be trained. Here is a wide field of work for the trade unions.

The foundation of our industrial successes has always been inflexible labour discipline. In war-time it is necessary to strengthen this still further, to fight against anyone who infringes it and to prosecute them according to war-time laws.

Trade unions must concern themselves with the needs of working people, by organising food distribution and attending to the general demands of employees. The efficient running of workers' restaurants, buffets, and canteens is the concern of the trade unions.

They must actively assist the front by helping to organise a large number of teams of nurses, medical assistants, and first-aid personnel. This work should continue ceaselessly. The care of the wounded and assistance to the field-hospitals are two responsible tasks of trade unions. They must also train the population in A.R.P. military duties, and prepare for the autumn mobilisation.

Most of the active trade unionists and organisers have gone into the Red Army. New men must be elected in their place. Every trade union has many active members on its list. These should be drawn into wider activity. Now, more than ever, it is necessary to carry on extensive educational work among the broad sections of the population.

People must be shown how they can help the Red Army and Navy. An active trade unionist is also a political worker. He must know how to use arms and explain their use to his colleagues and to other people.

Pravda, quoted in *Soviet War News*, 1941.

The first task of all nations and all States compelled to wage war against Hitlerite Germany and her allies is to bring about the speediest and most decisive defeat of the aggressor. For the full accomplishment of that task they must assemble and devote all their strength and resources, and determine the most effective ways and means of reaching their goal. It is the task which at the present time unites all the Governments which have sent their representatives to this Conference. Our countries face also the most important problem of laying the basis for the organisation of international relations, and of constituting the post-war world in such a way as to spare our peoples and our future generations the monstrous crimes of Nazism, incompatible with human culture. The U.S.S.R. is firmly convinced that this task will be successfully accomplished, and that as a result of complete and final victory over Hitlerism there will be laid the true foundations of international co-operation and friendship corresponding to the aspirations and ideals of freedom-loving people.

That is what all the peoples of my country are striving for. That is what inspires the Soviet Government in all its activities and in its foreign policy. The Soviet Union has applied and will apply in its foreign policy the high principle of respect for the sovereign rights of peoples. The Soviet Union was and is guided in its foreign policy by the principle of self-determination of nations. It is guided by the same principle which in fact embodies recognition of the sovereignty and the equality of nations in its dealings with various nationalities embraced within the frontiers of the Soviet Union. Indeed, this principle forms one of the pillars on which the political structure of the U.S.S.R. is built. Accordingly, the Soviet Union defends the right of every nation to the independence and territorial integrity of its country, and its right to establish such a social order and to choose such a form of government as it deems opportune and necessary for the better promotion of its economic and cultural prosperity.

The Soviet Union, which followed that principle in all its policy and in all its relations with other nations, has consistently and with full force denounced all violations of sovereign rights of peoples, all aggression and aggressors, all and any attempts of aggressive States to impose their will upon other peoples and to involve them in war. The Soviet Union has untiringly and resolutely advocated, and advocates to-day, the necessity of collective action against aggressors as one of the most effective means of bringing about the triumphs of those principles and advancing the peace and security of nations.

Striving for a radical solution of the problem of safeguarding freedom-loving peoples against all the dangers they encounter from aggressors, the Soviet Union has at the same time fought for complete and general disarmament. The Soviet Union is ready to give a fitting answer to any blow from the aggressor. At the same time, it has been and still is building its foreign policy upon the desire to maintain peaceful and neighbourly relations with all countries which respect the integrity and inviolability of its borders. The Soviet Union was and is willing to render all possible assistance to peoples becoming victims of aggression, and fighting for the independence of their native land.

In accordance with a policy inspired by the above principles, which have been unswervingly applied by the Soviet Union—a policy which, moreover, has been expressed in numerous acts and documents—the Soviet Government proclaims its agreement with the fundamental principles of the declaration of Mr. Roosevelt, President of the United States, and of Mr. Churchill, Prime Minister of Great Britain—principles which are so important in the present international circumstances.

Considering that the practical application of these principles will necessarily adapt itself to the circumstances, needs and historic peculiarities of particular countries, the Soviet Government can state that a consistent application of these principles will secure the most energetic support on the part of the Government and peoples of the Soviet Union.

Soviet Declaration at the Inter-Allied Conference, September 24, 1941.

Jewish brothers of the whole world! In the enslaved countries Fascism has introduced its "New Order" with the help of the knife, the gallows, fire, and violence. For the Jewish people bloodthirsty Hitlerism has outlined a programme for the complete extermination of Jews by all the methods known to the Fascist hangmen.

In Poland alone the Hitlerites have cruelly tortured and massacred over three million Poles and Jews. They have outraged daughters before their parents' eyes and split open the heads of children before their mothers. Those who have remained alive have been obliged to see their daughters forced into military brothels and their sons sterilised.

Jewish brothers! The Jewish people, scattered by fate throughout the world, have closely bound up their culture with the culture of the whole world. In the countries enslaved by the Fascists our unfortunate brothers were the first victims. The blood of Jews, tortured to death in the burned synagogues of Rotterdam, calls aloud to the whole world. So do the thousands of nameless graves in the towns of Poland, where the Fascist monsters buried their victims alive.

The blood which has been shed calls out not for fasts and prayers but for vengeance; not ritual candles but flames to consume the hangmen of humanity; not tears but for hatred and resistance to the monsters; not words but for deeds. It must be now or never.

In the tragic history of our long-suffering people, from the Roman Empire to the Middle Ages, it is impossible to find a time when there was such sorrow and misery as Fascism has brought to mankind, with particular ferocity for the Jewish people.

Intoxicated by blood and violence, the Fascist monsters have now attacked the one country where the Jewish people have found a real motherland which offered them a splendid life, freedom, and a flourishing national culture. Here, for the first time in thousands of years, Jews felt at home, equals among equals. In the fertile fields of the Soviet Union, for the first time the Jewish tiller of soil took his place at the wheel of a tractor. In the factories and mills Jews played their part. The doors of the universities were open to them, they entered the Red Army, worked in the mines, helped in the laboratories.

The Jewish people found a place for themselves in the great family of peoples in the U.S.S.R. All these peoples have, in a quarter of a century of fraternal collaboration, built up their security, their future, and their national freedom. Now their fields are being drenched in blood. Villages and towns which have temporarily fallen into the bloody clutches of the Hitlerite monsters are being destroyed. Highways are strewn with the graves of savagely tortured citizens.

. . . . . .

Jewish brothers of the world! As long as Fascism exists all mankind is in peril. Our call is to warn you. Our appeal goes out to you as a clarion call for resistance and vengeance. Let every day bring you closer to the hour of reckoning with the enemy. Let the sacred flame burn brighter in your hearts with every hour. Let every minute find you ready for action.

You must do everything in your power to disrupt the economic resources of the Fascists in whatever part of the world you are. Penetrate into the most vital branches of the death-dealing industries of the Hitlerites and paralyse them at all costs. Boycott their products everywhere. Proclaim aloud everywhere and in all tongues the outrageous atrocities perpetrated by the Hitlerite cannibals.

Act with the noble self-sacrifice of the indomitable guerrilla fighters. Not a single Jew must die without taking vengeance on the Fascists for shedding innocent blood. Develop everywhere widespread propaganda for solidarity with and active assistance for the Soviet Union, which is putting up a heroic resistance to the bearers of death and destruction. Mankind will be freed of the brown plague. Your duty is to help to exterminate it. Do your bit in this sacred war.

"To the Jews of the World," in *Soviet War News*, 1941.

The Fascists have drenched our peaceful fields in blood. They slaughter innocent women, old men, and children. Hitler is out to destroy learning and culture, to establish the Reich of barbarism and to exterminate the Moslem faith. The Central Moslem Ecclesiastical Board calls upon all the faithful to rise up in defence of their native land, to pray in the mosques for the victory of the Red Army and to give their blessing to their sons, fighting in a just cause.

An Appeal by the Central Moslem Ecclesiastical Board in the U.S.S.R., 1941.

I never had a chance to see Stalin at close range, only at demonstrations, when we saw him a long way off, standing on the tribune, looking just like he does in his portraits. Do you remember, Gregory, how whenever we went for a walk on spring evenings we always turned towards the Red Square, and longed to look beyond the brick Kremlin wall, to see Stalin? Somehow we always pictured him at his desk bent over books, papers, and maps.

We used to stand for hours on the vast deserted square, and it seemed to us that through the thick brick wall we felt the throbbing heart of this man. We felt his presence in our midst. And wherever I was I always had the feeling that he was with me. It is for Stalin that I go into mortal combat.

Since time began, youth has always been mankind's hope, flower, and pride. But the German youth is a misfortune for society, and a disgrace to the world. Reared in Germany's animal cages, tamed like beasts with a piece of bloody meat, corrupted by Hitler, this youth deprived of youth is only capable of plunder and murder.

Soviet youth has accepted the challenge, whatever the price may be. And it is to carry out this task that I go into battle.

> From a letter from a Soviet soldier to his friend (quoted in *Soviet War News*).

The nation which has trained such youth—the nation of Pushkin and Suvoro, Tchaikovsky and Kutuzov, Chkalov and Gastello, Lenin and Stalin—will never be brought to its knees.

Let us pledge ourselves to avenge all the victims of Fascism. And may this pledge be heard by every young man and woman in the Soviet Union, in Britain, America, and the Fascist-occupied countries. Let the freedom-loving youth everywhere rise up against the common enemy—German Fascism.

> NIKOLAI MIKHAILOV, Secretary of the Central Committee of the Young Communist League of the U.S.S.R., at the Anti-Fascist Youth Rally, Moscow, 1941.

I, a citizen of the Great Soviet Union, and a true son of the heroic Russian people, swear I will not lay down my arms until the last Fascist in our territory is destroyed.

I swear I will carry out the orders of my commanders without question and observe strict military discipline.

For damaging our villages and country, for the death of our children and for terror and tortures inflicted on my people, I swear to avenge myself bitterly, mercilessly, and ceaselessly on the enemy.

I will take an eye for an eye and a tooth for a tooth.

I swear I would rather die in a bitter fight than allow myself and my family or the Soviet people to become Fascist slaves. If by my weakness or cowardice or by ill fate I break this vow and betray the interests of my people, let me die a traitor's death at the hands of my comrades.

Oath of the Soviet Guerrilla Fighter.

Irrespective of your race, social status, religious and political views, we, the youth of the Soviet Union, appeal to you. Over us, the younger generation, hangs the threat of death. Our freedom, happiness, and our young lives are being menaced by the Fascist monsters who bring death and destruction. Hitler has enslaved and plundered Czechoslovakia, devastated Poland, mutilated Norway and Yugoslavia, trampled the fields of France, and burned the cities of Greece.

Listen to us, youth of the occupied countries. You had a native country. Fascism came and took it away. You had freedom. The Hitlerite bandits have taken that away and made you into slaves. You had your own national culture created by your fathers and grandfathers. The Hitlerite barbarians have trampled on it.

You had your happy homes. The Fascists have destroyed your nomes. You had a family. Hitler has broken it up. Some of them he killed, some he tortured, some he enslaved, others he dishonoured. You had great, fine hopes, such as a young person always has. The Fascists descended upon you like death and destroyed all your hopes.

German Fascism is preparing enslavement and misery for the youth of the whole world.

Youth of the world! Fascism is our deadly enemy. We now have a common task—to smash Fascism. Only the smashing of Fascism will give the peoples a chance of breathing freely, of building up their own States and culture.

Who, if not we, the young people, should go first into battle for the honour and independence of our people, for the cause of the whole of progressive mankind.

Students of the world! Students have always been a mighty

progressive force defending the freedom and independence of their peoples. In these days of historic battle, let every university become a mighty fortress of struggle for the people, let every student, wherever he may be, become a fearless fighter for the cause of his people. Forward, to battle! Lead on, Youth of the world!   *Appeal of Moscow Youth Rally*, 1941.

Despite the war, we have all the necessary conditions for continued fruitful work in the field of science, technique, literature, and art. This work never ceases for one day or one hour.

It goes on, more intense than in peace-time, both in the depths of our country far from the thunder of war and in the towns close to the front. In Leningrad and in Moscow our scientists, designers, and engineers stand firm at their posts, setting examples of determination and endurance to others.

The Soviet intelligentsia are the same flesh and blood as the people. Eighty to ninety per cent. of them have come from the heart of the workers, peasants and others sections of the working people. All they have received they owe to the people, the Socialist Revolution and the Soviet Government.

Workers in the field of literature and art bear the great and important responsibility not only of reflecting in the great historical works of our day all that is worthy of the heroes and the great epic of the war, but of imbuing the whole of our people with sentiments of supreme and self-sacrificing love of their fatherland, feelings of fearlessness and contempt of death.

The intelligentsia working in the field of science, technique, literature, and art are a great force in our country. All talents, all knowledge, all achievements must be subordinated to the one task—the crushing of German Fascism.

Pravda, quoted in *Soviet War News*, 1942.

Fascism has replaced the Humanism which characterises the spiritual development of peoples by the creed of eternal war and progressive marasmus, depravity and the enthronement of darkest reaction and the mass murder of the weak, the old, and the infirm. It is a deadly menace to the culture and science which are most dear and precious to us. In their common work for the conquest of nature, scientists throughout the world pay the greatest attention to the furtherance of the culture and welfare of the human race, whereas Fascism utilises the achievements of modern science and technology for destruction and extermination.

By their work in aero-dynamics, scientists have developed the mastery of the aeroplane which has given humanity the most powerful means of communication across oceans, deserts, and vast areas of land. . . .

What was for long a benefit to mankind has been turned into a deadly weapon. We scientists have the duty of avenging this abuse of our achievements. . . . We are convinced that this grim and difficult struggle of all the freedom-loving and progressive people of the world will achieve the destruction of Fascism. We must give all our knowledge and all our strength for victory in this most terrible war in history.

Appeal of Soviet Scientists to the Scientists of
the World, October 12, 1941.

To-day we mark the eighteenth anniversary of the death of Lenin, the creator of our Party and of the Soviet State. On this anniversary the Party and all our people take stock of their work.

Seven months ago the German imperialists attacked our country. They sent against us a colossal war machine. They wanted to destroy our people and our State and convert the workers and peasants of all the nations of the U.S.S.R. into the fettered slaves of German capitalists and landowners.

We have been subjected to the gravest trials, and it must be said that our people have come through these trials with honour. The Soviet rear was found to be worthy of its army. Our people did not waver or fall into panic.

The Soviet system founded by Lenin and Stalin turned out to be the most stable in the world, and in the course of war has become still stronger. It has been steeled in battle. This is the strongest proof that our Party under the leadership of Stalin has unswervingly and consistently put into operation the behests of great Lenin. . . .

Our motherland is a land of workers, peasants and working intellectuals, a country without capitalists and landlords.

When they started their attack, the Nazis supposed that they had merely to invade our country and then strife would break out between the Soviet workers, peasants, and intellectuals.

These hopes were dashed to the ground, like all their other stupid miscalculations.

Lenin instructed the Party to do its utmost to weld firmly the alliance of workers and peasants. In carrying out this instruction, the Party and the Soviet Government built up the collective farms. The working intellectuals helped in this matter. The collective farm system was victorious, and the peasants who have been given real human lives under the collective farm system will never again step off this road.

The German invaders wanted to restore capitalism in our country. They aimed at taking from the peasants their collective farms, seizing our lands and giving them to German kulaks, landowners, and barons. Never will this happen! Never will the German Fascists introduce their system on Soviet soil. Our peasants, who are happy in their prosperous, wealthy collective farms, will never be slaves to anybody.

The Soviet Union is a State of many nationalities. Supporting each other, helping each other, the peoples together built up and developed their own national culture. Our policy rejects inequalities among peoples. We have no higher and lower races. All nationalities within the Soviet Union have equal rights.

The Nazis reckoned on disunity between the peoples of the U.S.S.R. They thought that under their blows strife would break out among the different nationalities. Here again they miscalculated. The peoples of the Soviet Union are a united, indivisible camp. The armies of Ukrainians, Byelo-Russians, Azerbaijans, Cossacks, Georgians, Armenians, warriors of all the peoples of the Soviet Union, fought for the capital of our country, Moscow, and are fighting on to the final victory.

Our country had no intention of going to war. We were busy on peaceful work of construction. The foreign policy of the Soviet Government unswervingly followed the way of peace and constantly unmasked the aggressive plans of the Fascist imperialists. In this policy of peace we won the sympathy and support of all honest people throughout the world.

The land of Soviets has endured and resisted the heaviest blows of the German Fascists. Our people have strength and endurance enough to secure complete victory.

From a speech delivered by SHCHERBAKOV, Secretary of the Moscow Committee of Bolshevik Party.

The whole history of the peoples of the Soviet Union prepared them for the great historic mission of liberation they are fulfilling in the present war. But the greatest contribution to the country's preparedness for fighting and winning this grim war was made by the Bolshevik Party.

For decades the Party of Lenin and Stalin has forged generations of men and women ready for combat, for heroic exploits, for indefatigable endeavour and severe struggle. Stalin has said that life would be without meaning for him, were he not able to dedicate every day of it to improving the conditions of the working people. These words express the aim which is the essence of life for every one of us.

The Bolshevik Party has fostered in the Soviet people a profound respect for the peoples of other countries. It was this education in the spirit of equality of all peoples as opposed to the nationalist spirit and racial theories, as well as the constant concern shown by the Party for the consolidation of friendship between the peoples of the U.S.S.R. that produced our country's unbreakable moral and political unity.

Hundreds of thousands of Bolsheviks and millions of Young Communists are tirelessly cementing the ranks of the Red Army and conducting political and educational work among the soldiers and sailors. They daily explain to them the tasks facing the people, and give a constant personal example of fearlessness in combat. . . .

A profound sense of principle and ideological consistency; an iron Party discipline which Lenin frequently compared with military discipline; inseparable contact between the Bolsheviks and the masses at the front and in the rear; fearlessness in battle and contempt for death when the Socialist motherland is in danger; firmness as exemplified by Lenin and Stalin; implacability towards capitulators and faint-hearted, corrupt, and wavering elements; sterling morale,—all these qualities, fostered in the Party by Lenin and Stalin, are traits characteristic of the Bolsheviks whom history has charged with such serious responsibility in these days of war.

EMELYAN YAROSLAVSKY, in *Soviet War News*, 1942.

This evil has fallen on us all. The enemy is ruining our land with fire; his tanks scar our fields. He wants everything that is ours—that has been ours through the age-long centuries.

The fortunate and unfortunate gather together. Even he who hoped to hide like a cricket in a dark barn and chirrup away there till better times, even he now realises that alone one cannot save oneself. Our motherland prevails over all other feelings.

Everything we see around us, things that perhaps we hardly even noticed—or never valued—the smell of rye-bread in the smoke, the snow swirling round the cottage—all this becomes immeasurably dear to us. All faces, all eyes, reflect one single absorbing thought. We who live in this age are the guardians and caretakers of our motherland.

This movement of the people springs from the depths of the centuries and reaches out to the longed-for future in which they believe and which they create with their own hands for themselves and the coming generations.

Some day the various national streams will merge into one storm-free sea, into one single humanity; but this belongs to the future. At present our age is an age of grim struggle for our independence, for our freedom and for the right to build our society and our happiness according to our own laws.

Insane Fascism is the enemy of all national culture, including that of Germany. It strives to crush any national culture, to wipe it out. Its Pan-German idea of all the world for the Germans is the wily ruse of a big financial gamble in which countries, cities, and men are only a form of impersonal stock-exchange quotations flung into the total war.

ALEXEY TOLSTOY: *Motherland.*

In the whole course of history there has been no blacker apparition than Fascism. When it disappears, humanity will look back on it as a fantastic revolting nightmare.

GORKY: *On Fascism.*

Russia is a world, sheltering many peoples. A great power, she has never surrendered to a conqueror. She was first among the nations to proclaim the rights of labour and brotherhood.

The battle is for Russia—for the power built by labour and sanctified by the blood of many generations. The battle is for the light of Russian culture. In 1917 a great people launched a new era. They received as their heritage a beautiful, thrice-beloved country.

Now this country has been invaded by the greedy Germans. They want to kill Russia. . . . But Russia shall not pass under German rule. After they had finished with Kiev, Odessa, Smolensk, and Novgorod, the Germans drenched Donbas cities and quiet Cossack villages in blood. They are menacing Stalingrad. They are driving for Kuban. These stern days demand of us redoubled courage, redoubled determination.

If, reader, you are a soldier fighting on the Don, remember that the enemy must advance only over his own dead, that he must advance only to his death, that he must be halted. In the lull between the salvos of artillery, pause for a second to listen, and you will hear the quickened pulse of wrathful Russia. For to-day her destiny is being decided for years and perhaps for centuries to come. . . .

ILYA EHRENBURG, in *Soviet War News*, 1942.

The Nazis invaded our country during the twenty-fourth year of the existence of the Soviet State. Our peaceful tools of labour were exchanged for weapons of war. The tremendous work of creation was temporarily interrupted. The fate of everything built during this quarter-century depends on the outcome of the present struggle of the Soviet people and its Red Army against the Nazis.

But because we have Soviet power in our country, because Soviet power has trained a valiant generation, real heroes of labour and war, because during the twenty-five years of its existence the Land of Soviets has accumulated tremendous forces—that is why the Red Army fights on in the hardest conditions. It is precisely for those reasons that we are confident of our success.

EMELYAN YAROSLAVSKY, in *Soviet War News*, 1942.

O! Mighty Russia, thou that didst withstand
The furious onslaught of the Tartar horde,
Once more does Freedom gird thee with her sword
To keep inviolate thy holy land.

Strong bulwark—thine the immemorial fate
To shield the lamp of progress in the West—
The tyrant's spear is turned against thy breast,
Once more the savage foe is at thy gate.

. . . . . .

Rise in thy wrath, if thou wouldst still be free!
Arise and smite for all thou holdest dear!
A fiercer far than Attila is here,
Than Genghis or the Man of Destiny.

Sound forth the trumpet throughout all the land;
O'er steppe and desert let the echo roll,
From Caspia to the margin of the Pole,
From Yenisei to farthest Samarkand!

. . . . . .

O! Holy Russia—we who love thy song,
Thy people, and the magic of thy land—
Endure until we reach thy side and stand
At one with thee—endure, hold fast, be strong!

E. St. John Brooks.[1]

It needs no great effort to understand and to admire the price the people of Russia are paying for their liberty. It is true of Russia, as it is of China, that a people which can so exhibit its mettle compels some revision of the judgments passed by the West on its institutions. . . . A people that can make the kind of war that Russia has been making for thirteen weeks possesses the inspiration that Fox found in democracy; the challenge of the invader "arouses everything that belongs to the soul as well as to the body of man."

The Manchester Guardian, September 15, 1941.

To-day I and my peoples join with the peoples of the Soviet Union in whole-hearted tribute to the heroic qualities and magnificent leadership whereby the Red Army, in its struggle against our common enemies, has, by its resounding triumphs, written new pages of history.

[1] Written during the last war and published in *The Times*.

It was the unyielding resistance of Stalingrad that turned the tide and heralded the crushing blows which have struck dismay into the foes of civilisation and freedom. To mark the profound admiration felt by myself and the peoples of the British Empire, I have given commands for the preparation of a Sword of Honour, which it would give me pleasure to present to the city of Stalingrad. My hope would be that this gift might commemorate in the happier times to come the inflexible courage with which the warrior city steeled herself against the powerful and persistent onslaughts of her assailants, and that it might be a token of the admiration not only of the British peoples but of the whole civilised world.

> His Majesty King George VI, to M. Kalinin on the Twenty-Fifth Anniversary of the Red Army, February 23, 1943.

In the name of the peoples of the United States I wish to express to the Red Army, on the occasion of its twenty-fifth anniversary, our deep admiration of its marvellous achievements, unexampled in history. For many months, despite huge losses in material, means of transport and territory, the Red Army did not allow its powerful adversary to achieve victory. It stopped them before Leningrad, before Moscow, Voronezh, in the Caucasus, and finally in the immortal battles at Stalingrad.

The Red Army not only defeated the enemy, but launched the great offensive which is still developing successfully along the whole front from the Baltic to the Black Sea. The retreat that has been forced on the enemy is costing him dear in men and material and in territory, and reflects especially strongly on his morale. Such achievements could only be accomplished by an army that had skilful leadership, firm organisation, and the requisite training, and, above all, the determination to defeat the enemy without regard to its own sacrifices.

At the same time I wish to pay tribute to the Russian people from whom the Red Army springs and from whom it receives its man-power and equipment. The Russian people also gives its whole strength to the war effort, and is making the highest sacrifices. The Red Army and the Russian people have undoubtedly compelled the armed forces of Hitler to tread the path of final defeat and have won the admiration of the peoples of the United States for many years to come.

PRESIDENT ROOSEVELT, to Stalin.

In the course of the last few weeks the Army of your country has captured a number of famous towns one after the other, sweeping away the enemy robbers. In so doing your Army has made certain the complete rout of the robber bands of the Axis countries and still further confirmed the timeliness of an early counter-offensive of the United Nations.

For these brilliant military achievements we are wholly indebted to the heroic struggle of the Army and peoples of your country, under your wise and far-sighted leadership. I am filled with infinite joy at the news of your successes. On the occasion of the twenty-fifth anniversary of the Red Army of the Soviet Union, I, together with the whole army and people of China, convey to you my sincere congratulations. May the strains of the hymn of victory continue to ring in your ears!

In view of the fact that an essential premise for the stable establishment of complete peace in the world is the destruction of the armed forces of the Axis countries, both in the East and in the West, the destinies of the United Nations are linked into one whole, and the victory of one country is the victory of all. China and the Soviet Union should be imbued with the spirit of comradeship of people travelling on one ship and put all their forces into mutual action and mutual aid so as to lay the foundations as quickly as possible for a just peace throughout the world.

GENERALISSIMO CHIANG KAI SHEK, to Stalin.

Chapter Nine

SOVIET RUSSIA AND HER ALLIES

WE prize all these things that are "yours" for the very reason that we too have no less precious things which we call "ours," paid for likewise with the toil of centuries and millions of lives. We prize all this because to us Soviet people—above all such terms as "tribal" and "national," above such words as "yours" and "ours," not abolishing them, not detracting from their charm and value, but rather rendering them more poignant and profound—there stands the lofty and comprehensive concert of the *all-human*, the universal, that which belongs to all who are worthy of the name of "man."

It is these common values that we must now defend from unhumans, from these brown apes.

Hand in hand with you Englishmen we Russians are prepared to march to the end in this fight for the triumph of man over anthropoid, for Prospero over Caliban, for Faust over the spirit of darkness, reason over brute instinct.

We, Mr. Wells, are undaunted by this advent of Martians. We have joined battle with them and are confident of victory. Like the Time Traveller, we will batter in the skulls of these hideous morlocks besetting us. Once we destroy them we shall speed in your Time Machine towards the bright future.

       COMMANDER LEV USPENSKY, to H. G. Wells, 1942.

You cannot carry on a real struggle against Fascism if you do not render all possible assistance in strengthening the most important buttress of this struggle, namely the Soviet Union. You cannot carry on a serious struggle against the Fascist instigators of a new world-blood-bath if you do not render undivided support to the U.S.S.R., a most important factor in the maintenance of International Peace.

       DIMITROV: *The Soviet Union and the Working Class of the Capitalist Countries*, 1937.

The Coalition of the U.S.A., Great Britain, and the U.S.S.R. is a reality which will grow to the benefit of our common cause.
                                                           STALIN, 1941.

The Anglo-Soviet Agreement for joint action in the war against Germany, signed on July 19, 1941, marked a turning-point in relations between the U.S.S.R. and Great Britain. . . . In concluding this Agreement, the U.S.S.R. and Great Britain clearly realised that they were facing a strong and perfidious enemy possessing a powerful war machine, and that the merging of the efforts of all freedom-loving peoples of Europe and America would have decisive significance for his total defeat.
                                                           Izvestia, 1941.

Hitler knew that the Soviet people stood for something different and better than his policy of violence and enslavement. That is why Hitler decided that, in spite of his pledge, he had also to attack the U.S.S.R. without a warning.

Little he knew or understood of the intense love of their home and country which fills the hearts of the Soviet people.

He was so blinded by his own lust for power that he could not recognise the gallant strength of the Red Army, Navy, and Air Force. But now, as the third year of the war opens, he must look with different eyes upon the folly of his attack on the Soviet Union.

· · · · · ·

I send my greetings to the Soviet people and assure them that the British people will do their utmost to help them in every way they can. Our admiration for the magnificent achievements of the Soviet forces by land, sea, and air is unstinted. We acclaim the determination of every man, woman, and child to protect their homeland from the brutal invader, and we are confident that the spirit of courage and determination will bring our two countries to a final and successful issue in our struggle, when the world will once and for all be freed from the terror and suffering of Hitlerism.   SIR STAFFORD CRIPPS: A Message to the
                            People of the U.S.S.R., 1941.

In the days of the great fight against the Hitlerite hordes, the naval pilots of the Soviet Union warmly greet the naval pilots of Great Britain.

Comrades-in-arms, the historic task of freeing humanity from Hitlerite tyranny has fallen to the lot of the peoples of the Soviet Union and Great Britain. In the fight against Hitlerism, which seeks to drown the whole world in blood, naval pilots have shown fearlessness and great military ability.

We record with admiration the operation carried out by you at Taranto, the devastating blows on the battleship *Bismarck*, and your courageous fight for the destruction of military objectives and bases of the hated enemy.

The unshakable will of our peoples to wage the fight until complete victory over the enemy binds us naval pilots mercilessly to exterminate the Hitlerite monsters on sea, on land, and in the air. Our cause is a just cause. We are defending the freedom and peaceful labour of our peoples. We are defending the liberty and happy future of all humanity. Victory will be ours.

> From the Naval Pilots of the Soviet Union to the Pilots of the Fleet Air Arm of the Royal Navy, 1941.

We welcome the spirit of friendship shown to us by our valiant comrades of the Soviet Naval Air Force, and we look forward to the day when our combined efforts may bring that victory which we both so ardently desire.

The Naval Air Service reciprocates warmly the greetings and good wishes of the Soviet Naval Air Service, and wishes them good hunting and happy landings.

> From the Royal Naval Air Service to the Soviet Naval Air Force, 1941.

The trade union organisations send fraternal greetings to the representatives of 300,000 organised workers of the London Trades Council. The trade union organisations of Moscow warmly greet your decision condemning the act of bloody aggression of Hitlerite Germany against the Soviet Union and approving the fullest co-operation between the three great Powers—the Soviet Union, Great Britain, and the United States.

The workers of Moscow, with particular satisfaction, received your pledge to do everything possible in order, shoulder to shoulder with the Soviet people, to bring the war against Nazi Germany to a victorious end. This pledge is a token of the fact that the united front of the freedom-loving peoples is widening and strengthening, that the hour is not far off when bloody Fascism will be wiped off the face of the earth and hundreds of millions of people will be liberated from Fascist tyranny.

The workers of Moscow, like the whole Soviet people, are determined to fight against the modern barbarians to the last drop of blood, for their fatherland, honour and liberty, for independence and the democratic liberties of the peoples of Europe.

Let us unite our fighting ranks still closer, friends, in our common struggle. Let us strengthen our crushing blow on the Nazi bands. With united forces we will smash the enemy and victory will be ours.

From Moscow Trade Unions to London Trades Council, 1941.

The decision of the British Trades Union Congress to re-establish the Anglo-Soviet Trade Union Committee will undoubtedly meet with the approval of the working class in the Soviet Union. This Committee will make possible a close businesslike contact between the trade unions and the working class of the U.S.S.R. and Great Britain for joint practical action in mobilising the forces to combat Hitlerism. The statements of the Trades Union Congress and the British trade union leaders that the British working class is determined to render the necessary aid and support to the Soviet people in its heroic struggle against Hitler Germany, evokes satisfaction among Soviet workers. I regard this aid as a reply to the very serious aid which the Soviet Union is rendering Britain by diverting to the East the main German forces and thus freeing England of invasion and of German air raids on London.

As soon as the T.U.C. proposal on the Anglo-Soviet Trade Union Committee is received here, the Central Council of the Soviet Trade Unions will discuss it without delay and, for its part, will do everything possible speedily to organise the Committee and to ensure its fruitful activity.

From the Secretary of the Central Council of the Trade Unions of the U.S.S.R., 1941.

1. Unity of the trade unions of Great Britain and the trade unions of the Soviet Union for the organisation of mutual assistance in the war against Hitlerite Germany.

2. Every assistance to the Governments of the U.S.S.R. and of Great Britain in their common war for the defeat of Hitlerite Germany.

3. Strengthening of the industrial efforts of both countries for the purpose of the utmost extension of the production of tanks, aeroplanes, guns, shells, and other munitions.

4. Assistance in rendering maximum help to the Soviet Union in armaments on the part of Great Britain.

5. Utilisation of all means of agitation and propaganda—press, radio, cinema, workers' meetings, etc.—for the struggle against Hitlerism.

6. Every assistance to the peoples of the countries occupied by Hitlerite Germany, fighting for liberation from the Hitlerite yoke, for their independence and the re-establishment of their democratic liberties.

7. Organisation of mutual assistance and mutual information between the trade unions of Great Britain and the Soviet trade unions.

8. Strengthening of personal contact between the representatives of the trade union movements of the U.S.S.R. and Great Britain through the All-Union Council of Trade Unions of the U.S.S.R. and the British Trades Union Congress.

Agreement between British and Soviet Trade Unions, 1941.

Dear Friends,—Thank you for your kind greeting, transmitted to us through the Soviet Embassy in London. Through you we students of Moscow University greet all the students of the freedom-loving British people.

We are glad of the cordial feelings and associations which have become established between the oldest Universities of Great Britain and the Soviet Union in these days when both our great countries are waging a joint fight against Fascist barbarity.

Our Universities have always been united by a common aspiration towards science and progress; towards the struggle against barbarity and darkness. These ties will grow still stronger in the common fight against Fascism. Many of us students have joined as volunteers in the Red Army and in the People's Volunteer Force. Our girl students are working in hospitals and Red Cross ambulance brigades.

We are firmly convinced of our victory, the victory of truth and justice, the victory of reason and science, civilisation and progress —a victory over the dark forces of Fascism. This certainty in victory makes us ten times stronger. The knowledge that all progressive Mankind is with us, that the great British people and you, dear friends, are on our side, fill our hearts with still greater courage and confidence in victory. Let us unite our efforts for the war on two fronts—for the speediest possible defeat of the enemy of all Mankind—Hitler and Hitlerism.

History has entrusted the peoples of Great Britain and the Soviet Union with the momentous mission of rescuing world civilisation, science, and culture. Let us then give our all to this noble aim and honourably perform our duty to future generations. Victory will be ours!

From the Students of Moscow University to
the Students of Cambridge University, 1941.

Dear Sisters—Women of Birmingham,—Your warm and heartfelt words of greeting addressed to us women of Kiev have deeply touched and stirred us. Accept our deepest thanks for the book you gave us, every line of which is for us a witness of the friendship and ardent sympathy of the women of Britain for us women of the Soviet Union.

In these grim days, when all progressive mankind has entered into a decisive combat against death-dealing Nazism, we have linked our destinies. Side by side with you we are participating in the sacred war against the barbarians who have brought evil and death to the world. With you we are fighting against a sanguinary Hitler who is converting our towns and villages into ruins, who is destroying the great civilisation created throughout the centuries by the genius of Man.

Hitler is our common enemy—our mortal foe. There where his hordes have passed, women are turned into slaves and deprived of all rights of motherhood, their human dignities are trampled underfoot. We will never forget the unspeakable atrocities perpetrated by the Nazis on the women of Poland, France, Greece, Yugoslavia, Belgium, and Norway. We will never forgive the fiends for their mockery of mothers, sisters, and wives in the Soviet regions temporarily seized by them. Blood and tears cry for vengeance. And vengeance will be implacable. The sword of punishment will descend on the head of the tyrant Hitler, who, in his frenzied delirium, imagines himself to be the ruler of the world, and destroys this world.

We women of the capital of the Ukraine, who bear the brunt of the infuriated blows of the Hitler hordes, are filled with the resolution to crush the foe. From the first days of the war Soviet women patriots took up work in industrial undertakings and in the fields, replacing the men who had gone to the front. Soviet women have also left for the fighting lines and the war hospitals to help the wounded.

From the bottom of our hearts we wish you women of Birmingham still greater success in your unselfish work, in your heroic fight. We shall be victorious.

From the Women of Kiev to the Women of Birmingham, 1941.

Your letter [1] has found a response in the heart of every Soviet woman. For the sake of victory over the evil genius of humanity —Fascism—you have sacrificed three sons. Maternal feelings are the same everywhere; we know what it means to lose three sons. This turns the bravest hearts to stone, but you have as defiant a heart as the hearts of the Soviet women whom you praise. You prefer to turn your enemies into stone.

Your sons are dead, but you are sending fighters into the skies which they conquered, so that other sons and their mothers will be able to live in a liberated world. One of the fighters will be called "MacRobert's Salute to Russia." You have understood that no enemy can ever break the spirit of our people. Soviet women receive with pride this war greeting from their British sister, in recognition of the friendship between our great peoples which will lead to victory over our common enemy, Hitlerism.

From the Women of Moscow.

[1] Reference is to Lady MacRobert's letter to Sir Archibald Sinclair announcing her gift, in memory of her three sons, of four fighter aeroplanes to Russia.

A pilot's mother greets him as a son,
An eagle leading eaglet comrades bold.
On them she proudly wishes to confer
A weapon forged of wrath,
A holy wrath aflame within her,
Blazing up anew at every screaming siren's wail
And fanned by mute and piercing sorrow
At the loss of her beloved airman sons.

.   .   .   .   .   .

You Englishmen and we,
A warrior race,
Are making common cause
And will avenge one hundredfold their men that they
    have lost.
Many have perished beating back the hordes of evil
At Murmansk and at the gates of Moscow.
War brooks no delay.
The time has come to force a fighting union,
A battling comradeship which must increase
On land, at sea, and in the skies above.
In Arctic waters Soviet warriors,
With English comrades fighting at their side,
Are hammering the hated Hitler hordes.
Relentlessly and ceaselessly they guard
The freedom and the honour of their race,
Of both our races,
And—their mothers.
    ALEXANDER ZHAROV: *A Tribute to Lady MacRobert.*

Mothers hate war more than anyone else, for war spells death for their children, but mothers want to see their children free and happy, not slaves; therefore, mothers everywhere wholeheartedly support the just war of liberation against Hitler. They see their sons take up arms and inspire them to struggle and sacrifice. More—they themselves actively participate in the great struggle for liberty of their country. British women are proud to take their part in the auxiliary forces, they work in munition plants and courageously bear the sacrifices caused by war. Soviet women, who have experienced the endless brutality of Hitler's hordes, are writing pages of heroism and self-sacrifice in the annals of war. They know that there is no time for tears when the fate of their country is at stake. Every Soviet woman in town and village, every working woman and peasant, actress and scientist, stands prepared to fight for her liberty and honour, to defend the independence of her native land to the last drop of blood, to give her all, her knowledge, her energy and, indeed, life itself, for the cause of her people and her country.

The women of Russia have always played an outstanding rôle in the struggle for the liberty of their people, and to-day they are surpassing all examples of bravery hitherto known. They have proved themselves worthy of the unparalleled heroism of the Soviet Union's armies. In many occupied areas Soviet women are fighting hand-in-hand with partisans against Hitler's thugs.

They voluntarily offer their blood to save the lives of wounded soldiers. They have displayed marvels of heroism at the front lines. They are rescuing the wounded under fire of terrible bombings, amid bursting shells and the hail of machine-gun bullets. In industry, Soviet women and girls have taken the place of men in the forces. Often with superhuman energy they are surpassing the men's output in their patriotic zeal to provide the Army with all it requires for defence. They have shown themselves capable of working day and night. On collective farms they have greatly helped to gather in the harvest and are now preparing for the autumn sowing so that neither front nor rear shall suffer from a shortage of food. We are proud of our Soviet women—they evoke the admiration of their own people and are an example to the women of the world.

I appeal to all the women of the world, regardless of their political convictions, religious beliefs or social position, to show their effective solidarity with the Soviet and British women.

DOLORES IBARRURI: Speech, 1941.

We received your sincere message and are most grateful to you. The women of Moscow are working unselfishly in industrial undertakings, field hospitals, at the front, and in culture and art. There is no force that can break the will of Soviet women to achieve victory. In these historic days we are particularly stirred and moved by your pledge. We wish you success in your just struggle. We firmly believe that the close alliance of democratic countries will destroy Fascism for all time.

From the Women of Moscow to the Women of London, 1941.

This meeting of housewives of Moscow sends you, housewives of London, its affectionate militant greetings. We women of Moscow are helping the front by practical deeds, giving all our strength and labour for the annihilation of German Fascism, that wicked enemy of Mankind, which has drenched all Europe in blood, which brings to the nations mediaeval barbarism, rape, death to children, old people and women, hunger and destruction.

We call upon you, women of London, to wage an active struggle against German Fascism, to mobilise your strength for this struggle for the liberation of humanity from Hitlerism, for its complete destruction. We are sure that by the combined strength of the freedom-loving nations German Fascism will be destroyed.

From Moscow Housewives to the Women of London, 1941.

The women of Moscow send militant greetings to their comrades in arms, the women of London. History has placed on our nations a gigantic and important task—to save the world from the enemy of humanity, Hitlerism. The peoples of the Soviet Union are fighting a great and just war of liberation.

In these ten months all Soviet women have proved real patriots, devoted to their motherland. They are fighting heroically at the front and in the rear, in production, in A.R.P., in laboratories and institutes. Everywhere our work is dominated by one thought, one desire—to destroy the Fascist barbarians.

Dear Sisters, our friendship was born in the fire of battle, under threatening danger. It grew strong in the days of the heroic defence of Moscow, and will grow stronger still from day to day, because it is based on our common struggle.

Working relentlessly, not sparing our lives, let us direct all our efforts towards achieving the complete defeat of the Nazi

armies in 1942, and make 1942 the year of victory of the freedom-loving nations of the world. Victory will be ours!
> From a Message to the Women of Britain by an Anti-Fascist Rally of Women held in Moscow, 1942.

The Soviet Society for Cultural Relations with Foreign Countries warmly greets the Committee organising the Anglo-Soviet Friendship Week. The fact that the activities of the Committee are finding such splendid support among the most eminent representatives of one of the oldest centres of culture in England, the city of Cambridge, will still further strengthen the friendship between the peoples of Great Britain and the Soviet Union who are waging a common fight against a hateful Hitlerism.

We send our best wishes for the success of the Anglo-Soviet Friendship Week. The stronger the unity between the peoples of our countries the sooner will the common enemy, Nazism, be vanquished.
> From U.S.S.R. Society for Cultural Relations with Foreign Countries, 1941.

France knows that in the East people are defending civilisation from Hitler. The Soviet people are defending all that is dear to France, the right to smile, the right to think, the right to dream. Our revolution has not renounced its predecessors. We knew Rousseau, Voltaire, Diderot, and Mably. We loved St. Just; we loved the people of Paris, their merry laughter, incomparable heroism. We loved French literature and French history.

We loved the writers of France, Romain Rolland, Malraux. We are defending intrinsic civilisation, labour, human dignity, thought. We are paying for our liberty with our blood.
> ILYA EHRENBURG, in *Soviet War News*, 1941.

No honest person can henceforth dispute the tragic truth that mankind is faced with the immediate menace of a world war. In a number of countries war is already being waged. It is drowning Spain and China in blood. It has already engulfed one-quarter of the population of the globe. Nobody can any longer deny the criminal rôle of Fascism in the preparation and launching of a new world war.

In those countries where Fascism is in power, it means the most terrible economic exploitation, the most awful political oppression of the people; it means a brutal and bloody dictatorship, prison, concentration camps, the gallows, the scaffold. Fascism in the international arena means a policy of adventures and intrigues, of provocation and treacherous acts of violence. *Fascism means war.*

It was seen in the aggression of Mussolini against the Ethiopian peoples. It is to be seen in the onslaught of the Fascists of Rome and Berlin against the Spanish people. It can be seen in the aggression of Japan against the Chinese people. It can be seen in the alliance of the Aggressors—Germany, Japan, and Italy.

MAURICE THOREZ, 1937.

Collaboration with Hitler means helping the enemy of the French people to fight the peoples of the Soviet Union. The people of Soviet Russia, in defending their country, their liberty, and their independence are at the same time fighting for the liberty and the independence of all nations oppressed by German Fascism or threatened by it.

The Soviet people are fighting for our cause—for the liberation of France. To help Hitler would be to commit a crime against France.

The overwhelming majority of the French people refuse to be a party to such a crime. . . .

Never before have ardent feelings of sympathy and affection for the peoples of the Soviet Union—for its heroic Red Army and bold leaders, for Stalin, whose historic speech of July 3 evoked a profound response among our people—been so deep-rooted among the wide masses of France as they are to-day. On the day following Stalin's speech the walls of St. Etienne, the large coal and industrial centre of France, were plastered with inscriptions greeting the Soviet Union and acclaiming the Red Army. . . .

Our task is to unite and co-ordinate all the efforts for the success of this war. All honest Frenchmen, regardless of party affiliations or political and religious convictions, must unite.

They must rally in the fight against the invaders and their agents. Everything must be subordinated to one will, one thought—to drive the enemy out of France.

      A Broadcast by MAURICE THOREZ, 1941.

The Jewish masses of Palestine have heard with enthusiasm the appeal of Soviet Jews to world Jewry to mobilise all forces against Fascism. We stand shoulder to shoulder with the British armed forces ready to repulse any Fascist attack. Mass meetings organised in towns and villages and co-operative farms by the "Hashomer Hatsair" and the Socialist League declared their firm solidarity with the Red Army's heroic fight. Jews of the Soviet Union! Your brothers in Palestine acclaim your heroic resistance to Fascism.

      THE SOCIALIST LEAGUE OF PALESTINE, 1941.

We are indignant at the crimes of the Fascist hordes and admire the firmness and gallantry of the peoples of the Soviet Union in their struggle against them. The firm determination of the Soviet people to defeat the Fascists is a death sentence on the Fascists.

      GENERAL HO YING-CH'IN, Chinese Minister of War.

June 22, 1941, the day on which the U.S.S.R. entered the war for the freedom of the peoples, will for ever be a most decisive day for humanity. With my whole heart I share the enthusiasm of all freedom-loving people for the successful and heroic resistance of the Russian Army and nation against the merciless aggressor.

I, an old man now, wish nothing more ardently than to live to the day when all bells will toll and the people will embrace each other with the words: "The monster has been annihilated, the world is freed, a new life has begun and new happiness."

      THOMAS MANN, in a Message to Moscow.

It would be difficult to find another example when human efforts reached such favourable results in such a short period of time as the period of the Russian Revolution. The majority of the

inhabitants of our country are filled with admiration at the struggle which the Russian people have been waging for the last two years.
    DAVID LLOYD GEORGE, in a Message to Moscow.

At this moment, when the fate of the whole world depends on the selfless efforts of the Soviet people and on the heroism of the Red Army, all Spanish patriots, irrespective of ideology, again confirm the gratitude which binds them to the U.S.S.R., and their firm faith in the victory of the Army which is fighting for the progress and freedom of the world.
    JUAN NEGRIN, in a Message to Moscow.

Any nation that will fight and die like the Russians are fighting and dying must have a sense of eternity in their souls. To die for nothing does not make sense. To die for an ideal—that is a religion.   CHARLES CHAPLIN, in his Tribute to Russia.

There is no doubt at all that the imagination of the mass of people in this country has been fired by the epic battle of the Eastern front and by the grim resistance which the Russian armies and the whole Russian people have opposed to the German onset—a great national uprising on a scale which Hitler had not yet encountered within the confines of the European Continent. Eagerness to see that no effort is spared to bring about the maximum of effective co-operation between Great Britain and Soviet Russia was abundantly shown at the Trades Union Congress in Edinburgh earlier this week. Resolutions unanimously passed pledged the Trade Union movement to all possible assistance to Russia and approved the proposal to constitute an Anglo-Russian Trade Union Council, thereby laying the foundation for more fruitful collaboration in the future—a collaboration which can be made possible only by sympathetic understanding on both sides of points of agreement and difference. Mr. Churchill will doubtless take the first opportunity to make it clear that the British Government admits no qualifications to its resolve to co-operate with Russia to the fullest extent both in frustrating Nazi Germany's assault on the liberties of the world and in the measures of reconstruction which will be required when victory is won. No suspicion of half-heartedness marks the sympathy of the British people for our great Eastern Ally.

It is for the Government to translate this sympathy into prompt and vigorous action. If there is still the slightest hesitation in any quarter (though it seems incredible) to realise that the war on which Russia is engaged is our war, then the doubts—or the doubters—must be removed. If there are divisions of departmental function which impede the rapid organisation of aid to Russia in all its aspects, these too must be swept aside. The speedy settlement of such questions of competence under present conditions usually demands the personal intervention of the Prime Minister. In an issue whose intrinsic importance is so vast, and in which public opinion is rightly impatient and anxious, Mr. Churchill is assuredly not the man to tolerate a moment's unnecessary delay. *The Times*, September 6, 1941.

In this momentous hour we are united with you in one common aim—to smash the Nazi barbarians. The Nazis destroy civilisation and bring in their wake oppression and unhappiness. They torture, abuse, and murder wounded Red Army men. German planes bomb and machine-gun hospital ships. The past has not known such atrocities.

These Nazi crimes show the need for the great work of restoring to health men wounded in the fight against Hitler's hordes. Our soldiers fight for the interests of all progressive mankind. The closer and more united is the front of the U.S.S.R. with Great Britain, U.S.A., and all other freedom-loving countries, the more real and practical will be our mutual assistance, the quicker will come our hour of victory over Hitlerism.

From Moscow to Medical Workers in London.

I beg you to convey to the Government of Great Britain the warm thanks of the Soviet Government for their friendly congratulations and good wishes to the Soviet Union on the day of its twenty-fourth anniversary. Our thoughts and feelings are expressed in all their force and fullness in the speech of the Head of the Soviet Government, I. V. Stalin, on November 6, which sets out the aim of the Soviet Government in its implacable struggle with the German invaders for the freedom and happiness of the peoples of our country and of all freedom-loving peoples. We swear to go forward on this glorious road until we fulfil this world task, and we believe unshakably in the victory of our just cause. M. MOLOTOV, to Anthony Eden.

The people of Great Britain, to whatever school of political thought they may adhere, will desire to-day to pay warm and unanimous tribute to the Russian nation and to all the peoples of the Soviet Union, whose great-hearted resistance in face of overwhelming material odds has sealed the Anglo-Soviet alliance and won the admiration of the world. Nor is this tribute limited to words. It finds concrete expression in the fixed determination that every assistance which it is in our power to render shall be afforded to our allies....

The present war has transformed the issue of Anglo-Soviet relations by placing it in the right perspective. It has shown how numerous and fundamental are the points of agreement, and how sharply the common ground of agreement is differentiated from Nazi or Fascist ideals and doctrine. Above all, Russia is united with the English-speaking world in the belief that an ordered and peaceful international life must ultimately be achieved not through the military domination of a superior race or nation but through the recognition of a common interest and a common loyalty capable of turning to the best use the diversity of peoples. These common aims must lay the firm foundation of a united effort, both now and after the war.

The Times (Editorial), November 8, 1941.

I am fully convinced of the fundamental truth that on the main issue of international policy there is no reason for a conflict of interests between the Soviet Union and Great Britain. I felt that proposition to be true in 1935. It has certainly proved to be true in fact in 1941, and it will be proved true in the future. We in this country want the closest co-operation with the U.S.S.R. now and after the war, when our energies will be turned again to the cause of peace....

On July 12 we and the Soviet Government concluded an agreement for joint action in this war against Germany and we consecrated our alliance in a formal manner. Since then other events have taken place which have further strengthened our unity. The courage and endurance of the Russian soldier is traditional, and his qualities have never been more gallantly expressed than in the last five cruel months of Russia's ordeal.

Maybe Hitler thought—I said "maybe," because neither you, Mr. Ambassador, nor I are responsible for those thoughts—when he attacked Russia that the vast organisation which is the Soviet Union would collapse before his Panzer divisions. If so, he has been proved by the valour of Russia's sons to be completely mistaken. All the peoples of the Soviet Union can say with pride to-day that their national unity is complete.

Or it may be Hitler thought that by his unprovoked aggression on Russia he could divide public opinion here and in the occupied countries of our Allies and in the U.S.A., raising once again the spectre of the Bolshevik bogy. If so, then here again Hitler has been completely wrong. In this struggle there is only one cause, and in such conditions mutual help is self-help. Our resources are Russia's resources, and Russia's resources are our resources....

The consciousness of the people of Russia and of the people of the British Empire—they all are contributing to the same end, both are making sacrifices in a common cause—that is the best soil in which can grow those seeds of mutual understanding.

I can think of a number of spheres in which the interests of the Soviet Union and those of the British Commonwealth are complementary to one another. I can think of none where they need be rivals.

> ANTHONY EDEN, the Foreign Secretary, in a Speech to the Anglo-Soviet Public Relations Committee, November 21, 1941.

If backward, ignorant, serf-ridden Russia of the past centuries was able to crush the most powerful and civilised States of that time when they tried to destroy her independence, so much more confident are we that to-day we shall be able to annihilate Hitlerite Germany. For to-day the Soviet people are an enlightened people, and they are full of the highest spirit, generated not only by a primordial feeling of patriotism but also by the great enthusiasm for their political and social ideals.

In their resolve to go on until final victory is won, they are further reinforced by the thought that they are fighting not only for themselves, not only for their own fatherland, but also for the freedom and independence of all nations. . . .

The present war, regrettable as it is, must lead at least to a stable and just peace based on the principle of self-determination of nations and social security, a peace which guarantees to every country independence and liberty in arranging its internal affairs.

This implies the tremendous importance of the post-war organisation of peace. Perhaps the time has not yet arrived to discuss this very complicated problem in detail or to envisage the exact shape of things after the war. But one thing is clear already. Your country and my country, in friendly co-operation with the U.S.A., will be called upon to play a very great rôle not only in the fighting and eventual crushing of Nazi Germany, but also in the post-war reconstruction of Europe and of the world.

From this angle I warmly welcome Mr. Eden's announcement that the British Government would like to base its post-war policy on the principle of the closest possible collaboration with the U.S.S.R. I fully reciprocate this desire. My Government would like also to base its post-war policy on the closest possible collaboration with Great Britain. It would be futile to gainsay that there are still certain difficulties in the way of this being accomplished, but with good-will on both sides they can and should be overcome.

> M. MAISKY, the Soviet Ambassador, in a Speech to the Anglo-Soviet Public Relations Committee, November 21, 1941.

In leaving the Soviet Union after having spent eighteen months in your wonderful country, I would like to express my recognition of the generous attitude and friendship to myself which I have met with in your midst.

Having lived with you in the heart of the struggle, having witnessed the suffering endured with the patient conviction which has its roots in the righteousness of your cause, I have been the honoured spectator of the undying courage of your Red Army and Air Force, which, through long and anxious months, have slowly worn down the hitherto unbeaten armies of Germany and her allies. I have also been filled with admiration for the gallant exploits of your Red Navy in the face of numerically superior forces.

Against Hitler's "new order" of brutality you have pitted your age-old loyalty to your country, inspired by love of your homeland and of its great cultural heritage, by the achievements of your new system of planned economy, with its triumphs on farms, in factories, and in mines of your far-flung Republics—in a word, by the past and by the present.

The whole civilised world proclaims your victories, and we, your Allies, are proud to count ourselves as such. But the end is not yet. The power of the Nazis is shaken but not broken.

The alliance between our two great countries must be made firmer and stronger yet, so that together we may accomplish the task so well begun. Each one of us must be spurred on to still greater efforts. We must grasp with sure and strong hands the opportunity won for us by the valour of your armed forces and by the long and bitter vigil of Britain's Navy and Air Force which for two long years have fought to keep open the ocean highways—those highways by which help is now being brought to you from ourselves and our American allies.

Every man and woman in our countries must strain every nerve, on whatever work, however great the demand. Let us shorten the world's agony by the intensity of our effort.

When victory comes, of which we are so confident, our two nations will have the privilege of leading the peoples of Europe towards a civilisation of sanity and co-operation.

SIR STAFFORD CRIPPS, British Ambassador:
A Message to the Soviet People, January 20, 1942.

We are filled to-day with enthusiasm and gratitude for the magnificent exploits of the Soviet forces on the Russian battlefield, and equally admire the fine part that is being played by the young men and women, not only on the battle front, but on the industrial front, and on the farms and in the mines. Youth in Russia to-day has a burning zeal for its country and its institutions. It feels that it really is its country. It is that sense of their direct and vital interest in their own country that lies behind the enthusiasm of the Soviet Union. Whatever may be their difficulties and sufferings, they feel they are on the right road to a better future.

The great qualities that have been born in the young people of Soviet Russia have come to the rescue of the whole world. Past trials have steeled the youth of Russia, and from them have emerged a brave and resourceful people, and a confident and courageous youth, which is going to play not only a great part in the victory over Nazidom, but also in the construction of a new world civilisation after the victory.

In our own country we want just as courageous and resourceful a youth. Our goal may be the same as that of the Soviet youth, but the path by which we should reach it must be defined by our own environment and not by that of Russia or any other country.

    Sir Stafford Cripps, addressing a meeting of
      the Anglo-Soviet Youth Friendship Alliance,
    March 1942.

Russia has been reborn and regenerated through Lenin's leadership. He laid the foundation of an edifice whose solid strength, firmly based on a united and unshakable national spirit, has withstood the utmost fury of a rampant and hitherto victorious Hitlerism. And, more significant still, behind much in Lenin's teaching and career which was hostile both to the immediate interests and to the fundamental traditions of this country there lay a perception of the nature of the crisis upon which modern industrial civilisation was entering. . . . It was Lenin who first brought home to the consciousness of the Western world the truth that a civilisation based on the antagonism of capital and labour inevitably carried within it the seeds of its own destruction. He and his fellow-workers sought to solve the problem in revolution; others pursue their social ends by means that will maintain unimpaired the moral and material heritage of the past. In these ends there need be no incompatibility, and it is for the future to develop a way of collaboration that is not only desirable but imperative if the foundations of peace are to be made secure.

    The Times, on the occasion of the Unveiling of the
      Lenin Memorial Plaque at 30 Holford Square,
    London, 1942.

We are met in a world at war, when our two countries are

together at grips with the common enemy. Under the impact of war we have found that understanding which escaped us in the uneasy years of peace. The Treaty which we have just signed engages us to continue the struggle together until the victory be won. On behalf of my colleagues I give you the pledge that there will be no wavering in this endeavour on the part of the Government or people of these islands.

Such, then, is the first chapter of our task, the overthrow of Hitler and the destruction of all that his régime stands for. But there is a second chapter also to our Treaty. One day the war will end. One day the common enemy will be defeated and there will be peace again. We must see to it that this time peace endures. In the Treaty which we have signed we pledged ourselves to work together for this purpose.

Never before in the history of our two countries has our association been so close, or our mutual pledge for the future so complete. This is surely a happy augury. There is nothing exclusive in our agreement. We are seeking peace and security not only for our two countries, but for all the United Nations. But understanding between us is one of the foundations of peace, not for us alone, but for the world. We have signed our Treaty, and part of the work is behind us.

        ANTHONY EDEN, on the Treaty of Alliance between Britain and the Union of Soviet Socialist Republics, May 26, 1942.

The historical Treaty of Alliance between the U.S.S.R. and Great Britain, the ever-extending and strengthening collaboration of the Allied Powers with the United States of America, will provide a powerful stimulus for organising all the forces of the participants in the anti-Hitlerite coalition to intensify the heroic struggle which is being waged by the people of Europe enslaved by the Nazi invaders.

The news of the conclusion of the Treaty will be welcomed with great satisfaction by the peoples of the Soviet Union, who see in it one more living confirmation of Comrade Stalin's words that "the international connections of our motherland have recently grown and gained strength as never before."

        Pravda, on the Treaty of Alliance, quoted in *Soviet War News*.

There can be no doubt that an agreement of this kind will be of great significance to the entire future development of Europe. Both countries agree to work together after the re-establishment of peace "for the organisation of security and economic prosperity in Europe." The Treaty states that both countries "will take into account the interests of the United Nations in these objects, and they will act in accordance with the two principles of not seeking territorial aggrandisement for themselves and of non-interference in the internal affairs of other States."

These principles of the Treaty fully accord with the well-known pronouncement made by the head of the Government of the U.S.S.R., Stalin, on November 6 last year, when he said: "We have not, and cannot have, any such war aims as the seizure of foreign territories and the subjugation of foreign peoples, whether it be peoples and territories of Europe or peoples and territories of Asia, including Iran."

M. MOLOTOV, at the Session of the Supreme Council of the U.S.S.R., June 18, 1942.

As the Soviet Union enters the second year of the war I, as Prime Minister of Great Britain, which in a few months' time will enter on its fourth year of war, send to you, the leader of the great allied Soviet peoples, a renewed expression of our admiration for the magnificent defence of your armed forces, guerrilla bands, and civilian workers during the past year, and of our firm conviction that those achievements will be equalled and surpassed in the coming months. The fighting alliance of our two countries and of our other Allies, to whom there have now been joined the vast resources of the United States, will surely bring our enemies to their knees. You can count on us to assist you by every means in our power.

During the year which has passed since Hitler fell upon your country without warning, friendly relations between our two countries and peoples have been progressively strengthened. We have thought not only of the present, but of the future, and our Treaty of Alliance in the war against Hitlerite Germany and of collaboration and mutual assistance in the post-war period, concluded during M. Molotov's recent visit to this country, has been welcomed as sincerely by the British people as I know it has been welcomed by the Soviet people. That Treaty is a

pledge that we shall confound our enemies and, when the war is over, build a sure peace for all freedom-loving peoples.
> WINSTON CHURCHILL, to Stalin, June 1942.

The news of the conclusion and ratification of the Treaty of Alliance between the U.S.S.R. and Great Britain found me, together with a group of fellow scientists, in Kirghizia, Central Asia, where we had gone to do urgent work in connection with the mobilising of the resources of the Soviet East for defence.

In the name of all the scientists of our country, I am happy to convey hearty congratulations to you personally, and through you to all the scientists of friendly Great Britain. We are all convinced that this Treaty will be the greatest historical landmark on the road to further rapprochement between the two great democratic States.

Allow me to express my deep conviction that the Treaty will facilitate still further the strengthening of the friendship between the scientists of our countries, united for the struggle against Hitlerite Germany.

There is no doubt that the scientists of all peace-loving countries, and above all of Britain, the U.S.A., and the U.S.S.R., will give all their strength and knowledge for the speediest victory over our common enemy, which is the first condition of the further advance of science in the name of humanity's progress and happiness.
> PROFESSOR KOMAROV (President of the Soviet Academy of Sciences), to Sir Henry Dale (President of the Royal Society).

It is never easy for two peoples to arrive at a real understanding of one another. In the case of our Soviet Allies we have tended more to admiration than understanding. Many who now speak with the utmost enthusiasm of our Russian Allies have little, if any, understanding of their social, political, or economic life. Friendship that is based only upon admiration and lacks understanding is apt to be fragile and easily broken. We must therefore do our utmost to increase the understanding of the Soviet Union and its people among all classes of our society, and we must try our best to give the Soviet people a true picture of our country and our people. Real friendship between peoples depends as much on understanding each other's weaknesses as on appreciating each other's virtues. There is much the Russian and British people can learn from each other besides the art of war—if we are not afraid to learn—and there is much we can both contribute to a new philosophy and to new practices in the international life of the post-war world.

Sir Stafford Cripps, at an Anglo-Soviet
Demonstration, June 20, 1942.

Russia and the United States have now been drawn together, through and with Great Britain, in the affirmation of a joint purpose to create an expanding world trade on the basis of rising standards of living. There is nothing in such a purpose which contradicts the theory or the practice of the Soviet Union. The whole of Soviet domestic policy proceeds from the assumption of an expanding economy, and is geared to the conception of progressively rising levels of consumption and production. There is no doubt of the positive contribution which Soviet Russia can make to the realisation of the wider conception of progressively expanding welfare all the world over.

The qualities so outstandingly displayed in Russia during the ordeal of the past year by the Government and the High Command, by the armies in the field, and by the whole people—qualities of endurance, of adaptability, of ingenuity in innovation, of resolve to subordinate every accepted convention, every lesson, right, or interest to the single purpose in hand—have made a profound impression all over the world, and nowhere more than in Great Britain. But this impression is not limited to military achievements. It will not be effaced when the common victory is achieved, and will play its part in the building up of those common ideals which are as necessary as common interests if collaboration for peace is to be as confident and as effective as for war. *The Times*, June 22, 1942.

Amid all the anxieties and horrors of the time, on this twenty-fifth anniversary of the Russian Revolution, I feel above all a sense of gratitude to those men and women who, first in history, proved that the working class could take power, keep it, and with it build for themselves a new world.

For it was they who laid the foundations of that Soviet Union whose strength twenty-five years later was to save this country from the savageries of this most foul of wars, and which will ultimately save the world from Fascism and a Second Middle Ages. Because of what they did a generation ago I can still write and you still read.

From a country weak from years of war, isolated amidst hostile nations, with a bankrupt economy and a starving people, those men and women built a force which now stands against the might of Europe press-ganged for Fascist war. The sneers, the doubts, the suspicions, and the lies are swept away by the triumphs of this Soviet Power.

In this twenty-five years a new life blossomed out for scores of millions of people. Memories crowd on us this anniversary. The great Five-Year Plans, the flight to the Pole, Dnieprostroi, the grand education schemes, the Stalin Constitution. We recall the growth of the collective farms, a hundred million peasants meeting and mastering science, the Stakhanov movement. Countries of the old Tsarist Empire held in Asiatic bondage, oppressed, ignorant, and poor, saw a new world before them.

We remember the rôle of the Soviet Union in the sorry years of the last decade. Their attempt to build a sound system of collective security, Litvinov at the League, the help to Spain and China. Over all, we remember those men and women who, with little but their own faith and determination, were to give the free world its greatest bulwark against domination.

That new way of living is now in danger, and with it our old civilisation and our democracy. The farms, the great industrial plants, those new schools, are all threatened. Much has been lost. In occupied territory what has not been smashed in battle has been burnt by the people themselves. For these people fight as none have fought before. There is no secret in their fighting. They defend what is theirs. Twenty-five years ago they came into their own. To-day they fight to hold it. They blew up the Dnieper Dam. It was theirs. They destroyed the crops, burnt the farms, flooded the mines. All this was theirs. Now they fight not only for their factories and their homes, but for their way of life itself. They will win.

We in the British Labour movement, in sending greetings to our Soviet comrades on this anniversary, are determined that the time has gone when we shall merely applaud their heroism and salute their sacrifices. Twenty-five years ago they fought alone. Now they fight again—almost alone. They fight for us. For history in these twenty-five years has linked their destinies with ours and from now on we must fight—together.

JOHN HORNER, General Secretary of the Fire
Brigades Union, in *Labour Monthly*, 1942.

The people of Britain salute their Allies of the Soviet Union on this twenty-fifth birthday of their new State. . . . Your vast lands have been cultivated for the well-being of your people. Factories have been set up in the rear and far places of the Union. Great schemes of public works have enriched your country. Your peasant people have come to rank among the world's finest industrial workers. The Stakhanovite movement with its far-reaching influence on labour productivity sets an unrivalled example.

Into the last twenty-five years you have packed the development of a century: only the self-denial and the unceasing labours of your people made this possible.

We are proud to be your Allies. You have set the world new standards of heroism. In your country the front does not stretch only from the Arctic to the Caucasus; it reaches into every home and factory, farm and workshop. This is not only a military struggle: it is a war between peoples in which every sphere of activity is involved. The complete integration of your industry and agriculture with your military achievements is defeating the enemy. . . .

But, on this anniversary, we do not only hail an Ally powerful in war. We pay homage to your achievements in the field of culture and in the arts of peace. We honour your great progress in the education of your people. No shortage of buildings or books or teachers daunted your plans for making your 180 million people literate.

You have not only given them literacy; you have taught them that—in the words of Lenin—"the basic qualities of Soviet men should be valour and daring." This has inspired their activity in all fields of labour.

Our scientists have repeatedly acknowledged their debt to the great scientists of your country—to Kapitsa and Bogomolets, to

Michurin and Lysenko; Britain has conferred her highest scientific honour on Vavilov by making him a Fellow of the Royal Society. We have been thrilled by the exploits of your explorers, Schmidt, Papanin and Feodorov.

In developing the rich culture of your many nationalities, in giving opportunity to the creative genius of all your people, you have made an unrivalled contribution to the culture of the world.

The last twenty-five years have been for you a story of difficulties overcome, of hunger satisfied, of latent strength developed, of social progress achieved.

Now, in complete unity behind your great leader Stalin, there is no hesitation in your minds or hearts. Your example steels us all in our united determination to crush our common enemies. . . .

In the furnace of war is being welded an alliance between our peoples which is gaining constantly in strength and unity, which, long after the rattle of the machine guns and the scream of shells has died away, will continue its mighty contribution to the well-being and progress of mankind.

> From an Article in *British Ally*, issued in Kuibyshev
> by the British Ministry of Information.

On the occasion of the twenty-fifth anniversary of the foundation of the Soviet State, I send Your Excellency the congratulations of the Government and people of the United States. For the second time in a generation, our two countries stand side by side in the front ranks of the united peoples aligned against a common enemy. Collaboration in the fulfilment of the mighty task which confronts us must be a prelude to collaboration in the fulfilment of the mightier task of the creation of peace throughout the world.

The resistance of the free peoples has made possible the growth of the might of the United Nations. The Russian people and the Russian Army in their continuing struggle against the Nazi invaders are carrying the main burden of the concentrated forces of the Nazi onslaught, and the incomparable heroism of the Russian Army and people serves as a symbol of their determination and indomitable will.

> PRESIDENT FRANKLIN D. ROOSEVELT, in a Message
> to Moscow.

On the occasion of the twenty-fifth anniversary of the October Revolution I feel great satisfaction in sending to Your Excellency, and through you to the peoples of the U.S.S.R., my warmest greetings. China greets her valiant Soviet Ally, whose valour and determination in resistance to the invaders has secured for it eternal glory in history.

I am certain that the spirit which, a quarter of a century ago, gave birth to the revolution which inaugurated a new epoch will absolutely contribute to the accomplishment of our victory and lay the foundation of lasting international peace.

PRESIDENT LIN SEN, in a Message to Moscow.

Chapter Ten

THE NEW HORIZON

WE Russians, a people without traditions, and on that account bolder, more rebellious, and less bound by the prejudices of the past, have been the first to tread the path that leads to the destruction of the outworn conditions of capitalist society, and we are convinced that we have a claim on the help and sympathy of the proletariat of the entire world, and also of those who, even before the war, criticised sharply the present conditions of society. . . .

The New Russia proclaims to the workers and honourable men of the world: Follow us to a new life, for the creation of which we are working without sparing ourselves or anything or anyone else. For this we are toiling, erring, and suffering with an eager hope for success, leaving our acts to the just decision of history. Follow us in our struggle against the old order, in our work for a new form of life, for the freedom and beauty of life.
GORKY: *Follow Us!*

The Russians in no way despise life. The cult of death has not, and never had, any disciples in our country. From the ancient Russia of Kiev, from the life reflected in the icons of Roublev, to Pushkin and Tolstoy, and to our own times, Russian culture has always been impregnated with the triumph of life.

The Revolution meant not only a cruel struggle and a stern education. It meant, too, the earth's globe set in the hands of the nomad of yesterday, the student of to-day. It meant, too, the peasant recuperating in the sanatoria of the Crimea, parks of culture, libraries, stadiums—youth, vigour, laughter.

The people of our epoch are profoundly attached to life. If they march to death without fear, it is because they desire a life worth defending. One can love life with such fervour and passion as to sacrifice one's own life for its triumph.
ILYA EHRENBURG.

Russia—Thou? . . . I laugh, but, dying,
I glimpse a lucid gaze.
Thou art incredible, and yet
I love thy strangest ways.

Like scarlet poppies flashing bright
Before my eyes they gleam,
Like butterflies and flashing signs
They haunt my closing dream.

Receive my dumbly faltering hands
Weighed down with all thy gloom.
My reason wings its flight to thee
Amid thy martyrdom.

Oh, fill the chalice of thy days
With fate—Thyself—and drain
The chalice, and fill up thy soul
With lightning's purple rain.

I am in bliss and, as I die,
I glimpse thy gaze above.
And I know all . . . and I know naught. . . .
I love, I love, I love.

ANDREI BIELY: *Russia*.
(Trans. by Gerard Shelley.)

We are not alone, we are the flowing current. . . .
In the whirl of fiery suns,
Like a constellation, joyful and ardent,
In the mist of dead days we burn.

We are free as the wind in the field,
In bondage we will never be;
Aflame are the wires of steel
With the fire of our great will.

We bring light and revelation
To the world from the depth of the ages. . . .
We are the joyful hymn of redemption
In honour of depraved slaves.

> We have destroyed the prison vaults
> That we may see the glittering fields:
> All the peoples are united with us,
> The family of workmen throughout the world.
> ARSKY: The Collective Will.

To transform the school from an implement of the class domination of the bourgeoisie into a weapon for the complete annihilation of the division of society into classes. We make it an implement of the Communist regeneration of society ... the school should not only be the agent for applying the principles of Communism generally, but equally the agent of ideological and organisational education, influencing the proletarian, semi-proletarian, and non-proletarian strata of the toiling population. Its goal is to educate a generation which will be able completely to establish Communism.   *Communist Party Programme.*

To put this question (whether the procedure applied by the Communist in Russia may not be imitated) apart from the historically concrete situation, means not to understand the A B C of dialectical materialism. In various moments of economic evolution, in dependence on various conditions, political, national, cultural, social, etc.—various forms of struggle are brought to the forefront, because the chief forms of struggle and in relation with this, in turn are changed to the secondary, auxiliary forms of struggle. To attempt to answer "yes" or "no" to the question of a definite means of struggle, without examining in detail the concrete situation of a given moment at a given stage of its development, means to depart altogether from the Marxian ground.   LENIN: *Collected Works.*

Uneven economic and political development is an absolute law of capitalism. Hence, the victory of Socialism is possible first in several or even in one capitalist country, taken singly. The victorious proletariat of that country, having expropriated the capitalists and organised its own Socialist production, would stand up against the rest of the world, the capitalist world, attracting to its cause the oppressed classes of other countries. ...

I think that the deeds done by the Red Army, its struggle and history, will be of tremendously great importance for all the peoples of the East. It will show the peoples of the East that, however weak these people may be, however invincible may appear to be the power of the European oppressors who employ all the miracles of technique and the military art in the struggle, none the less if the revolutionary war being waged by the oppressed peoples succeeds in really arousing the millions of working people and exploited, it contains within itself such possibilities, such miracles, that the liberation of the peoples of the East is now a fully practical proposition.

LENIN: *Collected Works.*

We see that the first country to achieve this separation (from the imperialist system of States), the first victorious revolutionary country, has already won the support of the workers, of the labouring masses in general, in other lands. Without this support that country could not have held its own. Undoubtedly this support will grow and strengthen as time goes on. Further, the very development of the world revolution, the very process of separating a number of additional countries from the imperialist States, will be all the quicker and more thorough-going in proportion as Socialism shall have struck root in the first victorious country, in proportion as that country shall have transformed itself into the base whence the development of the world revolution can proceed, in proportion as that country shall have become the crowbar in getting a solid pry and setting the whole structure of imperialism rocking. STALIN: *Leninism.*

The New Soviet Constitution is, indeed, the Charter of Socialist civilisation. It is the sign of the intelligent progress of humanity through the power of the working class. It embodies the quintessence of the thoughts of our class in respect to the organisation of self-government. It marks the beginning of the New Order not merely in Europe but throughout the world. It is the legislative forerunner of the Constitution of the World Federation of Socialist Republics—the mighty Union of the peoples of the world—in which the men and women of all lands will be joined together, exchanging the products of their soil and manufactures, their ideas on work and play, and making known, one to another, their strivings and plans for a healthier, happier, and more cultured life. GEORGE HICKS, M.P., 1936.

WORKING MEN AND WOMEN OF ALL COUNTRIES:

The world possesses an unyielding support of the international struggle for our own, workers' cause. A powerful fortress exists at the fighting front of the whole of progressive mankind for liberty, peace, and Socialism. The millions of working people throughout the globe, in an indissoluble alliance with the peoples of the powerful Socialist State, constitute an invincible force. The achievement of this alliance imperatively demands the unification of the ranks of the international proletariat. Your unity is the most important condition for the victory of the working people, not only over Fascism but also over capitalism. Let your will to unity be stronger than all obstacles!
From a Manifesto by the Executive Committee of the Communist International, 1937.

> For the sake of the common fate of our brothers,
> You, the proletarians of all the world,
> With one strong will, one mighty effort,
> Rally to your great camp!
> Rush to the rescue of communards,
> Break serfdom's fetters,
> Let the tumultuous tide scatter
> At one sweep the old world. . . .   IONOV.

"You and I were born but yesterday. And even though our minds were ready to recognise the future, for which both of us are working, our feelings are still tainted with the colours of the present day. . . . After all, we are human beings," Riabiev pronounced excitedly, "and we cannot, of course, entirely resist that human part of us which completes us. And what completes you and me is the human part, the part we inherit from yesterday, but that human to-morrow, which we see with our mind, and which . . . Yes, and that is an advantage already that we see it with our mind, that it already has a place in our consciousness and has become our goal. That is already something."

"What then?" Tarpova said. "What are we to do, then? Sit with our arms folded and wait?"

No. In Riabiev's opinion there was no point in sitting with arms folded and waiting, and the Party was, of course, carrying out its own work. This was the work of cultural enlightenment; this was the struggle for that very thing which is called the "new life," "new culture," "new morality," "new man"; this was a struggle involving a whole sphere of questions which were linked to the conception of the "new man."

"We're not idle," said Riabiev, "we are, for example, liquidating illiteracy, we're building new dwelling-houses for workers, and we already have a Proletarian art. We are constructing workers' clubs and palaces of culture, we are building communal kitchens, we have emancipated women, and we have food now ... and many other things."

"Yes, many things," Tarpova gloomily assented.

"Listen," said Riabiev after a pause. "Listen, I haven't given all this much thought. But I do know one thing: there will be a new type of man, because there will be Socialism. And what if—on the way towards this new man—we are still faced with unsolved problems to-day? We shall resolve them, these unresolved problems, to-morrow; and to-morrow other insoluble problems will take their place, but we shall resolve them the day after; and so on, until the new man will step forth into a new world. ..."

S. SEMYONOV: *Natalia Tarpova.*

We have very little time, comrades, so I shall only be able to say the most important things. Andrei Trofimovich is going away again; he is off to Dnieprostroy, to other places where construction is being started, because, comrades, he hasn't come to the end of his run yet and his train goes on and on ahead. That run started nine years ago, in 1920, when Cherevko rushed his train full of Red troops to the front. He didn't know a single station on the way, he didn't even know when he'd return home. He only knew and believed that the road he'd taken was the right one and would lead him to Socialism. So for weeks and months on end he overtook the years in a broken engine, and what Comrade Cherevko and the Red Army men did at the front in those weeks was more than could have been done in years.

Why? Because they put time in harness and bridled it, comrades ... all those workmen from the workshops, the engines, and the mines ... and forced it to serve the Revolution. They got the better of time, comrades. They're masters of time.

Now their train is going farther. It's coming from the All-Union Congress of Soviets, comrades, where the Five-Year Plan for Socialist Reconstruction was set up—the Plan for the sake of which, ten years ago, our workers and peasants, the masters of the great October Revolution, fought and died.

IVAN KORCHERGA: The Secretary of the Party
in Masters of Time.

We are all masters of time. And because time is only what we ourselves put into it, and if we put into it all our enthusiasm and all our will to conquer, it will do for us what thousands of years and thousands of clever folk like this German cannot do for us. And when all the brief evanescent pleasures of those who live only for themselves have died, we shall still go on living for ever in the toil and happiness of regenerated humanity.

IVAN KORCHERGA: Lida in Masters of Time.

Dawn.
The train was traversing the Urals.
Through the windows the "Europe-Asia" obelisk can be seen
    flying past in a whirl from left to right.
A meaningless post. . . .
I demand its removal.
We shall never again be Asia.
Never, never, never!
In the puddles among the hills blow yellow flowers, downy as
    ducklings.
A tiny moon fades like a compact bud of lily of the valley in a
    green sky.
Klava hides her wet face in a moist bunch of lily of the valley. She
    peers out of the window through the bunch of the lily of
    the valley.
Branches of lily of the valley, out of all proportion, flash by like
    telegraph poles.
Children are selling lily of the valley at the stations. There is the
    fragrance of lilac everywhere.

Dawn is brimmed with an icy dew.
A harsh, glassy gurgle ripples in the clay throat of night.
Nightingales purl and purl through the night till dawn.
They are not afraid of the train.
A highway of lilies of the valley and nightingales.

Ufa, Saratov.
Clouds, elevators, fences, Mordavian sarafans, water-pumps, caterpillars, echelons, churches, minarets, collective farms, village soviets.

And on all sides, from right to left and from left to right, from West to East and from East to West, stride poles in diagonal, unfolding array, poles bearing high-tension currents.
Six-armed, six-legged, they stride like monsters, like Martians, casting barred shadows over forests and hills, over thickets and rivers, over the thatched roofs of villages. . . .
We shall never again be Asia.
Never, never, never.

VALENTIN KATAEV: *Speed Up, Time!*

Dawn was breaking grey and cold. Our lorries were waiting for us in the courtyard of the aviation school. We were leaving Zaporozhye.

Tracer bullets, gleaming green and red in the sky, indicated the movement of an enemy plane over the city. Then from the direction of the great Dnieper Dam we heard the booming of anti-aircraft guns.

Across the Dnieper river the steppes were made barren by the flames of war, steppes where but recently tall golden wheat swayed gently in the breeze.

Suddenly the morning stillness was broken by a terrific roar. We looked at each other in dismay. We knew what it meant, and none of us was ashamed of his tears at that moment. In that early hour the Dnieper Dam, the great creation of our epoch, was blown up.[1]

[1] Built under the first Five-Year Plan, and put into operation in May 1932. The hydro-electric station, the largest in Europe, had a capacity of 540,000 kilowatts, and served the aluminium, iron, and steel industries in the Dnieper region.

Memories flashed through our minds. We recalled the years when it was under construction. Our youth. The first blueprints on which, after years of hunger, bloodshed and war, our people began to create this, their beloved child. The joy of those years filled with hope. . . .

For about ten minutes we remained staring in the direction where the turbulent waters of the Dnieper were already rushing through the breach. Then one of our group broke the silence:

"Never mind, comrades," he said. "We will build a new one. We will build it better and faster. Our people have had experience now. The main thing is confidence. With that in our hearts we can build anything . . . new and even more gigantic dams."

In silence we walked to the waiting lorries and drove away.

V. LIDIN, in *Soviet War News*, 1942.

Those who hate the future of mankind also hate its past. It has sometimes been asserted that Fascism has "resurrected" the Middle Ages. This is an insult to our forefathers. There was much that the men of the Middle Ages did not know, but they desired knowledge. Epic poems and Gothic cathedrals are an encyclopaedic chronicle of this epoch, expressing their thirst for knowledge. But Fascism is the renunciation of knowledge. . . . We love the future. We thrive on it. That is why we do not renounce the past. . . . A great thing must have continuity. We shall not understand the grandeur of the past by renouncing creative endeavour and progress. . . .

Progress is a relay race. It is no easy race. History has known the invasion of vandals, the auto-da-fé of the Inquisition, the dull fanaticism of ephemeral rulers. But every new generation has received the torch from the bleeding hands of men of thought and light.

To-day this torch is firmly grasped in our hands.

ILYA EHRENBURG, in *Soviet War News*, 1942.

I shall ascend a mountain, turn my face to the East—fire, turn to the West—fire, look to the North—conflagration, and to the South—conflagration, fall to the Earth—it burns.

Where and what meeting, who will shape this blazing, unrestrainable fire—we-shall-burn-to-ash!

There, on the ancient stones, on the dear graves of Europe, a fiery heart will meet lucid wisdom.

And over Russia, spacious and parched, over the fire-wasted steppe and the menacing forest, will light lucid and faithful stars.

ALEXEI REMIZOV: *Fiery Russia.*

Flame, flame, elemental, fiery,
In pillars of thundering fire:
O Russia, my Russia, O Russia,
Rage madly, rage and consume me.

In the crash of your fateful ruins,
In your depths of deepest abyss,
Winged spirits with fluttering hands
Flash visions as piercing as light.

O weep not; but fall on your knees,
Then plunge into hurricane fires,
Into thunders of seraph songs,
Into torrents of cosmic days.

With beams of ineffable eyes,
The Christ that appears will illume
The vast arid deserts of shame
And seas of unquenchable tears.

. . . . .

Elemental, in roars of thunder,
Rage madly, rage and consume me,
O Russia, my Russia, O Russia,
Messiah of days that will dawn.

ANDREI BIELY.

The Soviet Union is the first country in history to apply the principles of Socialism to the economic and political structure of a State. One may like or dislike the principles, but nobody could dispute that in doing so the people of my country have clearly shown an audacity of mind and boldness of action unparalleled in human history. I would not try to speculate on how far the example and experience of the Soviet Union would influence the rest of the world in the coming generations, but I would emphasise only one thing. The State which they have built has been tested by the most severe and exacting tests that a State can undergo—the test of total war—and it has not been found wanting.

> M. Maisky, at the Opening Ceremony for a Short Course for Teachers on the Soviet Union, 1942.

The present stage of world history has confronted social science with problems which had not and could not have arisen during the lifetime of the founders of Marxism. Therefore, the correct answers to the questions raised by our epoch must be found by the creative application of the historic-materialistic method of research, the method tested by life.

There are periods in the life of peoples and States when in a brief space of time history traverses a path equal to many decades of normal peaceful development. These are milestones, turning-points in world history. In such epochs all the forces accumulated by society in the course of centuries are set in tempestuous motion. The former course of the historic development of society is disturbed, and events of a new character dominate the stage.

To-day mankind is experiencing precisely such a turbulent, crucial period. The grandeur of the events of our day is without parallel in history. The tension and pace of development of social life, the character and scope of the struggle of the freedom-loving democratic peoples of the world, headed by the Soviet Union, Britain, and the U.S.A., against German imperialism will exert an even greater influence on the destinies of peoples than the most important periods of past epochs.

> G. Alexandrov, at a Session of the Soviet Academy of Sciences, 1942.

It may now be considered indisputable that in the course of the war imposed upon the nations by Hitlerite Germany a radical demarcation of forces and the formation of two opposite camps have taken place: the camp of the Italo-German coalition and the camp of the Anglo-Soviet-American coalition. It is equally indisputable that these two opposite coalitions are guided by two different and opposite programmes of action.

The programme of action of the Italo-German coalition may be described by the following points: racial hatred; domination of "chosen" nations; subjugation of other nations and seizure of their territories; economic enslavement of subjugated nations and spoliation of their national wealth; destruction of democratic liberties; the institution of the Hitlerite régime everywhere.

The programme of action of the Anglo-Soviet-American coalition is: the abolition of racial exclusiveness; the equality of nations and the inviolability of their territories; the liberation of the enslaved nations and the restoration of their sovereign rights; the right of every nation to arrange its affairs as it wishes; economic aid to the nations that have suffered and assistance to them in achieving their material welfare; the restoration of democratic liberties; the destruction of the Hitlerite régime. . . .

It is said that the Anglo-Soviet-American coalition has every chance of winning and would certainly win, if it did not have one organic defect which is capable of weakening and disintegrating it. This defect, in the opinion of those people, is that this coalition consists of heterogeneous elements with different ideologies and that this circumstance will prevent their organising joint action against the common enemy.

I think that this assertion is wrong.

It would be ridiculous to deny the difference in the ideologies and social systems of the countries composing the Anglo-Soviet-American coalition. But does this preclude the possibility and expediency of joint action on the part of the members of this coalition against the common enemy who holds out the threat of enslavement for them? It certainly does not preclude it.

STALIN, on the occasion of the Twenty-Fifth Anniversary of the October Revolution, 1942.

> Above the world's long-reigning gloom,
> Where strife and pain for ever lour,
> In answer to the battle-cries
> The skies are flushed with new-born power.

And soon its rays as from a crown
Will pierce the darkness of the clouds,
And people hastening from the fight
Will seek its shining throne in crowds.

And we who knew but night and storms
Will glory in its royal rays,
And crumbling into dust, the world
Itself will pass down azure ways.
    ALEXANDER BLOK: *The New Power.*

Drum up the noise of revolt in the squares!
Up with heads of arrogant blood!
Our aim is to wash all the towns of the world
In waters that surge like a second flood.

Meek is the bull of the days.
Slow is the chariot of years.
Our god is in lightning ways.
Our heart is a drum without fears.

Like heaven itself is our gold.
The bullet may shorten our joys.
Our arms are our thundering songs.
Our gold is our boisterous voice.

Meadows, be covered with green,
Spread out a base for the days!
Rainbows, raise arches of years
For the steeds of our lightning ways!

Sing for joy, sing for joy, drink!
Spring is astir in our veins.
Beat to the battle, heart!
Drum in our breast with its strains.
    VLADIMIR MAYAKOVSKY: *Our March.*
    (Trans. by Gerard Shelley.)

NOTES ON RUSSIAN AUTHORS QUOTED

ALEXANDROV, Georgi. Professor. Chief of the Propaganda Department of the Communist Party of the Soviet Union; member of the Soviet Academy of Sciences.

ARKIN, David. Professor. Member of the Soviet Academy of Architecture.

ARSKY, Pavel Alexandrovich (1886-   ). One of the pre-revolutionary Russian poets who inspired the working classes with the concept of collectivism. From his youth he was fond of poetry. His favourite poets were Pushkin, Lermontov, Byron, Shakespeare, Goethe, Schiller and Heine. In 1905 he was arrested for spreading revolutionary propaganda, but after his escape from the prison he devoted his time to literary effort.

BAIKOV, Alexander. Professor (1870). Metallurgist. Member of the Soviet Academy of Sciences.

BEDNY, Demyan (pseudonym), Efim Alexandrovich Pridvorov (1883-   ). A poet and a soldier; was honoured with the badge of the Red Banner. His writings consist mainly of fables, satirical verse and stories, and in them he expressed grim determination of the proletariat to fight against the old order of things.

BELINSKY, Vissarion Grigorevich (1811-1848). Great Russian critic and philosopher. Son of a physician. By setting forth the theory of "art for life," Belinsky gave a criterion for literary criticisms. He exerted a considerable influence upon Russian literature.

BERDYAEV, Nikolai. Professor (1874-   ). Russian philosopher and theologian with strong Slavophil sympathies. Together with Struve he fought against all theoretical principles of Marxism. He was an idealist, and a follower of Kant.

BIELY, Andrei (1880-   ). Real name is Bugaev. In pre-revolutionary Russia he was regarded as one of the poets of Russian symbolism. In his prose works he describes the revolutionary epochs of New Russia.

BLOK, Alexander (1880-1921). Recognised as one of the outstanding Russian poets. After the Revolution he welcomed the birth of Soviet Russia "as a manifestation of a national impulse towards social and religious truth."

BOGDANOV (1873-1928). Real name is Alexander Malinovsky. A politician, philosopher, economist and literary critic. An organiser of the newspaper *Novaya Zhizn* (New Life). After the Revolution was a member of the C.C. of the Prolet Cult. Was a member of Communist Academy. He was the Principal of "Institute for the Fight for Longevity."

BURDENKO, N. Professor (1878-   ). Outstanding surgeon. Member of Soviet Academy of Sciences. Chief surgeon to the Red Army.

CHEKHOV, Anton Pavlovich (1860-1904). Son of a former serf. Studied medicine, but established his reputation as a writer of short stories in 1887. He also wrote several dramas. In most of his writings he describes with great force the hopeless condition of Russian society.

DIMITROV, Gregory. Bulgarian communist. Defied Hitler at the Leipzig Reichstag Fire trial; went to Soviet Russia and became a member of the Presidium of the Executive Committee of the Communist International, now dissolved.

DOBROLUBOV, Nikolai Alexandrovich (1836-1861). Son of a poor priest. He became one of the most brilliant critics belonging to the school of Belinsky.

DOSTOEVSKY, Fedor Mikhailovich (1821-1881). Son of a poor army surgeon. On the appearance of his first novel it was proclaimed as the work of a "new Gogol." Dostoevsky's writings are unsurpassed for the psychological analysis of human character.

EHRENBURG, Ilya (1891-   ). Soviet journalist and novelist. One of the most prolific writers of modern Russia.

ESSENIN, Sergey Alexandrovich (1895-1925). A peasant by birth; was educated in a Parish school. His first printed verse appeared when he was seventeen. By 1920-22 he became to be regarded as an exponent of the "Imagist Movement." He married Isadora Duncan. He hailed the advent of the Revolution with his poem *Inonia*.

FOMIN, Semyon Dmitrievich (1881-   ). A proletarian poet. He began to write at an early age, and his first verse appeared in the journal called *Novaya Volya* (New Freedom).

FRUMKIN, Alexander Naumovich. Professor (1895-   ). Member of Soviet Academy of Sciences. Gifted chemist.

GOGOL, Nikolai Vasilievich (1809-1852). Novelist. His father was a small landowner of more than ordinary culture. Gogol was recognised by literary critics of his time as forming a new school in Russian literature.

GORKIN, Alexander. Secretary of the Supreme Soviet of the U.S.S.R.

GORKY, Maxim (pseudonym), Alexei Maximovitch Peshkov (1871-1936). Novelist. Son of an upholsterer. Began his literary career under the guidance of Korolenko. Gorky's descriptions of workers, peasants and vagabonds surpass all previous attempts in literary craft.

GRIGOROVICH, Dmitri Vasilievich (1822-1900). Son of a landed proprietor. His writings attracted much attention because of his advocacy of emancipation of serfs and his realistic description of peasant life.

GRINEVSKAYA, I. (1850-   ). A well-known poetess.

HERZEN, Alexander Ivanovich (1812-1870). Son of a rich landed proprietor, but his mother was German. He began his career as a student of science and wrote a thesis on the *Historical Evolution of the System of Copernicus*. Herzen took a lively interest in philosophical and social themes, and gathered around him all the progressive forces of the younger generation. Both a political agitator and a man of letters, Herzen left a mark on Russian thought.

ILIN, M. (pseudonym), Ilya Yakovlevich Marshak. A young Soviet engineer, brother of Marshak, the Russian poet. Author of many popular scientific books.

IONOV, Ilya Ionovich (1887-). A proletarian poet. Was exiled to Siberia as a member of the fighting organisation of the Social-Democratic Party. After the November Revolution he managed the publication of the Petrograd Soviet.

JUSEFOVICH, J. Trade Union official in the U.S.S.R.

KAPITZA, Peter. Professor. Distinguished physicist. Director of the Institute for Physical Problems. Member of the Soviet Academy of Sciences; Honorary Fellow of the Royal Society. His research is mainly in the field of low temperatures and magnetism. Formerly Director of the Royal Society Mond Laboratory in Cambridge.

KATAEV, Valentin (1897-). One of the talented Soviet writers; served as a volunteer in the First World War. His writings were published before the Revolution, but he became widely known under the new regime. Kataev is perhaps most successful in the satirical novel. His *The Squaring of the Circle* is based upon Komsomol life.

KHOMYAKOV, Alexei Stepanovich (1804-1860). Soldier and author. In 1821 he ran away from home to join the Greek patriots in their struggle for independence; but his father prevented him from doing so. He then entered the Russian army. Khomyakov wrote patriotic and religious songs and left some excellent Russian prose.

KLUCHEVSKY, Vassili Osipovich (1841-1911). Son of a priest. Became Professor of Russian History in the University of Moscow.

KLUYEV, Nikolai Alexeyevich (1887-). A peasant poet. His love of Russia's Mother Earth is the keynote of his simple but penetrating verses. He first became known as a poet in 1912. He had a strong influence on Essenin.

KOMAROV, Vladimir. Professor. President of the Academy of Sciences of the U.S.S.R.; a leading Soviet botanist.

KONOVALOV, S. Professor. In charge of Russian studies at the universities of Oxford and Birmingham.

KORCHERGA, Ivan. A dramatist; author of *Masters of Time*.

KROPOTKIN (Prince Peter Alexeyevitch) (1842-1921). Author, geographer and revolutionary. His sociological theories are to be found in *Mutual Aid, Conquest of Bread*, as well as in his autobiography, *The Memoirs of a Revolutionist*. His anarchist philosophy largely agreed with the views held by the Narodniks. Exiled by the Tsarist Government; returned to Russia in 1917, settled near Moscow, and died on February 8th, 1921.

KRUPSKAYA, Nadezhda (1869-1939). Wife and active collaborator of Lenin; member of Central Committee of the Communist Party Supreme Council of the U.S.S.R. Rendered valuable service to the cause of education.

KUZMICHEV. A pre-revolutionary Russian poet. Through his spirited verses he proclaimed the beginning of a new life in Russia. The supreme needs of Russia were unity and common work in order to fulfil the promises of the Revolution.

LAVROV, Peter (1823-1900). One of the ablest revolutionary thinkers of the nineteenth-century Russia. Author of many books written as introduction to *The History of Thought*, which was never completed.

LENIN, Vladimir Ilyitch (1870-1924). Leader of the Russian Revolution. Son of a teacher, studied Law. As a strict Marxist he led the radical section of the Russian Socialist Party. Lived in exile from 1907 to 1917. Arrived at Petrograd in 1917 and took the lead of the Bolshevik Party. Lenin became President of the Council of People's Commissars. Died on January 21st, 1924.

LIDIN, Vladimir Germanovich (1894-   ). A well-known writer of the U.S.S.R. Began to write in 1915. He is a son of a merchant.

LITVINOV, Maxim (1876-   ). Now Soviet Ambassador to the U.S.A.; was until 1939 Commissar for Foreign Affairs of the U.S.S.R at the League of Nations. Played important rôle in maintenance of peace. Litvinov has been a diplomatic representative of the U.S.S.R. in Great Britain, Minister Plenipotentiary in Esthonia, Head of Soviet delegation at the Hague, Disarmament and London Economic Conferences.

LOZOVSKY, Solomon Abramovich (1878-   ). Real name Drydso. Son of a teacher, blacksmith by profession. One of the three Vice-Commissars for Foreign Affairs of the Soviet Union. Acted as spokesman for the Soviet Information Bureau in the critical months of the early part of the Soviet-German war.

LUNACHARSKY, Anatoly Vasilievich (1875-1933). Politician, author and dramatist. Joined the Bolshevik Party in 1903, and later the editorial staff of the Bolshevik *Vpered* (Forward). People's Commissar for Education of the U.S.S.R. (1917-29); organised mass education and encouraged development of the Russian stage.

LYSENKO, Trofim D. Professor. President of the Lenin All-Union Agricultural Academy. Born in the Ukraine, he studied at Kiev. He is one of the youngest Soviet scientists to win world distinction for his research on vernalisation.

MAISKY, Ivan Mikhailovich (1887-   ). Economist and journalist. Joined the revolutionary movement in 1899. Directed press department of People's Commissariat for Foreign Affairs, 1922-23. Counsellor of Embassy in London, 1925-27, in Tokyo, 1927-29. Minister to Finland, 1929-32. Ambassador to Great Britain since 1932.

MAISKY, Agnaya A., Madame. Wife of Ivan Maisky, Soviet Ambassador in London.

MALASHKIN, Sergei Ivanovich (1890-   ). A peasant poet. His verses reflect the deepest notes of the aims and aspirations of the Revolution, and sing triumphantly of "the universal victory of the proletariat."

MARSHAK, Samuel (1887-   ). Well-known contemporary writer of children's books. He is also a distinguished satirist, and frequently collaborates with the Kukriniksi trio of political cartoonists.

MAYAKOVSKY, Vladimir Vladimirovich (1894-1930). Poet. Son of a forester, was a member of the Social Democratic Party. After the Revolution he organised the Left front, equivalent to "Futurism at the service of the Revolution," and dedicated his energies and talent to the making of Soviet literature.

MIKHAILOV, NIKOLAI. Secretary of the Central Committee of the Young Communist League of the U.S.S.R. Very capable organiser.

MOLOTOV, Vyacheslav (1890-   ). At sixteen joined the Kazan Bolshevik organisation, and at nineteen was arrested and exiled for two years. In 1912 joined the Bolshevik newspaper *Zvezda*, and later helped to found *Pravda*. Appointed Chairman of the People's Commissars in 1930, and since 1939 he has become Commissar for Foreign Affairs.

NECHAYEV, Georgi Efimovich (1859-   ). Son of a glazier. His first verse appeared in print in 1891. He belonged to that group of the proletarians who realised that "their party, together with the political conditions of the country, was destroying their freedom, inner and outward alike. They became tired of living in twilight and longed passionately for a normal existence, consistent with full liberty of the soil" (George Z. Patrick in *Popular Poetry in Soviet Russia*).

NEKRASOV, Nikolai Alexeyevich (1821-1877). Poet. His popular verses which deal with the life of all classes of society, especially with the peasants, earned him the title of a notable lyrical poet.

ODOYEVSKY, Alexander Ivanovich (Prince) (1802-1839). A poet and one of the earliest representative Slavophil writers. Decembrist and friend of Ryleev.

OGAREV, Nikolay Platonovich (1813-1877). Writer of revolutionary songs. He was a close friend of Herzen.

OGOLOVETS, Alexander. A music critic in Soviet Russia.

PAVLOV, Ivan Petrovich. Professor (1849-1936). Famous physiologist. Member of the Soviet Academy of Sciences. His main research was on the problem of digestion and on cerebral activity and the theory of reflexes. Awarded Nobel Prize in 1904, and in 1928 was made an Honorary Fellow of the Royal College of Physicians in London. Died in Russia on February 27th, 1936.

PISAREV, Dmitri Ivanovich (1840-1888). Essayist and literary critic. His writings reflected the reaction of the early 'sixties against the opportunism of the previous decade.

PLEKHANOV, Gregory Valentinovich (1857-1918). Founder and for many years chief exponent of Marxism in Russia. Jointly edited *Iskra* with Lenin.

PLESHCHEEV, Alexei Nikolaevich (1825-1893). Poet. His writings were characterised by a militant spirit of liberty.

POGODIN, Nikolai Feodorovich (Stukalov) (1900-   ). Contemporary Russian dramatist. Author of *Kremlin Chimes*. Very popular.

PUSHKIN, Alexander Sergeyevich (1799-1837). The greatest Russian poet. His influence in Russian literature has not been surpassed by that of any other poet. Pushkin was descended, on his father's side, from an aristocratic family, and, on his mother's side, from Peter the Great's favourite negro, Hannibal. He was killed in a duel.

RACHMANOV,   . A dramatist; author of *The Deputy from the Baltic*.

REMIZOV, Alexei (1877-   ). A writer of folk-tales, legends and Russian history. In his writings about the Revolution he welcomes it as a purifier of national consciousness.

SALTYKOV-SCHEDRIN, Mikhail Evgrafovich (1826-1889). Novelist. Belonged to an ancient noble family. He became a writer of great distinction. His "provincial sketches" presented some extraordinary gloomy pictures of oppression and dishonesty in Tsarist Russia.

SEMASHKO, Nikolai A. Formerly Commissar of Health and author of *Health Protection in the U.S.S.R.*

SEMYONOV, Sergei (1893-   ). Son of a metal worker. He took part in the Revolution and held responsible military posts. From 1921 he became known as a promising literary novice, and his novel, *Natalia Tarpova*, published in 1927, made him a realistic writer of great reputation in Soviet Russia.

SHCHERBAKOV, Alexander. Colonel-General. Secretary of Moscow Regional and City Committee of the Communist Party of the Soviet Union. Assistant People's Commissar for Defence.

SHENSHIN, Afanasi Afanasevich (1820-1892). One of the most melodious of the minor Russian poets. His poems are short but contain much lyrical beauty. Wrote under pen-name of "Fet."

SHOSTAKOVICH, Dmitri (1906-   ). He is the most brilliant of Soviet composers. Has written operas, ballets, symphonies, concertos, and music for theatre and cinema. His Seventh Symphony, the Leningrad symphony, was written during the siege of Leningrad in 1941.

SPERANSKY, Michail Michailovitch (1772-1839). Son of a priest. Educated in an Ecclesiastical College (Seminary). Was Professor of Mathematics and Physics. Became a Minister in the Tsarist Government and served from 1809 to 1812.

STAKHANOV, Alexei Grigorevich. Ukrainian miner. Is the originator of the movement for higher productivity, which, starting with heavy industries, has now spread to other branches of economic activity. He is now a Deputy of the Supreme Soviet of the U.S.S.R.

STALIN, Joseph Vissarionovitch. Marshal (1879-   ). Premier of Soviet Russia. Joined the Socialist revolutionary movement in the Caucasian oilfields, and was repeatedly imprisoned and exiled to Siberia. After the Russian Revolution in March 1917 he became a member of the Political Bureau of the Communist Party under Lenin, and Commissar of Nationalities in the Soviet Government. Under his influence the Comintern was dissolved in 1943.

STALSKY, Suleyman (1869-1937). People's poet of Daghestan. Born in South Daghestan. His parents were poor peasants. He started work as a shop-boy and later became a labourer. The main feature of his poetry depicts the lives of the poor people of Daghestan. He was imprisoned by the Tsarist Government. In autumn of 1934 he visited Moscow for the first time in his life as a delegate to the All-Union Congress of Writers. There he met Gorky. He was awarded the Order of Lenin for his outstanding services to Soviet literature. The people of Daghestan nominated him for Deputy to the Supreme Soviet of the U.S.S.R., but twenty days before the election he died.

STERN, Lina. Professor. Member of the Academy of Sciences of the U.S.S.R. A noted neurologist. "A great deal of her work consists of investigations showing the peculiar and complex relations of the nervous system to the other systems of the body."

SUMAROKOV, Alexander Petrovich (1718-1777). A prolific Russian author. He has left odes, eulogies, fables, satires and dramas. He was highly valued in his day. In 1756 the Russian Theatre was created by a Decree, and Sumarokov was chosen as its first director.

TIKHONOV, Nikolai (1896-   ). Well-known poet. Stayed and worked in Leningrad under the siege of 1941-42. First Soviet writer to be awarded Order of the Patriotic War (1943).

TIUTCHEV, Fedor Ivanovich (1803-1873). Contemporary of Pushkin. Considered by some as Russia's second greatest poet.

TOLSTOY (Count), Alexey Nikolaivich (1882-   ). A leading Soviet writer. A member of Soviet Academy of Sciences. Deputy of the Supreme Soviet of the U.S.S.R.

TOLSTOY, Count Leo Nikolaevich (1828-1910). Novelist and essayist. Born of a noble family. He joined the army and went through the Crimean War, but later returned to his own estate and devoted himself to literary work.

TURGENEV, Ivan Sergyeevich (1818-1883). Novelist. His sketches from the life of the peasant made him famous in Russia.

USPENSKY, Lev. Commander of the Soviet Red Navy.

VOLYNSKY, Alexander L. An eminent literary critic; author of works on Leonardo da Vinci and Dostoevsky.

VOZNESENSKY, Nikolai. Chairman of State Planning Committee. Member of the Committee for State Defence.

YAROSLAVSKY, Emelyan. Professor (1878-   ). Member of the Soviet Academy of Sciences. An outstanding historian and author of several books dealing with the Revolution.

ZHAROV, Alexander (1904-   ). One of the younger Soviet poets of proletarian origin, influenced by Mayakovsky.

ACKNOWLEDGMENTS

I WISH to convey my gratitude to Mr. H. G. Wells for contributing a foreword to the book. When he visited Moscow in 1920, he referred to Soviet Russia as "this dark crystal." But he has always played the part of a candid friend to the Russian system. In his *Phoenix* (1942) he says: "There are grave defects in its necessarily experimental organisation, there are legacies from an autocratic past and there have been excesses of zeal, suspicion and vindictiveness, but I have never faltered in my conviction that the régime was enormously better and healthier on account of the elimination of private ownership in the material and apparatus of production and distribution. In 1914 Russia was three hundred years behind Western Europe, in a state of mediaeval ignorance and inefficiency; she is now leading the war."

I am indebted to the Society for Cultural Relations between the Peoples of the British Commonwealth and the U.S.S.R. for the use of its library; and to *Voks* in Moscow for the design of the jacket taken from one of its publications.

In every stage of the work, Baroness Moura Budberg and Miss Rose Herber have helped me with their advice and criticism. Without their encouragement I could not have succeeded in bringing out this anthology.

My thanks are also due to Miss Eva Landsberg for preparing the manuscript for the press, and to Dr. Sasadhar Sinha for translating two extracts from Rabindranath Tagore's *Letters from Russia*.

Now it remains for me to acknowledge my obligations to the following authors, publishers and editors who have assisted by giving permission to use extracts from their publications.

- Messrs. George Allen and Unwin Ltd. and Mr. Gerard Shelley for translations of two poems, "Russia" by Andrei Biely and "Our March" by Mayakovsky, from *Modern Poems from Russia*; also for a passage from Fridtjof Nansen's *Russia and Peace*.
- Messrs. Allenson and Co. Ltd. and Mr. John S. Hoyland for passages from *The New Russia*.
- Mr. E. St. John Brooks for a poem published in *The Times* in 1916.
- Messrs. Jonathan Cape Ltd. and M. Ilin for the extracts from *Moscow has a Plan*.
- Messrs. Chatto and Windus and Mrs. Garnett for extracts from Chekhov's *Cherry Orchard* and *The Three Sisters*.
- Messrs. J. M. Dent and Sons Ltd. for an extract from Kluchevsky's *A History of Russia*, and extracts from E. J. Dillon's *The Eclipse of Russia*.

East and West Ltd. and Mr. Frederick Richter for Dr. John Pollen's translations of *A Russian Scene* by Shenshin, *Te Deum* and *The Landlord* by Nekrasov.

The Editor of *The Anglo-Soviet Journal* for an extract from an article by the Editor, and to him and Messrs. Herbert Marshall and R. Magidoff for Gorky's "The Song of the Stormy Petrel" published in the *Journal*.

The Editor of *British Ally* for an excerpt from an article on the Twenty-fifth Birthday of the U.S.S.R.

The Editor of *Daily Worker* for a passage from Professor Haldane's article on Marxism.

The Editor of *Daily Herald* and Professor Harold Laski for an extract from his article on the Russian Revolution.

The Editor of *Izvestia* for an excerpt from its article on the Anglo-Soviet Agreement.

The Editor of *Labour Monthly* for excerpts from messages from Lord Horder, Dr. Aleck Bourne, and Mr. John Horner on the Twenty-fifth Anniversary of the U.S.S.R.

The Editor of *The Manchester Guardian* for a passage from an article on the Russo-German War.

The Editor of *News Chronicle* and Madame Maisky for a passage from her article on Children in Soviet Russia.

The Editor of *Pravda* for extracts taken from translations published in *Soviet War News*.

The Editor of *Soviet War News* for several extracts from articles on Russia and her Patriotic War.

The Editor of *The Times* for extracts from leaders on the subject of Anglo-Soviet Alliance.

Foreign Languages Publishing House, Moscow, for extracts from State Documents, Reports and Speeches by Commissars, and from *History of the Communist Party of the Soviet Union*.

Messrs. Victor Gollancz for extracts from Professor Semashko's *Health Protection in the U.S.S.R.*

Miss Rose Herber for translation of *A Song of a Tajik Farmer*.

The Hogarth Press for extracts from Chekhov's *Diary*, from *Reminiscences of Tolstoy, Chekhov and Andrev* by Maxim Gorky.

Messrs William Heinemann Ltd. and Mrs. Garnett for extracts from the work of Dostoevsky and Turgenev.

John Lane The Bodley Head Ltd., and Pandit Jahwarlal Nehru for a passage from his *Autobiography*.

Professor Harold Laski for an extract from his Foreword on the Soviet Constitution.

Messrs. Lawrence and Wishart Ltd. for a passage from *Memoirs of Krupskaya*; and for extracts from *Natalia Tarpova* by Semyonov, *Speed Up, Time!* by Kataev, and *Fiery Russia* by Alexei Remizov, in *Soviet Literature* compiled by George Reavey and Marc Slonim.

ACKNOWLEDGMENTS

Messrs. Longmans, Green and Co. Ltd. and Lord Passfield for an extract from Sidney and Beatrice Webb's *Soviet Communism*.

Messrs. Methuen and Co. Ltd. and Professor Janko Lavrin for an extract from *An Introduction to the Russian Novel*; and for an extract from *The Peasant* by Grigorovich.

Messrs. Macmillan and Co. Ltd., New York, for a passage from an article by Dr. Hans Kohn in the *Encyclopædia of Social Sciences*.

Mr. Herbert Marshall for a translation of a poem by Suleyman Stalsky.

The Marx-Engels-Lenin Institute for excerpts taken from the works of Marx, Engels and Lenin; also for an extract from a biography of Stalin.

The National Peace Council and Mr. Gerard Bailey for extracts taken from addresses at a Conference on *Britain and Russia in the New World Order*, April 1942.

G. P. Putnam's Sons, New York, for extracts from the writings of Sumarokov, Pleshcheev, Nekrasov, Ogarev and Alexander Blok taken from Dr. Wiener's *Anthology of Russian Literature*.

Messrs. Sheed and Ward Ltd. for an extract from Nicholas Berdyaev's *Russian Revolution*.

Sir Charles Trevelyan for two extracts from his essay on *Soviet Democracy*.

The University of California and Professor George J. Patrick for extracts from Poems by Arsky, Bedny, Bogdanov, Essenin, Fomin, Ionov, Kluyev, Kuzmichev, Malashkin, Nechayev.

U.S.S.R. Society for Cultural Relations with Foreign Countries (*Voks*) for extracts from *In Defence of Civilization against Fascist Barbarism*.

Visva-Bharati for translations of two passages from Rabindranath Tagore's *Letters from Russia*.

A. Volynsky for an extract from *Soul of Russia*, published in 1916.

Mr. H. G. Wells for two passages from Commander Uspensky's letter (1942) to him.

William T. Norgate Ltd. and Dr. J. G. Crowther for an extract from his *Science in Soviet Russia*.

I have taken the greatest care to trace the owners of all copyright material and I beg the forgiveness of those whose rights may have been overlooked.

N. G.

INDEX

Alexandrov, G., 263
Angell, Norman, 181
Anglo-Soviet Journal, 193
Aragon, Louis, 185
Arkin, Professor, 151
Arsky, 255

Baikov, Professor Alexander, 205
Barbusse, Henri, 159, 173
Bardina, Sofia, 36
Bedny, 89
Belinsky, 39, 55
Berdyaev, Nicholas, 68
Biely, Andrei, 254, 262
Blok, Alexander, 22, 265
Bogdanov, A., 66, 150
Bourne, Dr. Aleck, 193
Britain, Women of, 235
British Ally, 251
British and Soviet Trade Unions, 229
Brooks, E. St. John, 222
Burdenko, N. N., 142

Cachin, Marcel, 194
Campanella, Tommaso, 100
Carter, Rev. Henry, 123
Central Moslem Ecclesiastical Board Appeal, 213
Chaplin, Charles, 238
Chekhov, 39, 40, 41, 42, 48, 49, 59
Chiang Kai Shek, 224
Communist International Executive Committee, 257
Communist Manifesto, The, 101
Communist Party, 86
Cripps, Sir Stafford, 226, 243, 244, 248
Crowther, J. G., 114

Declaration of the Rights of the People of Russia, 77
Dillon, E. J., 28, 29
Dimitrov, 225
Dobrolubov, 52
Dostoevsky, 20, 31, 49, 50, 51, 52, 54, 55, 56
Dreiser, Theodore, 174

Eden, Anthony, 241, 245
Ehrenburg, Ilya, 207, 221, 235, 253, 261
Engels, 101
Essenin, 67

Feuchtwanger, 191
Firlinger, Zdenek, 192
Fomin, 48
Fourier, 100

George, David Lloyd, 238
George VI, 223
Gogol, 45
Gomez, Jose Royo i, 186
Gorkin, Alexander, 123
Gorky, Maxim, 41, 44, 53, 57, 59, 62, 64, 74, 87, 115, 135, 169, 197, 220, 253
Gregory, Sir Richard, 145
Grigorovich, 47
Grinevskaya, 208

Haldane, J. B. S., 184
Head, Nancy, 93
Herzen, Alexander, 31, 54
Hicks, George, 257
History of the Communist Party, 104
Hitler, Adolf, 196
Horder, Lord, 193
Horner, John, 250
Hoyland, J. S., 173, 175, 187

Ibarruri, 233
Ilin, 23, 95
Ionov, 257
Izvestia, 226

Jusefovich, J., 99

Kalinin, 223
Kapitza, Professor Peter, 144
Kataev, Valentin, 260
Khomyakov, 55
Kiev, Women of, 231
Kluchevsky, 27
Kluyev, 92
Kohn, Hans, 183
Komarov, Professor Vladimir, 145, 206, 247
Konovalov, Professor, 121
Korcherga, Ivan, 259
Kropotkin, 101
Krupskaya, 75
Kuzmichev, 80

Lampert, Evgheny, 122
Land-Decree—Peasants' " Nakaz " 1918, 83

Laski, Harold, 112, 182
Lavrin, Janko, 149
Lavrov, 58
Lenin, 41, 64, 65, 66, 69, 70, 75, 76, 79, 81, 86, 108, 109, 110, 124, 127, 134, 158, 255, 256
Lidin, V., 261
Litvinov, 160, 161, 162, 163, 164, 166, 167, 172, 200
Lozovsky, 154
Lunacharsky, 86

Maisky, Madame, 143
Maisky, 128, 155, 171, 200, 242, 263
Malashkin, 91
Manchester Guardian, 222
Mann, Heinrich, 188
Mann, Thomas, 237
Marshak, S., 196
Marshall, Herbert, 96
Marx, Karl, 102, 105, 106, 107
Masereel, Frans, 187
Mayakovsky, Vladimir, 265
Medical Workers in London, Moscow to, 239
Mikhailov, Nikolai, 214
Molotov, 112, 153, 168, 170, 198, 240, 246
Moscow Housewives, 234
Moscow Trade Unions, 228
Moscow University Students, 230
Moscow, Women of, 231, 234
Moscow Youth Rally, Appeal of the, 216

Nansen, Fridtjof, 174
Narodnaïa Volia, 34, 37
Naval Pilots of the Soviet Union, 227
Nechayev, 72
Negrin, Juan, 189, 238
Nehru, Jahwarlal, 185
Nekrasov, 21, 22, 24, 45, 53
Netchayev, 57
Nevsky Star, 40
Nicholas II, 72
Nikoleyeva, Klavdia, 208

Odoyevsky, 31, 54
Ogarev, 57
Ogolovets, Alexander, 152

Palestine, Socialist League of, 237
Pavlov, 113
Pisarev, 62
Plato, 100
Plekhanov, 58
Pleshcheev, 46, 59
Pogodin, Nikolai, 136
Pososhkov, 23

Pravda, 76, 95, 118, 120, 136, 143, 203, 209, 216, 245
Pushkin, 27, 31

Rachmanov, 78
Rakoshi, Matias, 190
Rassulayev, The Mufti Abdul Rahman, 129
Remizov, Alexei, 262
Resolution at Peasants' Congress 1918, 83
Resolution of the Sixteenth Party Congress, 89
Resolution on the National Question 1917, 80
Resolution of the Third World Congress 1921, 110
Rolland, Romain, 174, 175, 176
Roosevelt, F. D., 224, 251
Rousseau, 100
Royal Naval Air Service, 227
Russian Liberals, The, 37
Russian Workers' Petition to Nicholas II, 38

Saint Simon, 100
Saltykov, 23
Semashko, N. A., 40, 141, 142
Semyonov, S., 258
Sen, Lin, 252
Shapiro, Henry, 207
Shcherbakov, 218
Shenshin, 20
Shostakovich, Dmitri, 207
Sinclair, Upton, 182, 183
Song of a Tajik Farmer, 95
Soviet Declaration at Inter-Allied Conference, 211
Soviet Guerrilla Fighter, Oath of the, 215
Soviet Scientists, Appeal of the, 217
Soviet War News, 121, 127, 133, 135, 139, 140, 157, 206, 207, 213, 214
Speransky, 25
Stakhanov, Alexei, 137
Stalin, 70, 73, 87, 88, 89, 90, 91, 111, 114, 115, 124, 125, 126, 128, 132, 136, 137, 138, 164, 165, 168, 170, 171, 172, 199, 201, 202, 204, 205, 226, 256, 264
Stalsky, Suleyman, 96
Stead, W. T., 62
Sumarokov, 32, 33
Swinburne, 30

Tagore, Rabindranath, 177, 178
Thorez, Maurice, 236, 237
Tikhonov, Nicolai, 99
Times, The, 239, 240, 244, 248

Tolstoy, Alexey, 119, 205, 220
Tolstoy, Leo, 55, 57, 60, 61, 62
Trade Unions Central Council, 228
Trevelyan, Sir Charles, 126, 129
Tse-Dun, Mao, 184
Turgenev, 42

Uspensky, Commander Lev, 195, 225
U.S.S.R. Society of Cultural Relations, 235

Volynsky, A., 67
Voznesensky, N., 138, 144

Walling, William, 64
Webb, Sidney and Beatrice, 179, 181

Yaroslavsky, Emelyan, 219, 221
Ying-Ch'in, Ho, 237

Zharov, Alexander, 232

For Product Safety Concerns and Information please contact our EU
representative GPSR@taylorandfrancis.com
Taylor & Francis Verlag GmbH, Kaufingerstraße 24, 80331 München, Germany